THE ANCIENT NEAR EAST

Frontispiece. Terracotta plaques representing diverse subjects, such as demons, cyclops, animals and musicians, are widespread in Old Babylonian contexts (see p. 90), and seem to be typical of the period. Comparable with them is this plaque representing a winged nude female with ferocious talons, flanked by owls and holding short lengths of cord, commonly associated with Lilith, goddess of death, the 'screech owl'.

THE ANCIENT NEAR EAST

CHARLES BURNEY

Cornell University Press

ITHACA, NEW YORK

To Brigit, Roderick and Sarah

First published 1977 by Cornell University Press

Published in Great Britain and the British
Commonwealth under the title *From Village
to Empire*

International Standard Book Number 0–8014–1080–0
Library of Congress Catalog Card Number 76–55483

Printed in Great Britain by
Cox & Wyman Ltd, London, Fakenham and Reading

Contents

Preface

The artist constructing a mosaic may have only a partial vision of the whole work before its completion. So it was with this book which critics may be fully justified in claiming as foolhardy to attempt, at least within an imposed limit. The author must thank the publishers for their tolerance of a book which exceeds the length originally envisaged. He need not, however, apologise for the inevitable omissions. Some aspects, some sites, have been discussed at fair length; others have received little or no mention. Stress has, on the whole, been laid on the less familiar at the expense of those areas better known to the general public and to the student alike. No two writers would ever arrive at the same proportionate emphasis on the different regions and periods involved. Almost certainly, if this book is ever revised or rewritten, the space allotted to Iran, Syria, Arabia and perhaps also Anatolia will be increased, for these are the lands where the major archaeological discoveries of the next twenty years in the Near East are most likely to be made.

The aims and methods of archaeology in the Near East have of course changed radically since the days of Botta and Layard, although the ability of archaeologists to convey the essence of their discoveries and conclusions to the wider public has not kept pace with their technical expertise. Indeed, some might say that it has declined. One problem is the vanishing common background of knowledge of the Hebrew and Classical roots of western civilization. Another is the fear of the specialist of venturing out of his home ground. Yet another is the ever-growing volume of publications—preliminary reports on excavations, final reports, articles in a proliferating array of journals and tomes of varying bulk and value—to be mastered or at least skimmed through. This last is perhaps a problem especially severe in the context of the ancient Near East: the prehistorian in Britain or Europe, for example, may have time to build interpretative schemes, if the material records from a site comprise plans, sections and a handful of sherds. The archaeologist in the Near East is more likely to be overshadowed by the mass and complexity of his material. Simplification is all the more tempting, but also all the more perilous.

There have been many excellent books and articles on methodology and on the processes, or mechanisms, of cultural change; but this is not one of them. Its purpose, perhaps more humble, is to guide the newcomer to the more significant aspects of a bewildering landscape which lacks the unity to be found within one homogeneous civilization, such as that of Egypt under the Pharaohs. To have attempted more than the briefest reference to processes of change would require a second book, probably very much longer than this one. The writer anyhow believes that a wide acquaintance with the material evidence is essential before any worthwhile efforts towards its explanation in terms of cultural process can be made. He also believes that human history, before or after the advent of written records, can seldom be explained primarily in statistics or equations.

Chronology has become a subject of considerable discussion, even controversy, within and beyond the orbit of the ancient Near East. The more extravagant claims of *ex oriente lux* have rightly been discredited, though it has not been generally admitted that radio-carbon dates, calibrated as they may be, can often be made to support the line of argument desired. The gap between prehistoric Europe and the Near East was narrower than formerly appeared, but it cannot be eliminated without selective use of evidence. Recent changes have pushed back the absolute chronology of parts of the Near East, such as Anatolia, and have tended to reduce the role of Mesopotamia as the centre of all progress; but the general framework of comparative chronology remains substantially the same. In this book such matters can be given little more than a passing glance from time to time.

If the text, illustrations and bibliography of this book encourage the reader to a deeper involvement in the study of the ancient Near East, including the more recent discoveries, it will have achieved its purpose. Inevitably it is incomplete, not entirely up-to-date and stamped with the writer's choice of emphasis. It would not be human if it were otherwise.

Charles Burney
MANCHESTER 1977

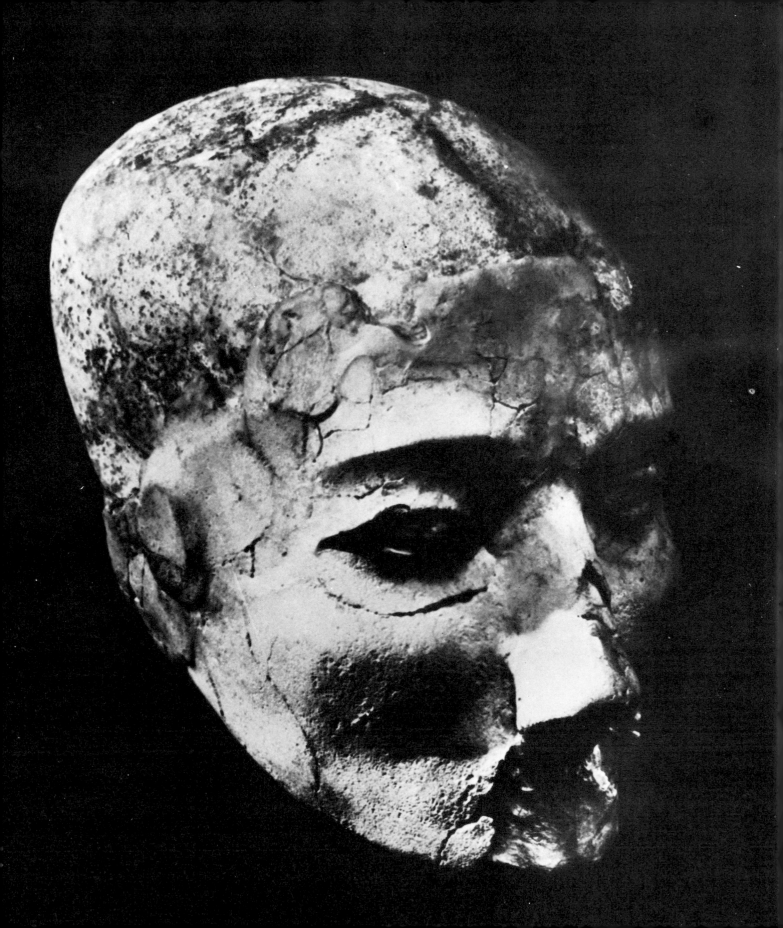

The Neolithic Revolution in the Near East

This first chapter attempts to outline the salient features of a continuing process in widely differing regions of the Near East: man's hesitant but on the whole growing mastery of his natural environment. The age of glib explanations of the transition from food-gathering to food-producing has passed for ever: the more becomes known, the greater must be the recognition of the complexities of the problems surrounding early agriculture and stock-breeding.

It is self-evident that the morphological changes apparent in animal bones of presumably domesticated species must have required thousands of years to develop. Changes in cereals must likewise have covered a long time-span. Pressure of population created, as much as resulted from, the conditions favourable to the emergence of permanent, perennial villages. Much of the credit given to Neolithic man should go to his Upper Palaeolithic ancestors.

Local factors account for the appearance of phenomena such as Jericho and Çatal Hüyük, each probably serving a wide hinterland. Defence became a paramount necessity wherever fertile land and, above all, a reliable water supply were available within a restricted area: hence the Pre-Pottery Neolithic A (PPNA) defensive wall and tower of Jericho. Çatal Hüyük seems to have served as a gathering centre for the wide Konya Plain. The earliest settlements in western Iran and upper Mesopotamia can now be seen as the forerunners, at least indirectly, of the later urban communities.

Trade must not be given a disproportionate significance in these early phases, though at least it proves that there was, even in Neolithic times, no such thing as total isolation. A common Upper Palaeolithic inheritance lay behind an advance by no means uniform, but now to be seen in the context of the greater part of the Near East. The identity of separate centres of Neolithic development has proved largely illusory, the outcome of inadequate investigation. Geographical distinctions cannot, however, be ignored.

THE ENVIRONMENT

The questions of why, where and when ancient man turned from the gathering to the production of his food become ever more complex as evidence increases and methods of investigation improve. Consequently, no simple answers, only broad lines of approach, can be indicated.

Recent research suggests that the Near East in the closing stages of the Pleistocene era, and in the millennia immediately following the last glaciation, was to some degree colder and drier than today, though north Africa was wetter. The former theory of climatic deterioration, of increasing aridity, with its corollary that the Near East enjoyed the benefit of the Atlantic depressions which now cross Europe, must therefore be abandoned. Pollen analyses suggest that the distribution of trees, apart from the maritime forests fringing the southern

1. Opposite: The famous plastered skulls of Jericho provide contemporary evidence of the appearance of the Proto-Mediterranean race inhabiting the town during the seventh millennium BC. Even the detail of the use of cowrie shells for the eyes appears also at Çatal Hüyük, emphasizing the wide extent of this ancestor cult and the readiness of Neolithic man to travel long distances.

shores of the Black Sea and the Caspian, was more restricted before *c*. 8000 BC than in the subsequent millennia. Recent contraction in the areas of woodland has been the outcome of human interference. In the environmental conditions of the parklands of the Levant, however, trees continued to flourish in the late Pleistocene era. Any simple generalizations about the climate of the Near East ten thousand years ago are sure to be misleading, for within quite short distances there were sharp variations dependent on local peculiarities. These are not yet sufficiently understood: they certainly decided whether the environment of each area was more or less favourable to early pastoralism and agriculture than at the present time. For example, in contradiction to the theory of greater aridity in Neolithic times, the situation of certain early settlements in Palestine and Jordan hardly suggests less rainfall than today. Evidence of erosion, however, indicates aridity over most of the year. Annual precipitation could have been greater than today without being any more evenly distributed through the year, thus providing no better conditions than those of the present time. Total annual precipitation by itself should not be over-emphasized.

The concept of the Neolithic Revolution is still valid in its stress on the significance of the change from the gathering to the production of food, if not in the implications of this term for the mechanics of that change. The available evidence still indicates the Near East as the birthplace of agriculture and pastoralism. Recent upward adjustments of radio-carbon dates in Europe need to be set against corresponding modifications for the Near East. Moreover, no such adjustments affecting the absolute chronology of prehistoric Europe can alter the presence of sites large enough to bear the description of town at Jericho and Çatal Hüyük before *c*. 6000 BC, as outlined below. Whatever the ultimate end of these communities, Neolithic man in the Near East seems to have achieved a very high degree of control over his environment, to the limit of his economic needs.

The Neolithic Revolution in the Near East was no sudden event, even if it can be dated in many areas within the period *c*. 9000–7000 BC. The control of the environment by stock-breeding and cultivation must have led to a growth in population; but it would be a mistake to suggest that the Upper Palaeolithic hunters and fishermen were wholly unorganized and at the mercy of environmental changes or the related movements of wild animals. Just as these, both herbivores and carnivores, have their own territorial limits, so too the Upper Palaeolithic ancestors of the Neolithic population assuredly hunted within certain generally recognized boundaries. Leisure time was abundant in the long millennia of the cave-dwelling hunters and their contemporaries living in humble shelters in the Russian steppes, nor was their diet inferior to that of the later farmers. It was the impetus to rapid change which was lacking before the advent of food production: with that economic revolution came the will to achieve further technological advances, together with the ever-widening influence of trade.

The Upper Palaeolithic background has immediate relevance to the Neolithic communities of the Near East, if only because the most recent opinion suggests pressure of population from the favourable hunting habitats into the more marginal areas as the stimulus ultimately leading to food production. The broadening of the diet of Upper Palaeolithic groups to include molluscs, fish, fowl and a variety of vegetable foods seems the only possible explanation for improved health and expectation of life, and thus for growth of population. Moreover, the evidence of physical anthropology indicates ethnic continuity.

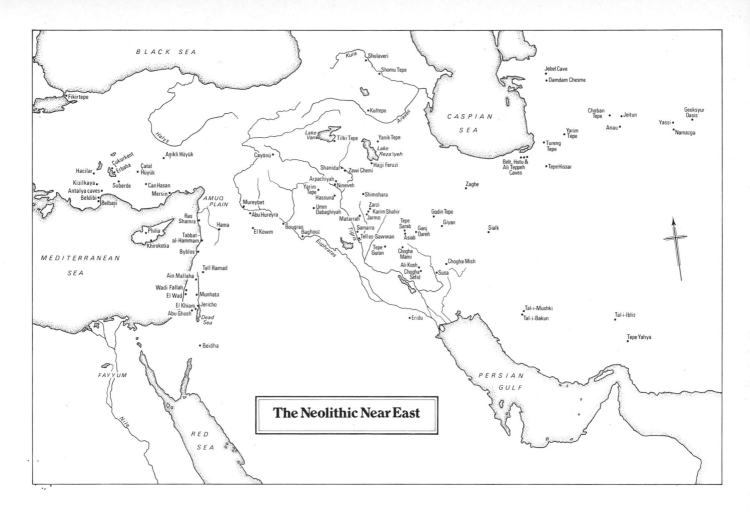

2. Map showing Neolithic sites in the Near East.

The Levant and Anatolia at least were occupied by people of common ancestry, sharing such a significant tradition as the detachment of the skull from the body before burial. This practice has been found, in variant forms, at Jericho, Beidha and Tell Ramad in the Levant and at levels at Hacilar not yielding any pottery (aceramic), and at Çatal Hüyük in Anatolia [1]. Obsidian most clearly illustrates trade, through analyses of impurities traceable to defined regions, if less plausibly to precise sources. Migratory movements may be suggested, if hardly proved, by the arrival of alien plants in a new habitat, exemplified perhaps by the appearance of einkorn wheat, of northern derivation, in Jericho Pre-Pottery B (see p. 18).

Environmental factors and their relatively slow changes deserve first place in any enquiry into the period in which the economy of a given region underwent the transition towards food production. Any search for the first 'inventors' of agriculture or stock-breeding is sure to end in disappointment. The Neolithic Revolution was not achieved in any single centre, subsequently spreading over the rest of the Near East and beyond. Nor is it the origin of an 'invention' which the archaeologist should seek: it is better for him to study the emergence of food production as a gradual, even haphazard, change in its early phases, and perhaps hardly, if at all, accelerated by deliberate human intent.

The improvement of wild strains of cereals may have been a natural outcome of reaping, without any conscious selection by early farmers. Wild wheat has been found growing in areas such as the upper Tigris valley around Diyarbakir in south-eastern Turkey and in other parts of the piedmont country bordering the Fertile Crescent, in more than sufficient abundance to have supported village settlements. Here there would have been little stimulus to develop improved strains through domestication. Such an incentive was far more likely to exist on the periphery of an area where cereals grew wild, where conditions for their survival were only marginally favourable, with fluctuations from year to year according to rainfall. If cereals were to remain a staple food, some improvement on mere collecting of wild grain had to be evolved. In such areas, therefore, were the conditions for the domestication of wheat and barley. The distribution of wild emmer, einkorn and two-row barley in the Near East is thus unlikely to coincide with patterns of Neolithic settlement.

The origin of domestication of animals is a problem related to that of the cultivation of cereals in that it has rightly been emphasized as a mainstay of Neolithic settlements. But evolutionary processes already set in motion, therefore originating in Palaeolithic times, may have been at least partly responsible for osteological changes in sheep, goats, pigs and cattle too readily attributed to the effects of domestication. Animal bones from excavations can indicate the diet of a community and elucidate its standard of living and perhaps also its health; but efforts to differentiate wild from domestic species may frequently prove vain.

Food collecting may therefore have merged imperceptibly into food production, from the first limited gathering of wild wheat and barley and the earliest coralling of cattle, sheep and goats by Upper Palaeolithic hunters in the Near East to the systematic exploitation of animal and plant resources by Neolithic villagers and by the inhabitants of the first towns. Imperceptible as this development may have been, however, there came a time when a proportion of the population abandoned the life of the nomad, or the hunter living in caves or rock shelters or temporary camps, and began to build themselves permanent or seasonal settlements in the open air, normally close to fresh water. In different regions of the Near East the manner and date of this transition will become clearer as a result of the growing number and thoroughness of excavations devoted to a solution of this problem. In the Zagros highlands of Iraq and Iran and in the Natufian cultural province in Palestine much has already been achieved to this end. Once communities began to live in open-air settlements of a perennial character the Neolithic Revolution was in effect completed, since the demands of agriculture had in most places, though not in all, come to surpass in economic importance those of hunting. Stock-breeding by itself would not necessarily have resulted in sedentary populations. Not till this change in living habits had come about was hunting, the old way of Palaeolithic life, set on its slow but irreversible decline. Meanwhile in many areas, even in the sedentary communities, it continued to flourish. Thus it is best to regard the early villages of the Near East as being sustained by a mixed economy.

The ability of man to control his environment, for better or for worse, was to have far-flung effects only with the spread of two activities which began, with the probable exception of Jericho, not at the beginning of settled life but some time afterwards. The first of these was irrigation, by which is meant the diversion of any river or stream, whatever its size or speed of flow, from its natural course, in order to water the largest possible area of cultivable land in any region with insufficient rainfall for dry farming. Irrigation may require communal organization, as in the flood plain of Mesopotamia; or it may be easily achieved by a few families, as in the oasis of Jericho [*Pl 1*]. The distinction is surely important enough to account for the separation of three millennia between the foundation of Jericho as a town (*c.* 8000 BC) and the establishment of the earliest Sumerian cities. But whatever its scale the effects of irrigation were often permanent and always far-reaching, both ecologically and socially. In some parts, such as south-western Iran (Khuzistan), crop yields may have increased by half over those from dry farming; and a reliability of food supply impossible with the simpler method was achieved. At least in Mesopotamia the larger mammals, such as the aurochs and deer, were driven to the fringes of the cultivated land, if not made locally extinct, within the first centuries of an urbanized economy. By this period, some time after the Neolithic Revolution, plant life had also been irretrievably changed, with the proliferation of crop weeds.

It has aptly been observed that any reconstruction of the Upper Palaeolithic environment in the Near East, whose balance had thus been upset, must depend on pollen samples and on bone debris. The social effects of irrigation in Neolithic times have been demonstrated by comparison with conditions in the Near East today, where until recent reforms the very small percentage of the total land surface accessible to irrigation, thus yielding the greater part of the food supply, tended to be in very few hands. This encouraged the stratification of societies into rich and poor, landowner and serf.

The second activity of man which greatly affected the natural environment, almost entirely for the worse, was the felling of forests. This became widespread only when the demands of building on a large scale and of shipbuilding had reached a significant level. From the late fourth millennium BC onwards, as recounted in written sources or implied by archaeological discoveries, the extraction of cedar-wood from the Amanus mountains and from the Lebanon for Mesopotamia and Egypt respectively became an enduring economic and political factor in the Near East [*Pl 2*].

Thus the natural environment of the Near East came to undergo permanent changes, which, once started, could scarcely be reversed. Deforestation has had disastrous consequences; and irrigation, when practised to excess, or without provision for drainage, has caused progressive deterioration of the soil through increasing salinity, especially in the alluvial plains. There is no need to seek explanations for the Neolithic Revolution in the Near East in climatic changes for which the evidence is at best conflicting, at worst negative. In this delicately balanced ecological zone, subdivided into many local environments, the effects of human activity were slow but eventually immeasurable, once they had gathered momentum. The initial slowness of any impact on the environment was related to the small size of populations. The narrower but surer basis of the economy, in cultivation of cereals and in breeding of sheep and goats and later of cattle, marked a radical change from the wide Upper Palaeolithic variety of diet through hunting and collecting. It was this innovation which in due course created renewed pressure on the relatively limited areas of suitable land and thus further environmental changes.

THE LEVANT

In the Levant the mixed oak woodlands had apparently supported a thriving Upper Palaeolithic population. Indeed the stimuli to change were perhaps less strong than in some other parts of the Near East, the people of the Natufian

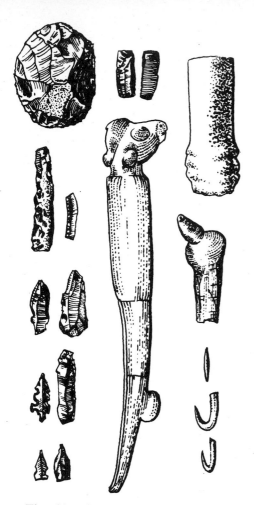

3. The chipped- and ground-stone industries and the bone industry provide evidence of daily life in Natufian communities. (above) The carved bone haft of a sickle illustrates their artistic skill and the bone fish-hooks a means of livelihood. Flint and chert, but not obsidian, were used for implements, sickle blades being common and set in bone hafts. (opposite) The flint lunate microliths (top row) and the bone harpoon head and awls give added evidence for the economy.

culture in Palestine subsisting for a long time on intensive collection of wild cereals, in some places supplemented by fishing, which was the main diet at Ain Mallaha (Eynan) beside Lake Huleh. The Natufian communities were only semi-sedentary, but it is with them that the Neolithic Revolution may justly be said to have begun in the Levant. The high radio-carbon dates for Lower Natufian Jericho and the continuity, or at least length of occupation, at a number of settlements from this early period into the full aceramic Neolithic culture are two good reasons for beginning the regional discussion of the Neolithic Revolution in the Levant, even if its highest attainments and most far-reaching effects were manifested elsewhere.

This culture has been variously subdivided into Lower, Middle and Upper Natufian and into Natufian I–IV. There is good reason to judge the Natufian I phase as the most creative. Ain Mallaha, Wadi Fallah (Nahal Oren), Jericho and Beidha have all yielded Natufian I remains, showing the wide distribution of this culture even in this earliest phase. But the terraced slopes of El Khiam in the Judaean desert have yielded no Natufian I material, suggesting that the Natufian culture originated in the more favourable areas of the Levant, only its later phases being represented at El Khiam.

The most impressive evidence of the Natufian culture has been excavated at Ain Mallaha, an open-air settlement covering half an acre, with about fifty huts in use at any one time. These range in diameter from 2.5 to 9 m. and were grouped round an open area, suggesting a hut compound, with many plastered bell-shaped storage pits. Three levels were distinguished and three types of burials, all within the settlement and often sprinkled with red ochre: individual burials, collective burials in pits and collective secondary burials after decomposition of the flesh. The most remarkable burial in the second level, presumably of a chieftain, contained two skeletons, extended and with legs removed and out of position: one was an adult male, the other probably a woman, with a head-dress of dentalium shells, found also at Mugharet el Wad, one of the caves on Mount Carmel. Earth, a stone pavement, a hearth, more earth and another pavement were successively laid above these burials, the circular tomb being five metres in diameter, probably the round house formerly used by the dead man. A plastered, red-painted parapet surrounded the whole tomb. Evidence of Natufian burial customs comes also from Wadi Fallah: detached skulls occur at both sites. Most of the Natufian burials at Wadi Fallah were surrounded by stones, with others beneath the skeleton. One grave contained a complete skeleton and four skulls, together with reliefs, engravings, stone beads and bone implements. This site had large terrace walls and two Natufian occupation levels, a camp site and then an oval building of stone construction.

The stone industry at Ain Mallaha was more advanced than in the Mount Carmel caves; but even there no arrowheads occur, an innovation not found until the declining stages of the culture (Upper Natufian). Microliths of lunate form must have been used for composite weapons. Picks, chisels and engraving tools, the last commonly called burins, suggest cultivation of the soil and the carving of wood and bone, the latter for fish-hooks and harpoon-heads [3].

Not all Natufian sites reveal continuity of occupation into the Neolithic periods. At Beidha, near the ruins of the Nabataean city of Petra, Natufian implements were found stratified beneath 3.5 m. of wind-blown sand. This chipped-stone industry included lunate microliths, blades, points and scrapers; but the most characteristic implement was the notched blade, with a variety of notches, suggesting the importance of woodworking and thus the presence of trees. Otherwise this industry resembles that of Mugharet el Wad Level B2. The chipped-stone industry of Jericho until the end of the eighth millennium (Pre-Pottery Neolithic A [PPNA]) period was in the same tradition, but displays a lack of variety, the only common forms being burins, borers, small bifacial chisels and adzes.

Jericho must have pride of place both for the length of its occupation and for the size and importance of the PPNA settlement. Near the north end of the mound a structure was excavated, where the natural clay, a foot thick overlying the limestone bedrock, had been retained as a low platform, the rock being exposed by removal of the clay in the surrounding area. A stone wall enclosed this space, which measured 6.5 × 5.5 m. The clean condition of the clay platform, with debris on the surrounding rock, added to the impression that this may have been a shrine, though this can scarcely be proved. This was the earliest occupation at Jericho, dated by microliths and a bone harpoon-head, such as occur only in the Natufian I levels at Mount Carmel. This was the period of expansion and of artistic talent in carving of stone and bone by the Natufian people.

The story of Jericho continues with the period termed Proto-Neolithic, represented by remains discovered in only one part of the site and forming a small mound concealed by the later levels. This mound comprises four metres of numerous successive layers, with remains of flimsy structures revealed by floors with slight humps marking the walls. These are of interest for the development of building methods, for they were at least partly constructed of lumps of clay of a size to be held in the hand. A minimum duration of several centuries seems likely.

Then one of those dramatic changes, often so hard to explain in man's past, occurred at Jericho. This was marked initially by the appearance of a distinctive architectural form, the round house, by its very shape suggesting nomadic origins in flimsier tent-like structures. Soon afterwards the settlement was enclosed by a formidable defensive wall, built to protect the greatly expanded community, traced in three excavation trenches and thus evidently surrounding an area of about four hectares, comparable with that of the Early Bronze Age town about five millennia later. These defences can be attributed to a date around 8000 BC, and include a massive round tower of water-worn stones set in hard clay [4]. This demonstrates the presence in the surrounding country of potentially hostile people, without whom the necessity to build these defences would scarcely have arisen. The generally accepted explanation that this expansion of Jericho resulted from rapid improvements in agriculture and domestication of animals in the fertile oasis, with the communal organization involved in irrigation, is probably correct, even though the palaeobotanical evidence and the animal bones hardly yet prove this. Clearly such defences, built after the first expansion of the community, were not the work of a population solely dependent on hunting and fishing. Trade certainly played a part, Jericho commanding salt, bitumen and sulphur from the Dead Sea; but it is hard to believe that it can have been on a large enough scale to provide a major proportion of the livelihood of the inhabitants, who probably numbered up to three thousand. The tower lasted through four phases; the third was marked by its incorporation in a completely rebuilt defensive circuit, with a ditch laboriously hewn out of the natural limestone, a considerable feat in the absence of metal tools. The rock chippings were used as the backing, against the earlier perpendicular wall, for a massive revetment wall with a pronounced batter. The fourth and final phase comprised the

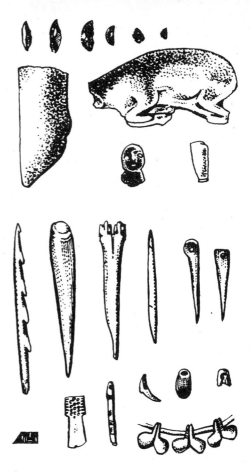

4. The tower and defences of Jericho lasted through four phases, in the first being associated with a perpendicular, free-standing wall. In the second phase it was reinforced by an outer skin of stonework; against the north segment of the tower were structures with thin, in-curving walls, having no doorways and presumably serving for storage. Probably at the end of this second phase came an attack on the town, since several bodies were found hurriedly pushed inside the entrance passage giving access to a staircase, but by then largely silted up.

rebuilding of this wall, reusing the bottom courses of the preceding phase. The store-rooms had also been rebuilt. Whether the tower was unique or one of a series at intervals round the defensive perimeter is quite uncertain. Impressive as these defences are, they must not obscure the fact that their construction shows more ingenuity than technical skill: the stones used in the defences were carefully laid but not dressed, only split; and the available stone tools were scarcely sophisticated. Other crafts besides the working of stone and bone and the weaving of rush mats and baskets are but meagrely attested.

The typical round house of this period at Jericho was of beehive plan, with an incurving wall of mud-brick, probably roofed with wattle-and-daub. Some had an entrance passage; others were semi-subterranean, with steps down into the house from outside. The bricks used were of a distinctive shape, plano-convex. Other sites of the PPNA period, at Jericho approximately equivalent to the eighth millennium BC, are few.

The stone industry of Wadi Fallah, a settlement on Mt. Carmel of the PPNA period, appears to suggest the arrival of northerners, who did not reach Jericho until the following period, and who had affinities with the Tahunian culture of southern Syria. There are variations in the chipped-stone tools in different huts: it may be that the smaller huts were inhabited by one man or woman, the larger by a man and woman together. South of Lake Tiberias two sites have remains of the PPNA period: this is indicated at Munhata especially by the stone industry of the two lower levels; and at Sheikh Ali by round houses in the lowest level and by the stone industry.

It seems likely that the PPNA period represents a stage of only incipient agriculture and stock-breeding. Gazelles may have been rounded up and kept in captivity, as the abundance of their bones suggests. Only the goat may have been truly domesticated. Moreover, it has been claimed that the territory surrounding a number of sites, including Wadi Fallah, comprised mainly rough grazing, with only one fifth of the land being potentially arable. But such restrictions must have been overcome in later periods.

The Neolithic village of Beidha was aceramic, with seven levels, not corresponding precisely to the sequence at Jericho, perhaps because it was more open to influences from the north. After polygonal houses (Beidha VI), the architectural traditions of the PPNA culture were preserved in the development of curvilinear houses, round in Level V and sub-rectangular with gently curving walls in Level IV. In Beidha III, when the Pre-Pottery Neolithic B (PPNB) culture had become firmly ensconced, there came a radical change in architecture, with the first 'corridor buildings', comprising a central passage about six metres long with three rooms off each side, the whole structure being so massive as to suggest an upper storey. The external contacts of Beidha are exemplified by obsidian imported from Anatolia, partly at least in exchange for cowrie shells. The wealth of the community was indeed clearly based on manufactures and on trade, the former evident in its workshops and the latter made understandable by its geographical situation, giving it the same advantages as those much later enjoyed by Petra as a caravan city.

Eventually the defences of PPNA Jericho fell, either gradually into decay or more probably to attack. The site was then abandoned long enough to leave traces of weathering and even of a turf line. When it was reoccupied the material culture had radically changed. But just as the discoveries at Beidha demonstrate the blending of elements of both cultures, PPNA and PPNB, so do burial customs indicate a strong line of continuity, presumably drawing on a tradition common to a wide zone, well beyond Palestine. In PPNA Jericho two groups of skulls attest an ancestor cult: a circle of skulls facing inwards and three sets of three facing in the same direction. These are clearly prototypes of the famous plastered skulls, and show a precocious ability to model the human face, variously embellished with bivalve or cowrie-shells for the eyes and by touches of paint for a moustache. Without these the people of Jericho and other communities of this culture would appear devoid of artistic talent, at least as applied to durable materials. The plastered skulls were found in a building directly above a level filled with poorly preserved human remains, mostly fractional burials, with bones thrown in after the bodies were largely decomposed; the intact burials were in a crouched position. Many of these bodies lacked a skull, as with contemporary burials at Beidha, but retained their mandible (lower jaw), except in one instance. The same funerary custom has been discovered in Tell Ramad II, south-west of Damascus, where red-plastered skulls occur.

It seems that Tell Ramad may lie in the homeland whence the newcomers bringing the PPNB culture arrived in Palestine. Their chipped stone industry was Tahunian, including a considerable proportion of arrowheads, some of

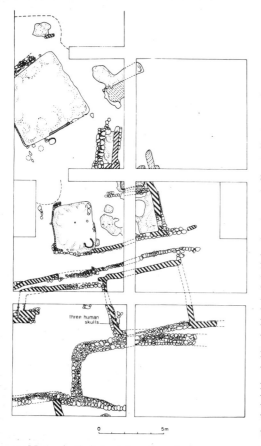

three human skulls

0   5m

5. Not only their burial customs but even more so their architecture distinguished the PPNB people. Rectangular house plans and plastered walls and floors, often with red paint for decoration and with corners and ends rounded, gave a recognizable character to a style of building known from many sites widely scattered through the Levant, including Ras Shamra VC-B, Hama M and Tell Ramad I–II, with traces northward into Anatolia. At Ras Shamra VB the first pottery appears, but otherwise the cultural tradition continued, with rectangular houses also in VA, in the early sixth millennium BC.

obsidian, and many flint denticulated sickle-blades. The Upper Natufian affinities of this industry are the surest indication that the newcomers may not have arrived from farther north than central Syria. The similarities between earliest Ras Shamra (Ugarit) V (see p. 114) and Jericho PPNB are less close than between the latter and Tell Ramad, where Level II dates to about the earlier half of the sixth millennium BC. However, before PPNA Jericho and other settlements had been overrun, the Tahunian people seem to have inhabited caves and camping sites in Palestine. Thus the cousins of the PPNB settlers remained with an economy not far removed from the Mesolithic. This was a foretaste of a perennial theme in the history of Palestine: conflict between settled peasants and townsmen, on the one hand, and restless nomads, often wishing to settle, on the other [5].

Jericho again is the most fully representative site of PPNB, demonstrating both the advanced layout of the town and the long duration of this period, with twenty-six phases in one part of the site. The houses are grouped round a courtyard, with smaller rooms for storage off the main room, contrasting with the haphazard arrangement of the PPNA houses. The plaster on floors and interior wall-faces was carefully smoothed, special stones being used to give the floors a high polish: these stones, often shaped like a cake of soap, were found in large numbers. That this architecture was introduced to Jericho from outside rather than developed locally is clearly discernible in the presence of a large building in the earliest level of this period, having a rectangular central room, 6 × 4 m., with a finely plastered hearth or basin in the middle. Other houses had large rooms, which, like the major buildings of Beidha III–II, must have required long beams for roofing. The bricks used were of a distinctive form, cigar-shaped, up to 50 cm. long and with two rows of thumb-impressions. The possibility that this was a more peaceful period than PPNA is suggested by the lack of any convincing evidence of a town wall. Two walls described as such seem to have served simply as revetment walls, and are hardly comparable with the defences of the earlier period. The group of skeletons connected with the skull cult must, however, point to violence of some kind. It is inherently improbable that Jericho remained entirely undisturbed throughout the seventh millennium BC.

The agricultural basis of the economy is demonstrated by grain, querns, rubbers and sickles; heavy stones pierced with a hole were probably used as digging sticks. Querns were frequently reused for the foundations of walls. The denticulated sickles may have been used to pull the ears off the wheat stalk rather than for cutting.

Apart from the obvious significance of the ancestor cult, Jericho did not reveal much evidence of the religious beliefs and cults of its inhabitants. There was, however, a building evidently serving as a shrine for some kind of pillar cult, presumably of chthonic significance, for in a niche with a stone pedestal at one end of a room there had originally been set a carefully shaped volcanic stone, fitting the niche exactly.

BYBLOS

The easiest routes for trade and movement from the Levant to Anatolia lay inland, away from the malarial swamps and river barriers of the narrow coastal plain. Nevertheless, a distinct cultural province is discernible here, commonly called the Byblos Early Neolithic, and combining features found in the Levant in the PPNB culture and in Anatolia in Çatal Hüyük VI (c. 6000 BC). At Byblos itself houses were built on their own, of rectangular plan and of mud-brick or reeds plastered with mud; the floors were of lime plaster, like those of Tell Ramad and Jericho. Houses had a main room and often also a store-room; hearths and benches or platforms were normal features. Although obsidian was rare, the elements paralleled at Çatal Hüyük VI include flint pressure-flaked dagger-blades and tanged arrowheads, clay stamp-seals and clay figurines. From Tabbat al-Hammam in the north to Beirut in the south settlements of this culture were thick on the ground. Axes for tree-felling are characteristic of those sites situated in the hills. Thus even in this period of several centuries, ending in about the mid-sixth millennium BC, the stretch of the Levant coast eventually to become the Phoenician homeland was already asserting its individuality.

In the lower Jordan valley the artistic traditions persisted, though in modified style, in the final phase of PPNB Jericho, in which there were at least three levels of buildings of rough, undressed stones, with earth instead of plaster floors, yielding a number of flat, disc-like heads, not modelled over skulls though with shells still used for the eyes. A complete head and bust, the head being very stylized and spade-shaped, was found in the latest surviving PPNB level. Jericho, and with it all Palestine, had entered on a long decline from which it emerged only in the late fourth millennium BC.

Khirokitia, on the south coast, is the most significant of the earliest settlements of Cyprus (Neolithic I): with three levels, it spanned much of the sixth millennium BC [6].

6. Khirokitia was a village of solidly built beehive houses, some with an upper storey, and workshops extending along a cobbled main road. Intramural burials have yielded a variety of personal ornaments and other grave goods. Vessels of andesite with spout and relief decoration are distinctive.

THE ANATOLIAN PLATEAU

Until the first major archaeological survey was carried out in 1951–2 over a very extensive southern zone of the Anatolian plateau, from the Konya Plain westwards, the general belief among archaeologists was that this was territory totally beyond the pale in terms of material culture until the advent of the Bronze Age. Nothing has changed more in the last two decades of archaeology in the Near East than the understanding of the achievements of the most advanced Anatolian communities from the seventh millennium BC onwards, even if their earliest antecedents remain obscure.

The current knowledge of Palaeolithic man in Anatolia is most inadequate, with scattered finds making only a fragmentary picture. One exception is the Antalya region, where a sequence of chipped-stone industries attributable to the Lower, Middle and Upper Palaeolithic periods, with traces of Neolithic habitation, has been distinguished at the Kara'in Cave. A phase termed Mesolithic, transitional between Upper Palaeolithic hunters and Neolithic hunters and farmers, is represented at Belbaşi near the Mediterranean coast, with a chipped-stone industry including tanged arrowheads but lacking obsidian. This strongly suggests that at this stage there were few contacts with the Anatolian plateau, where obsidian is abundant in certain areas. A sequence unique in Turkey, from Upper or even Middle Palaeolithic to early Neolithic, occurs at a rock shelter at Beldibi, though almost certainly it was not occupied continuously throughout those long millennia. The use of such shelters may anyhow have been seasonal. Rock-paintings, engravings and painted pebbles occur at the Antalya sites, especially Beldibi [7]. At the cave of Kurtun Ini, near the Konya Plain, are paintings of animals resembling ibex. The Antalya sites were not entirely isolated, however, for the Mesolithic stone industry of Beldibi has affinities with the Natufian of Palestine, as does the Upper Palaeolithic industry with that of Mount Carmel (Mugharet el Wad). Moreover, obsidian was imported into the Antalya district in Upper Palaeolithic times from Çiftlik near Niğde, or from some other source of obsidian with the same trace elements.

Clearly there was a chronological overlap between the Neolithic layers in the Antalya caves and shelters and the earliest levels of Neolithic villages on the Anatolian plateau; but by then the Antalya district must have been relatively backward. The immediate origins of the sophisticated cultures of Çatal Hüyük and Hacilar, doubtless represented also at numerous unexcavated sites, must be sought elsewhere, in all probability on the plateau.

At Hacilar, in south-western Anatolia and situated near Lake Burdur and just north of the Taurus mountains, a small mound comprising seven levels of houses with rectangular plans, built of mud-brick, was found concealed by the remains of the Late Neolithic and Early Chalcolithic village of the sixth millennium BC. The admittedly slender evidence of one radio-carbon sample suggests a date just before c. 7000 BC. Carbonized grain and clay storage boxes imply, though scarcely prove, that agriculture was at least one mainstay of the economy. A distinctive, if negative, feature of this village is the absence of pottery. Connections with distant parts of the Near East are revealed by the discovery of human skulls, buried without any trace of the rest of the skeleton, a manifestation of the widespread Neolithic ancestor cult. Another feature widely found in the earliest settlements is red-painted plaster on walls and floors. With the end of this aceramic village the site of Hacilar was deserted throughout the seventh millennium BC.

Another site perhaps earlier in its beginnings than Çatal Hüyük was Aşikli

7. The engravings at Beldibi, including a bull and a deer, are in a naturalistic style, partly covered by the paintings, and thus earlier and presumably Upper Palaeolithic. The paintings, in the same reddish-brown pigment as used for the pebbles, are in a conventionalized style. Illustrated here (above) are a bull from Öküzlü'in, human figures and cruciform and other motifs.

Hüyük, near the south end of the Salt Lake, not yet excavated; but six metres of deposit have been exposed by a river, showing red-painted plaster low down in the section. The chipped-stone industry could be earlier than that of Çatal Hüyük or merely a regional variant: the painted plaster suggests the latter probability. The obsidian industry was largely for the killing of animals and the cleaning and preparation of hides. Projectile points are curiously scarce, in contrast with the abundance of lanceheads at Çatal Hüyük. But different types of hunting weapon were required for different fauna. The microliths from Suberde, a small site with permanent dwellings beside Lake Suğla, about sixty miles west-south-west of Çatal Hüyük, could hardly have dispatched the great aurochs (*Bos primigenius*) so typical of the Konya Plain. Yet this was a community still mainly dependent on hunting, domesticated species being unrecognizable among the 25,000 animal bones collected by the excavator. Agriculture was practised, perhaps merely as a supplement to hunting.

Cultivation of food plants was clearly well established over many parts of the Near East, including much of the Anatolian plateau, by the early seventh millennium BC if not before. Moreover, three widely separated sites—aceramic Hacilar V, Beidha VI and Bus Mordeh in Khuzistan—all suggest a consistent order of importance of cereal crops: the first being hulled two-row barley, followed by cultivated or wild emmer wheat, indigenous especially to the Levant, and then by wild einkorn wheat, typical of the highlands forming the outer north and east perimeter of the Fertile Crescent. Lentils, peas and vetch were also important elements of diet. Among many foods gathered wild were pistachio nuts and acorns.

Thus in the Konya Plain and other regions of Neolithic occupation in Anatolia there was the necessary basis, by *c.* 7000 BC, for the support of communities choosing to abandon the nomadic habits of their forefathers. Much of the Anatolian plateau remained, however, beyond the zone of the Neolithic economy, the limit of which seems to have passed not far north of Aşikli Hüyük, with the later Hittite homeland within the great bend of the River Halys (Kizil Irmak) lying beyond. Towards the Black Sea the earliest settlements may not antedate the fourth millennium BC, though the perishable nature of buildings constructed of timber makes this far from certain.

The environment of Çatal Hüyük was, perhaps, especially lush; and the community may have achieved a degree of domination over a very wide tract of the Konya Plain, with far-flung trade providing a motive for such expansion of power or influence. With the lack of any site of comparable size or sophistication Çatal Hüyük remains something of an enigma, a precocious phenomenon, testifying at the very least to the ingenuity and imagination of its people. Its sheer size, thirteen hectares, three times as large as Jericho, puts it in a class by itself among sites of comparable antiquity. The art and architecture of Çatal Hüyük invite speculation, justifiable if kept within limits. Precocious workmanship in a wide variety of materials must necessarily demand a radical reassessment of the abilities and cultural level of Neolithic communities in the Near East and beyond. The old simplicity of dependence on stone and metal artefacts and pottery to distinguish successive periods of human advance, from the Palaeolithic to the Iron Age, has long been abandoned: the first criterion to be modified in the Near East has been the presence or absence of pottery, which occurs only rather meagrely at Çatal Hüyük.

The prosperity of the people of Çatal Hüyük seems to have been based not so much on any improvement in diet over that of previous generations as on the

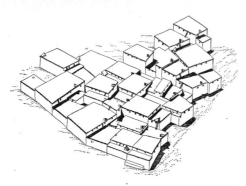

8. Architecture was conservative at Çatal Hüyük, with houses terraced up the sides of the mound, having no doorways at ground level but with access from the roof by a ladder set against the south wall. A simpler cellular layout has been uncovered at the mainly aceramic settlement of Can Hasan III, also in the Konya Plain.

9. In the hunting shrine of Level V the scenes show men clad in leopard-skin loincloths leaping and dancing around animals: the north wall was dominated by a bull, found in that position in a number of shrines from Level IX upwards. A frieze of wild asses runs along the lower register of part of the west and north walls; above, on the west wall, are two deer, one originally having its head modelled in relief, and a wild boar which two miniscule men are trying to ensnare in nets. Surrounding the bull on the north wall are men armed with bows, clubs and axes, some acting in an extraordinary way, leaping on the bull's back or trying to pull its tongue.

greater stability compared with the life of hunting groups. Trade must have played a significant role in accumulating the resources to support the craftsmen and perhaps also the priests and priestesses of the town. Agriculture and the unusual supply of meat from the herds of aurochs created enough surplus to support a minority not bound to spend all working hours in obtaining food. The art of the shrines, the reliefs and especially the figurines makes the primacy of the female in this society a strong probability, although the paintings, with their hunters and dancers and the absence of agricultural scenes, tend to emphasize the role of the male. It seems that the expectation of life for women increased, implying a better resistance to disease. Equally important was the greater availability of time for child-bearing, a major factor in the growth of population. Thus the evidence from the skeletal remains recovered in the excavations adds direct testimony to the general impression of a community very well adapted to the most advantageous exploitation of its environment.

Whether or not the shrines discovered in the excavated area extended over much or most of the remainder of the site, it is idle to speculate. These rooms, in their mural decoration, design, movable contents and burials, reveal most of what is known of Çatal Hüyük, and enable the archaeologist to approach as near as ever possible to an insight into the minds of a prehistoric people without written records. Naturally no precise label can be attached to the population, although their physical remains suggest mixed ethnic origins, comprising an older Proto–Mediterranean and a newer round-headed (brachycephalic) element.

Two of the shrines, in Levels III and V but perhaps only fifty years apart in date, provide the clearest evidence of the importance of hunting, which was probably still a major means of subsistence or at least a significant memory; and this evidence is reinforced by the numerous obsidian lanceheads, surface examples of which contributed to the first recognition of the potential distinction of the mound. If any animal was hunted purely for the excitement and prestige of the chase it was the leopard, probably even then more at home in the Taurus foothills than in the plain surrounding the town: one shrine in Level VII had

two leopards in plaster relief, replastered some forty times, as its focus. Leopard-skin headdresses as well as loincloths are frequently represented; and some of the female statuettes described under the general heading of goddesses are shown holding leopard cubs, supported by leopards or wearing a leopard-skin dress. Similar female statuettes in Hacilar VI provide an element of continuity with the slightly earlier art of Çatal Hüyük II and also the basis of the excavator's claim that they can be compared with the 'Mistress of Animals' of Classical times. Continuity over many millennia is very possible in popular Anatolian religion [9].

Agriculture and stock-breeding probably played an increasing part in providing the means of subsistence for the population of Çatal Hüyük as the life of the town continued. Sheep and goats seem to have been domesticated from the earliest known levels. The palaeobotanical evidence is rather surer, revealing that at least fourteen food plants were under cultivation by the time of Level VI, some probably used for their oil. The grape and the olive appear not to have been cultivated before the fourth or third millennium BC. Sugar was presumably obtained from honey, whose use may be implied by a wall-painting showing insects and flowers. Picks and hoes for breaking the soil seem to be absent from the otherwise varied stone industry: implements made solely of wood may have been used. The women must have borne much of the burden of work in the fields and outside their houses, where they would have used the many querns, pestles and mortars.

At Çatal Hüyük houses were entered from the roof [8]. Climate and security alike made this access advantageous, the gloomy interiors being cool in summer and snugly warm in winter, conforming with subsequent traditional design in the Near East. Only the eyes of those working indoors would have suffered: these may have included the women and girls, who spent the long winter nights weaving the *kilîms* (woven rugs) which hung on many of the walls, or woollen cloth for garments. Methods of building were not static, however, since the earlier fashion of construction around a timber frame with flimsy filling of mud-bricks was by Level II completely supplanted by construction in brick, with mud-brick piers replacing the vertical posts [10]. Reeds served as roofing material, then as today in Anatolian villages, bundles being placed on matting across the supporting beams, with a layer of mud on top of all. The local availability of these materials has made this the traditional method of roofing in much of the Near East, though nowadays the beams can be rather costly, being less easily obtainable. The chief disadvantage is the weight, which eventually cracks the beams and is a danger in an earthquake. Modern parallels suggest that the walls of both houses and shrines had to be replastered annually, in the spring, and indicate that the buildings of Çatal Hüyük could have had a long lifetime, provided that they were regularly repaired. The worst threat to exterior walls, erosion of the foundations by rain, was minimized at Çatal Hüyük by the arrangement of houses and shrines in blocks or *insulae*. White earth was used for plastering walls, floors and ceilings: in Çatal Hüyük VII there were 120 layers of plaster and in VIB up to 100 layers, with fewer in the other levels, but with the number of layers of plaster approximately the same in buildings of the same level [11].

Interior layout was fairly standardized. Fixed beds along the walls were used as seating in daytime. Light must have come from clerestory windows. The kitchen with its hearth and oven was always next to the stair ladder on the south side, to allow heat and smoke to escape. The good preservation of houses and

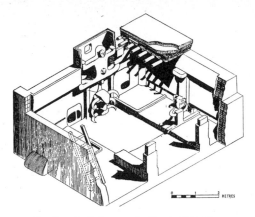

10. Earlier buildings of Çatal Hüyük were weakened by the way in which the walls were stepped in, a survival from lighter structures of wood and reeds, creating stresses which the lower part of the walls was hardly able to sustain. This is exemplified by this shrine.

11. The use of reeds is directly attested by this wall-painting at Çatal Hüyük which depicts a four-gabled building, from the representation of human skulls and headless skeletons evidently a charnel-house.

shrines, which share common features, has made reconstruction of the original appearance of the excavated area much more reliable than at most sites of this early date.

There is no evidence that any defences were ever built round the town, Çatal Hüyük perhaps being secure enough through the continuous and blank façades presented by the *insulae* of houses and shrines; and marshy ground may also have provided natural protection.

The fame of Çatal Hüyük rests largely, and surely in most spectacular form, on its numerous and often enigmatic wall-paintings, whose unexpected discovery initially presented very serious problems of recording and conservation. An outstanding difficulty is that the shrines were normally repainted at frequent or even regular intervals, either repeating the earlier picture or altering it wholly or in part. Reliefs too were recurrently replastered. In spite of the picture of a town [12], landscape as such was of little interest to the artists of Çatal Hüyük, who depicted scenes of hunting and its associated rituals in a concise style,

12. A unique wall-painting seems to depict a town such as Çatal Hüyük with a volcano, perhaps Hasan Dağ, in eruption in the background.

without distracting attention from the *dramatis personae*. The concept of art for art's sake is irrelevant in any context in the ancient Near East: this is true of Çatal Hüyük both in relation to the mural paintings and reliefs and to craftsmanship on a small scale. Artist and craftsman were one and the same, and both were circumscribed by the limitations of the materials and implements at their disposal and the injunctions and taboos of cult, ritual and magic, which will always be largely beyond our comprehension. For paints a variety of minerals was used, including iron oxides, copper ores, mercury oxide, manganese and galena. Different shades of red are predominant, from iron ore, cinnabar and perhaps also haematite. Pestles and mortars were used for grinding the colours; and brush strokes visible in some paintings show the use of very fine brushes. Modern analogies in the Konya Plain suggest that plain red panels, more characteristic of houses than of shrines, were rendered by using a rag dipped in paint.

So numerous are the works of these artists that it is possible to see what themes were foremost in their repertoire and so probably also in the minds of those who saw their masterpieces. One theme was the moment of birth, in the context of a shrine, with all that it implied to the community: the effect was usually achieved with the help of the third dimension, either by plaster relief alone or with massive bulls' horns or other, smaller animal skulls or tusks [*Pl 4*].

The artists of Çatal Hüyük did not confine themselves to painting but used relief in plaster, painted or left plain, especially in the earlier shrines, in one of which (Level VII) only reliefs occur. Paintings may have originated as early as reliefs, but did not attain their full popularity until Çatal Hüyük VIB. In a shrine of Level X, bulls' heads with enormously long horns suggest a phase not long after the beginnings of this artistic form. Reliefs went out of fashion after Level V, and at about the same time stone began to give place to clay as the commonest material for statuettes. Repairs to some of the stone statuettes suggest that they were closely connected with the cult of the shrines, though a male statuette with leopard-skin headdress evokes comparison with the dancers in the paintings of Levels V and III, and thus may represent a priest rather than a god. The female or matriarchal element was, however, by far the more dominant in the shrines.

Side by side with naturalistic statuettes were others crudely modelled in clay and aniconic stone figures, possibly inspired by collections of stalactites. Thus stylistic analysis in any attempt to discern a progression in skill will be sure to fail. Stone carving was also used for statuettes preserved from earlier shrines, when the time came to destroy and rebuild them, and when the fixed images on the walls were deliberately defaced. Only the discovery of workshops could provide a stratigraphic sequence of such statuettes. Towards the end of the history of Çatal Hüyük, however, a certain stylistic development is apparent: in one shrine of Level II were found nine statuettes, eight of clay, exhibiting parallels with the slightly later examples of Hacilar VI. By the early sixth millennium BC, therefore, a common artistic tradition, at least in sculpture in the round, had spread over much of the southern Anatolian plateau. This was the aspect of the art known at Çatal Hüyük most likely to become widely disseminated, if only because the statuettes were so easily portable. The paintings and reliefs can hardly have been seen by so many outsiders, who anyway may have been debarred from entering the shrines.

The combination of wall-paintings, reliefs, cattle horns set into benches, rows of bulls' heads, cult statuettes, human skulls on platforms and ochre burials

15. Opposite: Hands, shown here with a net, appear often in the paintings, usually the right hands of adults but sometimes of children: these are either painted by the artist or stuck on after dipping the hand in paint or left in reserve. In the modern village close to Çatal Hüyük such hands appear on either side of some doorways; and the hand is widespread as an amulet to ward off the evil eye or evil in general. These hands could represent a muster of the faithful or the act of those seeking strength from the walls of the shrines or from their images.

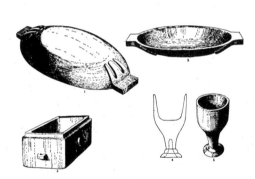

13. A variety of wooden vessels and boxes was recovered from Levels VIB–VIA at Çatal Hüyük, preserved in houses and burials by carbonization. Neither nails nor glue were used by the woodworkers. Soft woods for vessels were gouged out with obsidian scrapers and other implements, the final smoothing being effected with emery and sand.

differentiates the shrines from the houses, which seldom contain any of those. Birth led on to life and death to burial, these being the central themes of the art, and so also presumably of the cult, of these shrines. Each aspect of the life cycle had its own place, birth being represented on the west wall and death on the north and east walls, where the burials lay within the platforms. Bulls or cows occur on the north wall alone, the bull in later periods in Anatolia being associated with the weather god and storm god. Apart from the problems of the iconography of the shrines, there is the question of who were the worshippers and how they approached. Given the evidence of their duration, the shrines do not contain enough burials to be more than those of a few select persons [15].

The grave goods with burials in the shrines were richer than those in the houses, suggesting a priestly caste. Women were normally buried with a variety of jewellery and occasionally with an obsidian mirror; and men with hunting weapons, especially a dagger, and occasionally a belt with bone fasteners surviving. These, with the obsidian mirrors, were restricted to burials in the shrines. The people of Çatal Hüyük were as concerned as their contemporaries elsewhere in the Near East with the afterlife and with due provision for the dead [14].

The technical achievements of the people of Çatal Hüyük, whether professional craftsmen or householders exercising acquired or inherited skills, can scarcely be overestimated. Stone, clay, wood, bone, textiles and even metals were worked. Containers for domestic use and storage were made not only of pottery but also of wood, skins, basketry and stone. Pottery occurs right down to Çatal Hüyük XII, where straw-tempered and cream burnished wares were found: heavy bowls with a wide flat base and thick section. Such forms can be termed primitive; but the origins of pottery on the Anatolian plateau have yet to be traced. Stone vessels are rare, being laborious to make. The evidence for woodworking is more abundant than at any other site of comparable antiquity in the Near East. Soft woods were used for vessels and the harder woods, oak and juniper, were used in building for beams and posts, being squared with axes, adzes and chisels of greenstone: thus began the long Anatolian tradition of construction in wood [13].

The chipped-stone industry represents, in general terms, a development from earlier Upper Palaeolithic traditions; but grinding, polishing and drilling were also used in the manufacture of tools, weapons, statuettes, ornaments and vessels of stone. The obsidian mirrors were polished by an unknown technique. Maceheads were large enough for their perforation to present no great difficulty; but smaller stone beads, including some of obsidian, have perforations too fine for

14. These paintings in a shrine of Çatal Hüyük VII showing vultures attacking headless corpses illustrate not only the stripping of all flesh from the bodies, but also the prior removal of the skulls for separate burial, though this was not the normal custom at Çatal Hüyük. Red ochre was applied to the skull only or else to the whole skeleton in twenty-one excavated burials. Green paint was found with a few of the richest graves.

a modern steel needle. Copper drills can hardly have been used; but the discovery of both copper and lead, from Çatal Hüyük IX upwards, must indeed compel a reassessment of the technology of the most advanced Neolithic communities. Hammering and rolling of small pieces of native copper is hardly remarkable: far more significant is the possibility of smelting of copper and lead. Çatal Hüyük was not unique in this respect, for there are earlier hints of metallurgy from Çayönü, near Diyarbakir in south-east Turkey. A copper awl was found at Suberde. The absence of metal artefacts from Çatal Hüyük may therefore be fortuitous.

Another industry which seems to have flourished at Çatal Hüyük was that of weaving woollen textiles, both for clothing and for *kilîms*, these largely for hanging on walls. The carbonized fragments of cloth are evidently of wool, not linen, and include some of remarkably fine two-ply yarn spun from two very fine threads of wool. Fringes and knotted fragments occur; a plain weave is most common, and there is a looser weave, suitable for shawls. Vegetable dyes were used, including madder (dark red), woad (blue) and weld (yellow). These are, however, more perishable than the mineral pigments of the wall-paintings. Materials presenting no difficulties in their use were straw and rushes (for baskets and mats) and bone, carved and polished into spatulae, belt-fasteners and miniature vessels, also made from antler.

Imported materials include a variety of stones, indicating trade. Cowrie-shells found associated with a skull provide a clear parallel with PPNB Jericho: these shells came from the Red Sea, and may well have been obtained in exchange for obsidian from the Hasan Dağ region. Stamp-seals suggest the idea of ownership, and thus indirectly the organization of trade.

There seems no good reason to seek an origin for the culture of Çatal Hüyük beyond Anatolia, even if knowledge of the Early Neolithic period outside this site remains regrettably meagre. A backward contemporary of Çatal Hüyük was Can Hasan III, near Karaman, with very crude pottery from the latest levels but none beneath, an obsidian industry, and hulled barley among the plant remains. Far to the west, the site of Hacilar, long deserted after the end of the aceramic village, was reoccupied in the Late Neolithic period (Hacilar IX–VI), immediately followed by the Early Chalcolithic levels (V–I), after which the site was permanently abandoned. Near Beyşehir, and thus intermediate between Çatal Hüyük and Hacilar, is the mound of Erbaba, with at least two levels, characterized by plaster floors and, in the upper level, houses built of uncut limestone blocks. One significance of this site is its attribution to the early sixth millennium BC, overlapping the end of Early Neolithic Çatal Hüyük and Late Neolithic Hacilar. It thus provides a sequel to the Early Neolithic sites of the Lake Beyşehir region, known only from surface exploration, among them Çukurkent and Alan Hüyük on the shores of the lake. The environment of the Anatolian Lake District was evidently very favourable to early settlement. The pottery and obsidian industry of Çukurkent suggest parallels with Mersin (see p. 28), a variety of human and animal figurines of stone and clay also being found. At least five levels were distinguished in a cut at Alan Hüyük, some with traces of red-plastered floors. Farther west a few sites on either side of the Taurus range above Antalya are distinguished by the Kizilkaya culture, with pottery comparable with that of Çatal Hüyük and Late Neolithic Hacilar, which it may only just have preceded. In the Marmara region Menteşe, south of Lake Iznik, had red-plastered floors; Fikirtepe is the most important known site of this cultural province.

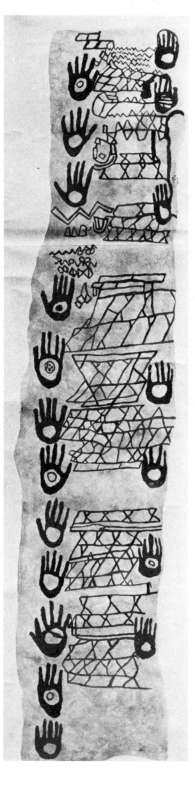

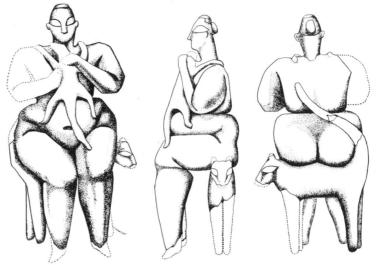

16. The finest of all these Hacilar VI statuettes is one of those classified as the Mistress of Animals, showing the goddess seated on a leopard and holding a leopard cub in her arms. This type, though better modelled, is in direct line of descent from the similar statuettes at Çatal Hüyük, scarcely earlier in date. But the variety of pose and subtlety of modelling put these statuettes in a class above any from Çatal Hüyük.

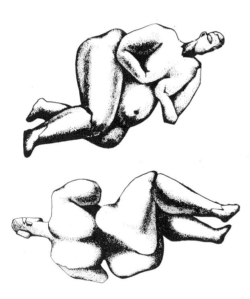

THE LATE NEOLITHIC IN THE ANATOLIAN PLATEAU: HACILAR AND MERSIN

Radio-carbon dates suggest a brief time-span for the whole Late Neolithic period of only about one century (*c.* 5700–5600 BC) at Hacilar IX–VI, the only other excavated site being Mersin XXVI–XXV. A very large cultural province extending from Lake Eğridir and Lake Burdur in the east across to the estuary of the Maeander River and northward along the Aegean coast almost to the Troad can now be distinguished by pottery of the fine quality and high burnish typical of Hacilar IX–VI. This was the earliest major westward extension of Anatolian influence to the Aegean coast to be widely attested. To the east, in the Konya Plain, Çatal Hüyük was abandoned, with a hiatus in the history of settled life represented by the deeper, unexcavated levels of Çatal Hüyük West. In the Cilician Plain Mersin XXVI–XXV form the culmination of the long succession of Neolithic levels, with some evidence of a decline in the role of hunting and a corresponding development of agriculture.

Hacilar remains the most significant site for the Late Neolithic period, distinguished by its architecture, pottery and clay statuettes. Hacilar VI was the most prosperous phase, when the village expanded to a size unsurpassed even by Hacilar II, and may have been fortified. The inhabitants relied less on hunting than their predecessors to the east at Çatal Hüyük, perhaps partly because the Burdur district was less rich in game. Dry farming was the mainstay of the community. Emmer, einkorn, bread wheat and some barley were cultivated. Cattle and sheep must have been domesticated. The people of Hacilar included two dolichocephalic groups, the widespread Proto-Mediterranean and a tougher Eurafrican element; the brachycephalic group present at Çatal Hüyük, probably as newcomers, is not in evidence.

Pottery and statuettes alike indicate the indigenous character of the Late Neolithic culture at Hacilar. There was a continuous ceramic development from the largely cream or light grey burnished ware of Hacilar IX–VIII to the pink to dark red ware of Hacilar VI, nearly all highly burnished and commonly with two or four vertical lugs. Oval bowls and theriomorphic vessels occur in Hacilar VI, when a little painting also appears, the origins of the painted pottery of the Early Chalcolithic levels. Successive fires did not destroy the cultural traditions of the community. Some of the clay statuettes were unbaked, thus necessarily made on the spot. Normally they were modelled round a core, finished with a fine red- or cream-slipped and burnished surface and with a separately made head with a peg for insertion into the body; coarser figurines of baked clay had wooden peg heads. In subject matter there is an obvious emphasis on fertility and childbirth, no adult males being represented; boys or youths are quite subordinate, as son or lover. Different ages and ranks, if not different ethnic groups, are represented among the statuettes, whose heads were of minor significance, no portraiture being intended. Aprons, bodices, robes and headgear of the high, conical, *polos* type all occur, though most women are shown unclothed. The largest of the statuettes is 24 cm. high, but most are little more than half as tall. In three adjoining houses was found the majority of the statuettes, though not so numerous that any full-time specialist workshop is suggested [16].

The common denominator of all the cultures called Early Chalcolithic, a useful term if not taken literally, is the appearance and development of painted pottery, a phenomenon found from the Aegean to Iran. In Anatolia two cultural provinces, exemplified by Hacilar V–I and by Çatal Hüyük West with Can Hasan IIB, yield evidence of local development from earlier beginnings. Only in the Cilician Plain, anyhow as closely linked with north Syria as with the Anatolian plateau, does Mersin XXIV–XX suggest strong outside influences. Hacilar provides older phases of the Early Chalcolithic period than those yet known from the Konya Plain, which are contemporary only with Hacilar I (c. 5250–5000 BC).

Hacilar V–III were less completely excavated than were the later levels. Hacilar III and IIA were partially burnt; Hacilar IIB was violently destroyed. Hacilar II had been enclosed by a perimeter wall; but Hacilar I was built on largely new lines, on a terrace dug out of the side of the mound. There were two phases (IA–IB), during which there was a massive mud-brick defensive wall, both ending in fire, followed by two phases of reoccupation (IC–ID) by impoverished squatters. The site was then finally abandoned. Clearly southwestern Anatolia suffered unsettled conditions in the Early Chalcolithic period, in the end succumbing to incomers from the north.

The most important building of Hacilar IIA may well have been a shrine, with a sliding door or screen dividing the main room into two halves: in the east part was a deep alcove with a broad, shallow recess at the back. This was empty, yet a similar but smaller recess in the north wall contained a smooth stone slab set upright, a hint of a cthonic cult, with many pots in front. Burials beneath the floor were the first found at Hacilar, where extramural burial must have been the rule. The painted pottery is the most distinctive feature of this period, unlike any found elsewhere in the Near East, with high burnish adding lustre to the colours and patterns, some of which could be derived from *kilims* or other textiles. Wide bowls in Hacilar V–III continued in II, but were largely displaced by the most typical form of that level, an oval cup with pinched mouth. Oval vessels were characteristic of the pottery of Hacilar V–I; there are also sub-rectangular forms [17].

In Hacilar IIA, in the middle of the village compound, three adjacent buildings clearly served as potters' workshops, and were stocked with painted cups, bowls and jars respectively, suggesting that each type of vessel was made by different potters. Many cakes of red and yellow ochre, used for paint on the pottery, were found on the floors, as well as quernstones with traces of these pigments and stone pounders, mortars and palettes [18, 19].

17. From geometric patterns of chevrons and triangles (Hacilar V–IV) the potters evolved the curvilinear, bolder decoration of the next phase (Hacilar III–II); motifs included the 'Japanese wave'.

18. In Hacilar I, perhaps rebuilt by newcomers, there was a change in the pottery, with the introduction of new forms yet without any complete break with the traditions of Hacilar V–II. Pots became larger, less imaginatively decorated and with linear patterns, largely imitating basketry.

19. At Çatal Hüyük West the earlier of two styles of painted pottery has continuous linear patterns, and corresponds to a phase when the culture of the Konya Plain was exerting an influence on that of the Cilician Plain (Mersin XXIV–XXII).

In Hacilar I a small proportion of vessels with white-painted decoration suggests the earliest origins of a tradition destined to reach its climax in the third millennium BC in Anatolia. The baked clay steatopygous statuettes of Hacilar II, larger than those of VI but less lifelike, were succeeded in Hacilar I by anthropomorphic 'goddess' vessels with obsidian eyes, all too attractive to the private collector.

Hacilar I can be put in its wider context more easily than the preceding Early Chalcolithic levels (V–II), for it is roughly contemporary with the Early Chalcolithic I–II phases in the Konya Plain, as they are with Mersin XXIV–XX and Amuq B in north Syria. The most significant advance in Can Hasan IIB in the Konya Plain was perhaps in metalworking, exemplified by a copper bracelet and macehead: as at Hacilar, copper occurs in all the Chalcolithic levels, suggesting a major role for Anatolia in the first stages of metallurgy. The fine meander motif on some of the painted pottery was reproduced on fragments of wall-paintings [20]; but the variety of themes of the mural art of Çatal Hüyük did not recur. Basement rooms are suggested by massive walls, internal buttresses and the absence of doorways at ground level: there is a general resemblance to Hacilar I. The culture of the Konya Plain, however, had a character of its own, influenced by Anatolian and Syro-Cilician traditions. It was to persist into the fifth millennium BC, without the break in continuity found in south-western Anatolia. There, after the final abandonment of Hacilar, soon after c. 5000 BC, an inferior culture appeared at Beycesultan, developing slowly through the long succession of Late Chalcolithic levels (XL–XX).

THE ZAGROS HIGHLANDS

The Zagros highlands of western Iran and Iraqi Kurdistan have for some years been widely regarded as one of the most significant zones in the emergence of settled, food-producing communities in the Near East. There are, however, no sites providing a stratigraphically continuous sequence comparable with those found in the Levant. There are probably still gaps in the sequence obtained by correlations between different sites, and the concentration of effort since 1960 in this zone has perhaps given it a prominence which may eventually be modified as discoveries are made in less well investigated parts, especially of Iran. Nevertheless, there is an accumulation of evidence to suggest that the change from complete dependence on food-collecting to a mixed economy, with an ever-increasing significance of agriculture and stock-breeding, began in some areas in the early ninth millennium BC, even though no settlements like those in Syria and Palestine based solely on food-collecting have so far been found in Iran. This intermediate stage was thus perhaps less protracted than in the Levant. Population seems to have increased sufficiently in the upland valleys of the Zagros highlands to explain migrations into new, hitherto unsettled lands. It seems very probable that a movement in the eighth millennium BC resulted in the first settlement of the plains of Khuzistan. By the later seventh millennium BC some seasonal sites in the Zagros had developed into perennial settlements. During the sixth millennium BC there appeared Neolithic villages in widely scattered regions of Iran and beyond, from the Urmia basin to Kashan, Fars and eastwards to Soviet Turkestan and north Afghanistan. It would be premature to assert, on present evidence, that the wide expansion of the Neolithic economy originated in the Zagros region. The connections of the earliest settlements of Khuzistan and the Urmia basin with the Zagros sites seem, however, indisputable. Some areas remained backward and still largely dependent on hunting: such were the rain forests of the south Caspian shore, with the Belt Cave and Hotu Cave.

The immediate precursors of the first food-producers in the Zagros are best exemplified by rock shelters in Iraqi Kurdistan, at Zarzi, Palegawra and Shanidar (Level B2). At this last a radio-carbon determination suggests a date around 10000 BC for this Zarzian culture. Other caves and shelters also yielded Zarzian material, including backed blades and end- and round-scrapers. The chipped-stone industry comprises microliths and larger blade-tools, and is in a general way comparable with the approximately contemporary Kebaran industry of the Levant. The Zarzian culture extended at least into the Kermanshah region, where it is represented at Gar Wawasi. It is possible, though not certain, that these Zarzian food-collectors, the last heirs of the Upper Palaeolithic traditions, had arrived from the Russian steppes to the north. The occurrence of some obsidian indicates relations with the region around Lake Van. There is a possibility that the Zarzian groups, though inhabiting caves and rock shelters, were already making tentative attempts at domestication of plants and animals; but they were primarily hunters and gatherers. This culture thus marks the first phase of the transition from the Palaeolithic way of life, traced in the Zagros back as far as the Mousterian culture. The Shanidar Cave gives the clearest sequence: in Level C an Upper Palaeolithic blade-tool industry, the Baradostian, preceded the Zarzian of Level B, with a hiatus between the two.

Other groups dependent on hunting and gathering, their diet including seal and red deer, have been investigated in the Belt and Hotu Caves above the south-east corner of the Caspian Sea. Farther east a similar way of life is evident from remains left by hunters of gazelle, ox, wild sheep and goat, who were also fishermen, and found at Damdam Cheshme and Jebel Cave, east of the Caspian in Turkmenia, and at the Snake Cave on the Balkh River in the northern foot-hills of the Hindu Kush. Collection of wild barley and wheat became in due course an element in the subsistence of these cave-dwellers, though radio-carbon determinations suggest that this did not emerge until c. 7000 BC, well after the period of the earliest villages in the Zagros highlands. These cave-dwellers were almost certainly not pioneers but late developing groups, clinging to Palaeolithic ways while gradually absorbing Neolithic imports, including soft-fired pottery. It is therefore tempting to speculate whether there may not have been more advanced groups already living in open, seasonal settlements at the same time as the known Zarzian groups were inhabiting their caves and shelters.

In the next phase the juxtaposition of an open settlement to a cave is well demonstrated by the village site of Zawi Chemi Shanidar, four kilometres from Shanidar Cave. Three phases of round huts, about four metres in diameter, were built of river boulders and whole or fragmentary querns, mortars and grinding stones; towards the end of the lifetime of the village buttresses and orthostats were used in construction. The great quantities of animal bones show that hunting was the major support of this community, with red deer the commonest bones in the lowest level; sheep also occurred, becoming more prominent and—as far as this question can be determined with any certainty—apparently domesticated in the upper levels, where bones of wild goat also occur. Carbonized grain is lacking, although the appearance during the lifetime of this village of a varied ground-stone industry, together with bone sickle-hafts, demonstrates preparation of vegetables. Herding of gazelle, sheep and goat may already have been practised by the inhabitants of Ali Tappeh Cave, above the south-east Caspian, so that it could have become far more widespread at this

20. The later phase, best known from Can Hasan IIB, has thinner and even better fired wares, mostly white-slipped, the finest Early Chalcolithic II pottery being decorated in dark brown paint on white or cream. Red-on-cream ware is also characteristic. At this time the direction of cultural influence was from the Cilician Plain (Mersin XXI–XX), with painted carinated bowls similar to some Early Halaf pottery occurring at Çatal Hüyük West, apparently before the time of Mersin XIX, the first of the three Halaf levels at that site. The role of these eastern elements in Cilicia and the Konya Plain should not, however, be exaggerated.

21. Ganj Dareh—to which these buildings belong—is outstanding not for its size, modest compared with Jericho or Çatal Hüyük, but for its evidence of architectural and technical achievements far beyond those of any other site of the eighth millennium BC, save only Jericho (PPNA).

23. Opposite: Plain and painted pottery from Tepe Guran. The earliest pottery at Tepe Guran is plain and straw-tempered, accompanied from the next level (Guran R–O) by an archaic painted ware, with rather poorly adhering red ochre paint on an orange-buff surface. The standard painted wares which soon appear are of three varieties of decoration, comparable with Jarmo (Guran O–H), Sarab (Guran L–D) and the later Hajji Mohammed wares of south Mesopotamia, with comparable wares in Khuzistan (Guran J–D). In the latest levels (Guran H–D) a red-burnished ware eventually includes omphalos-based bowls paralleled at Tepe Sialk I, approximately dated 5600 BC.

early stage, around 9000 BC, than the scattered available data might at first sight suggest. At Zawi Chemi Shanidar the Upper Palaeolithic liking for molluscs was continued in a taste for snails. Although this village cannot be directly connected with the later sites on either side of the Zagros ranges, the evidence of external trade provided by obsidian, bitumen and native copper, whatever the precise source of the last, suggests that this remarkable settlement should not be regarded as an isolated phenomenon. In due course further discoveries in Iraq and Iran are sure to reveal a widespread pattern of similar settlements only just beginning to experiment with food production, and likewise attributable to the early ninth millennium BC.

For centuries to come settlements were only seasonally occupied, an explanation of the generally modest depths of deposit. Some, such as Karim Shahir, were more seasonal than others. Elsewhere, as at Tepe Asiab near Kermanshah, there are pits suggesting tents or reed huts, a summer encampment; goats were being domesticated, shellfish gathered for food.

In the earliest period (E) at Ganj Dareh, not far east of Kermanshah, a similar camp site, seasonal and with pit dwellings, has been excavated. Unlike Tepe Asiab, however, this was followed by four successive levels of a significantly more advanced culture (Ganj Dareh D-A), attributable to c. 7500–7000 BC. The preceding millennium remains very poorly represented in the known archaeological record, although from Ganj Dareh D onwards a reasonably continuous sequence is becoming apparent from different sites in the Kermanshah region, Luristan and Iraqi Kurdistan. The discoveries at Ganj Dareh make it one of the four or five most significant Neolithic sites in the whole Near East [21]. Plano-convex mud-bricks (cf p. 66), mud slabs, ordinary terre pisé, rubble and stones were used for the buildings, which were rectangular in plan. In some buildings of Ganj Dareh D beam-holes indicate the wooden floor of an upper storey, the ground floor comprising small cubicles probably used largely for storage, provision for which was a universal feature of early village sites. The settlement was destroyed by fire. In one cubicle was a niche, at the very centre of the mound, with two skulls of rams, probably wild, attached to the wall, one above the other. Here is a clear parallel with the rather later shrines of Çatal Hüyük, surely a pointer to common religious traditions extending perhaps throughout the Near East in the formative phases of the Neolithic Revolution. The implications of this discovery should not be under-estimated. These buildings have that cellular plan already observed at Çatal Hüyük and Can Hasan III, and probably designed for security. Conflict with less advanced neighbours would not have been unique to the Zagros zone. The chipped stone industry was of flint, the absence of obsidian suggesting cessation of former contacts with the Van region. Blades with the sheen found on sickles were quite common in Ganj Dareh D-A, less so in E. Polished stone bowls were made. Most significant is the occurrence of large pottery vessels, built in situ in the cubicles, unfired until the destruction of Level D. Clay rims were found built round the edges of large boulder mortars. Some miniature pots were also found, and in Level B some small simple vessels. Here, then, at Ganj Dareh, is the earliest pottery known in the Near East or indeed anywhere, some of it fired at a low temperature at the time of fabrication. Nowhere else have the first beginnings of pottery been revealed. The economy of this village was partly dependent on domesticated goats, thus resembling Tepe Asiab; but there was a variety of other animals slaughtered, including cattle, deer and pig. Pounding and storage of plant foods are demonstrated by mortars, pestles and clay bins, but there is as yet no explicit evidence of agriculture. It is not certain that this settlement was inhabited all the year round, but one argument in favour of perennial occupation is the burial of the dead within the walls of the buildings, albeit with few surviving grave goods; one mandible was recovered facing a pair of hands severed from the arms and lying palms upward. The skeletal remains may cast light on the ethnic affinities of this early community. Ganj Dareh suggests that the Kermanshah region was perhaps the most advanced of the whole Zagros zone, although the comparable date of the first (Bus Mordeh) phase in Khuzistan could well imply the existence of contemporary and geographically intermediate settlements, not necessarily so advanced.

In the Hulailan Plain of north Luristan the small site of Tepe Guran, a mound with eight metres of deposit, has eighteen levels (D–V) of Neolithic occupation, the bottom three levels (T–V) being aceramic. This early phase, continuing up to Level Q, is distinguished by the meagrely preserved traces of flimsy huts, discernible in the dark outlines of rectangular or slightly curvilinear rooms. Its situation in a lower intramontane valley, at an altitude of 950 m., makes it very likely that Tepe Guran began its history, perhaps very early in the seventh millennium BC, as a winter headquarters for a hunting group which herded goats and moved north in the summer months to the higher altitude (1350m.) of the Kermanshah Plain. By Guran P the first permanent house, of *terre pisé* with stone foundations, appeared side by side with a wooden hut; not till Guran M did the houses completely supersede the huts. Some of the floors of these houses were carefully laid with pieces of felspar set in clay coloured with red ochre; red or white gypsum plaster was used to face some walls. Tepe Guran was never a large community, but its long history and connections with other areas give it a special significance. It carries the story of early village farming communities in the Zagros well into the sixth millennium BC. From Guran P onwards the economy changed, with querns, mullers and sickle-blades, absent in the earlier levels, providing evidence of the local development of agriculture, barley being cultivated. An increase in the quantity of bones of wild animals, and thus of hunting, was simply the outcome of the change from seasonal to perennial occupation. This change occurred in the later seventh millennium BC, at a time when the relatively primitive village of Tepe Sarab near Kermanshah comprised more temporary structures, suggesting the persistence of a semi-nomadic way of life.

Meanwhile in Iraqi Kurdistan the village of Jarmo, originally up to one and a half hectares in area, was flourishing, if scarcely in the forefront of the Neolithic Revolution. It was a community in contact both with the Mesopotamian Plain and with the Iranian plateau, yet probably contributing little to areas beyond the relatively remote foothills of its own district. Its chief claim to celebrity is that it is perhaps still the earliest known settlement in Iraq with evidence of fully developed agriculture, with cultivation of einkorn and emmer wheat and hulled two-row barley, morphologically close to their wild forms. Human figurines, especially numerous in the later levels, hint that the people of Jarmo shared the widespread Neolithic religious traditions [22].

For the cultural relations of the Zagros sites in the late seventh and early sixth millennia BC, however, it is best to return to Tepe Guran, with its succession of ceramic styles. These suggest both the priority of this site compared with Jarmo and Tepe Sarab and the diffusion of the village farming economy over wider regions of the Iranian plateau [23].

During the sixth millennium BC the number of settlements in the Zagros

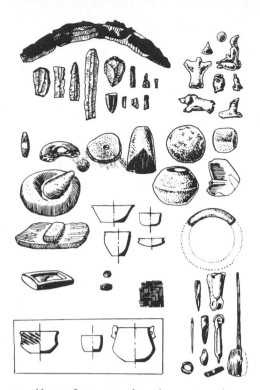

22. Above: Jarmo may have begun as early as *c*. 6750 BC, with its sequence of eleven aceramic levels. Towards the close of the seventh millennium BC pottery appeared, and the occupation continued with five ceramic levels. Much obsidian was in use; the ground-stone industry includes stone bracelets.

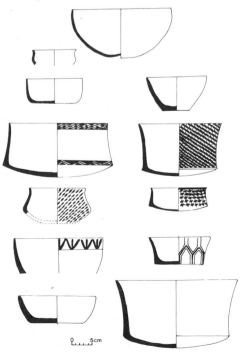

Pl. 1. The fertile oasis of Jericho possessed a constant water supply from its spring, requiring little effort or skill for dispersion into fields and gardens.

Pl 2. In the highland zone, exemplified by this village in eastern Anatolia, the tree cover may have survived in places until the Christian era. This valley is in remote Hakkâri province.

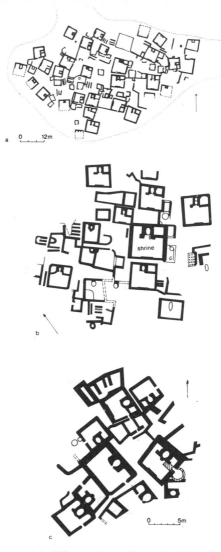

24. (a) Village plans of the Neolithic Jeitun culture. Jeitun itself was an open village with nineteen excavated houses, their walls of *terre pisé* and floors thickly plastered with lime, sometimes coloured reddish-brown, a parallel with Tepe Guran, Ali Kosh in Khuzistan and other sites farther west. (b) Pesseji Depe. (c) Chagylly Depe.

highlands increased, with a transitional phase perhaps immediately following the end of Tepe Guran, and represented by Bog-i-No, in the area of Khurramabad, with other sites in western Luristan. The next phase is exemplified by Tepe Giyan VA, Tepe Siabid and Godin Tepe VII–VI, from Kermanshah eastwards. There was a steady extension northwards to the Urmia basin and beyond the Araxes of early village communities, best exemplified at three sites: Hajji Firuz, the earliest of five excavated sites in the Solduz Plain; at Yanik Tepe, near Tabriz; and at Ṣomu Tepe in Soviet Azerbaijan. The painted pottery of Hajji Firuz suggests possible influence from the Hassuna culture of north Mesopotamia. The radio-carbon samples from all three sites indicate progressively later dates in the sixth millennium BC. It seems that by this time the settlements of the central Zagros may have reached an economic stability which provided no stimulus to further advance but insured an equilibrium for several millennia, leaving other regions to take the lead.

EASTERN IRAN AND KHUZISTAN

In Iran beyond the Zagros sites in the southern province of Fars occupied by *c.* 5500 BC included Tepe Djari: other sites—Tal-i-Mushki, Tal-i-Bakun, Tal-i-Iblis—were occupied later; all are characterized by plain, soft-baked pottery. On the central plateau Sialk 1 had been established by *c.* 5750 BC, if not earlier; and Sialk II likewise falls within the sixth millennium BC. To the northeast, Tepe Hissar dates back in its earliest phase (IA) to shortly before *c.* 5000 BC.

Much of eastern Iran, including Khorassan, remains virtually unknown for these early periods, although the Neolithic Jeitun culture of Turkmenia extended into the Gurgan Plain, at Yarim Tepe and Tureng Tepe. The Caspian Cave sites and the Snake Cave have yielded evidence of an aceramic phase (*c.* 7000 BC), with collection of wild barley and wheat, hunting and fishing. While it is possible that this phase provides the background to the Jeitun culture, the relative backwardness of the later, ceramic Neolithic culture of the caves makes this open to question. Among signs of incipient domestication are paintings in the Shakhta Cave of dogs at work in a hunt.

In Turkmenia, in the favourable environment between the Iranian plateau to the south and the black sands of the Kara Kum Desert to the north, the Jeitun culture emerged soon after *c.* 6000 BC [24]. The villages of Jeitun and Choban Tepe, with their open plan, are comparable in this respect with those of Nea Nikomedeia and Karanovo I in Macedonia and Bulgaria rather than with the cellular or agglutinative plan of Ganj Dareh or Çatal Hüyük. This difference suggests a contrast between Near Eastern traditions and those of the northern steppes, extending westwards into the Balkans. Such a distinction should not, however, be over-emphasized, for there is repeated evidence from the Jeitun culture and its successors, the Anau IA and Namazga I cultures, of contacts with central Iran: in the bone sickles with flint blades of Jeitun and the painted pottery of Anau IA and Namazga I, all paralleled in Sialk I. Mixed farming, with cultivation of barley and wheat, was a major element in the economy of the Jeitun culture: already most meat came from domestic goats and sheep; but hunting continued, with onager, wild pig, sheep, fox, cat and wolf as the quarry. By the later Jeitun phases cattle had become domesticated, and hunting declined. In the Namazga I culture of the later sixth millennium BC domestication of cattle, goat, sheep and pig was all the more apparent. By then two-row barley had become far the commonest crop, with little wheat, perhaps suggesting desiccation or, more probably, increasing salinity of the soil. Comparable evidence of changes in crops appears in rather later phases at Tepe Yahya, in the Kerman province of south-eastern Iran. Mud-bricks, large and thin, in two sizes, now first come into use, with the architectural tradition of the Jeitun culture continuing: buildings are arranged on an open plan, the square houses having a hearth and raised platform on the opposite side of the room. Metal now first occurs in the Namazga I culture, in the form of copper knives and awls. At Yassa Tepe and Anau IB wall-paintings appear, perhaps in shrines, imitating woven textiles in patterns of squares and triangles: red-brown, black, red, pink and white pigments were used. Steatopygous 'mother goddess' clay figurines are often decorated in white paint; bull and goat figurines also occur.

Remote as these cultures of Turkmenia may seem to be, this sequence, starting with Jeitun and continuing through the Anau IA and Namazga I–III cultures, shows the importance of this region as one of a rich autochthonous tradition, for the most part independent yet sharing certain features with the Near East and ultimately originating in Iran, if the present inadequate evidence is correctly interpreted. The sequel to the earlier phases in Turkmenia witnessed the first development of urban life in the later Namazga II culture (mid-fifth millennium BC), including fortified settlements at Yalangach and Mullali Tepe, in the Geoksyur oasis, and the extension of its influence into the Oxus basin, in the Kelteminar culture. By the time of Namazga III (late fourth millennium BC) Turkmenia was exerting an influence on lands to the south-east, evident in parallels with Shahr-i-Sokhte I and Mundigak, and underlining the wide extent of this civilization.

Far to the south-west, the influence of the earliest settlements of the Zagros region may also be discerned in the first village cultures of Khuzistan (Susiana), the hot lowlands of south-west Iran. The archaeology of this region is significant for three reasons: first, for its light on the Neolithic Revolution over the whole Near East; second, for the antecedents of the Urban Revolution in southern Mesopotamia; third, as the prelude to Elamite civilization. Only the first aspect will be discussed at this point. Clarification of the early phases is not made easier by the terminological tangle created by reports on successive excavations, especially at Susa, the most important site. Here, as elsewhere, archaeologists have generated many of their problems [25, 26].

At Tepe Ali Kosh three phases of the cultural sequence in the Deh Luran Plain have been distinguished, all representing development of an economy increasingly supported by dry farming and dependent on the rather unpredictable rainfall. In the first (Bus Mordeh) phase, hunting gazelle, onager, wild ox and wild boar and systematic collection of wild plants were of major importance. Goat herding played a leading role, as in the early Zagros sites; sheep, perhaps also domesticated, were much fewer. The presence of thousands of carbonized seeds indicates, among other things, the cultivation of emmer wheat and two-row hulled barley, rye-grass and einkorn occurring less abundantly. These cannot have been merely collected, since they are not native to Khuzistan. Thus it is hard not to believe it possible that agriculture emerged earlier in lowland Khuzistan than in the highland plains of the Zagros, if the excavators' dating of the Bus Mordeh phase to *c*. 7500–6750 BC is correct, since Ganj Dareh was not indisputably agricultural. Against this, however, is the rather improbable length of fifteen hundred years attributed to the Bus Mordeh and Ali Kosh phases: a date of *c*. 7000 BC for the beginning of the Bus Mordeh phase may be more acceptable. Even this makes the claim of priority in agriculture for the Zagros

Pl 3. The depiction of one theme in the paintings at Çatal Hüyük was usually achieved with the help of the third dimension, either by plaster relief alone or with massive bulls' horns or other, smaller, animal skulls or tusks.

Pl 4. At Çatal Hüyük movement was mainly confined to painting and thus to two dimensions. The dancers of Level III may be judged the climax of this sequence of mural paintings. This relief of the goddess, with its painted ornament, is by contrast static.

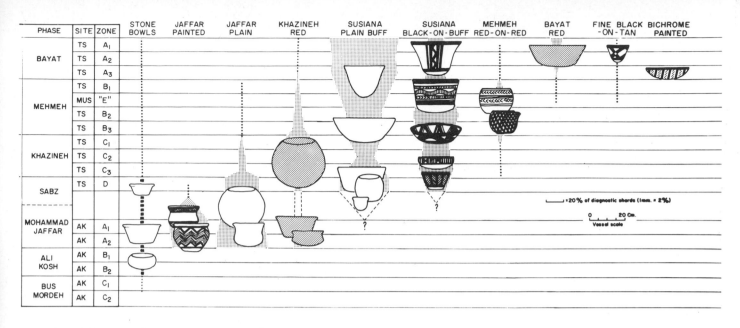

PHASE	SITE	ZONE	STONE BOWLS	JAFFAR PAINTED	JAFFAR PLAIN	KHAZINEH RED	SUSIANA PLAIN BUFF	SUSIANA BLACK-ON-BUFF	MEHMEH RED-ON-RED	BAYAT RED	FINE BLACK-ON-TAN	BICHROME PAINTED
BAYAT	TS	A₁										
	TS	A₂										
	TS	A₃										
MEHMEH	TS	B₁										
	MUS	"E"										
	TS	B₂										
	TS	B₃										
KHAZINEH	TS	C₁										
	TS	C₂										
	TS	C₃										
SABZ	TS	D										
MOHAMMAD JAFFAR	AK	A₁										
	AK	A₂										
ALI KOSH	AK	B₁										
	AK	B₂										
BUS MORDEH	AK	C₁										
	AK	C₂										

= 20% of diagnostic shards (1mm. = 2%)

0   20 Cm.
Vessel scale

25, 26. In Khuzistan a long sequence of seven cultural phases has been distinguished in one area, the Deh Luran Plain, though the most important site is Susa to the south-east, with Tepe Jaffarabad a few miles away. The accompanying tables clarify the natural environment, domestication of animals and development of pottery.

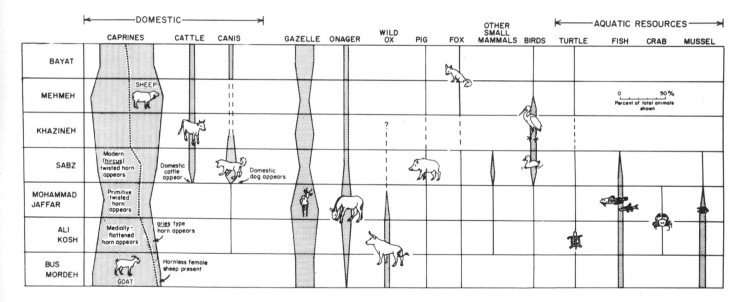

sites a matter for debate. Building methods were also relatively advanced in the Bus Mordeh phase, with slabs cut from the natural red clay. Cultural relations with the Zagros sites and beyond are demonstrated by the plant types, the chipped-stone industry (with its many end-scrapers paralleled at Karim Shahir), a few sickle-blades and the presence of obsidian of Van type. These people may have occupied Ali Kosh only in the winter months, since summer crops were little in evidence. Summer grazing would have been in the Zagros, facilitating contacts farther afield.

In the second (Ali Kosh) phase, Tepe Ali Kosh was the only site in the Deh Luran Plain certainly occupied, measuring about one hectare in area and numbering not more than one hundred inhabitants. Both the hunting of large ungulates and the cultivation of winter-grown cereals increased; but the cultivation of legumes decreased. Architecture became more sophisticated, with larger houses of sizeable mud-bricks, having walls up to one metre thick. Crafts are more apparent, in floor-mats, baskets and more varied and numerous stone bowls, though still no pottery. There are many more grinding stones, the stone industry being generally comparable with that of aceramic Jarmo. Wider trade was carried on, evident not only in obsidian from the Van region but also in sea-shells from the Persian Gulf, copper in the form of a tubular bead and turquoise from north-eastern Iran, near Nishapur. Burials were intramural, contracted and wrapped in a mat sometimes stained with red ochre; some bodies had been disinterred and later reburied.

The third (Muhammed Jaffar) phase, the last at Tepe Ali Kosh, is important for the first appearance of pottery in this region, both plain straw-tempered ware and painted ware of a distinctive style. Moreover, at this time the Deh Luran Plain and neighbouring areas of Khuzistan witnessed the beginning of a marked increase in population, with new settlements at Tepe Sabz in the Deh Luran Plain and at Tepe Jaffarabad and Chogha Mish. This phase spans the earlier sixth millennium BC (c. 6000–5600 BC), and is marked at Ali Kosh by a striking change from arable farming to overwhelming dependence on stock-breeding, especially goats. This was, however, accompanied by further architectural improvements, the mud-brick houses having stone foundations and plastered and red-painted walls. The chipped-stone industry exhibits parallels with ceramic Jarmo, Tepe Sarab and Tepe Guran: the scarcity of sickle-blades agrees with the change in the economy.

At Chogha Mish the Archaic period has three phases, distinguished by different varieties of painted pottery, beginning with burnished-painted ware in the earliest phase (Archaic 1) not far removed in date, if at all, from the pottery of Jarmo. The final phase (Archaic 3) has elements continuing in the following Susiana A period, just as, in spite of a gap in the Deh Luran sequence after the Mohammed Jaffar phase, the distinctive painted pottery appears also in the next (Sabz) phase, in the lowest levels of Tepe Sabz. This discontinuity was anyhow the result of the interpretation of material from two sites alone: since then a third site, Chogha Sefid, has partially filled this hiatus, with at least three ceramic phases, the first two with painted pottery and the third with a red unpainted ware.

Thus there was a steady progression from the transhumant farmers of the Bus Mordeh phase to the growing settlements of the Sabz phase, the first of the four phases distinguished at the site of Tepe Sabz. The botanical evidence suggests irrigation was now first introduced on a limited scale. Another innovation was the domestication of cattle. Changes in settlement pattern, perhaps the result of irrigation, heralded a radical and relatively rapid transition to denser population and the first emergence of urban life. Dry farming persisted, however, in many villages. This is the first phase (Susiana A) in a sequence for Khuzistan originally based on pottery alone. The great value of the excavations in the Deh Luran Plain and the recent surveys in the region is the publication of evidence ending the exclusive dependence on styles of painted pottery for elucidating the conundrums of the early cultures. The results from Chogha Mish have emphasized links with Mesopotamian sites, those of the Sabz–

Jaffarabad–Susiana A phase being especially comparable with Samarra and Eridu. The later phases in Khuzistan are discussed briefly in the next chapter. The question of how much Khuzistan owed to southern Mesopotamia or vice versa is not as easily answered as once seemed likely.

THE MIDDLE EUPHRATES VALLEY

The region intervening between the Levant, the Anatolian plateau and the Zagros highlands is centred on Syria and upper Mesopotamia, and includes the Amuq (Antioch) Plain and Cilicia in the west. Cyprus may for convenience be linked with these, though its connections were partly with Anatolia and partly with the Levant littoral around Byblos. This is a region given early prominence when it was thought that the 'dark-faced burnished ware'—best known from the first phase in the Amuq Plain (Amuq A) and from the Early and Late Neolithic levels at Mersin (XXXIII–XXV)—represented the earliest stage of village communities in the Near East. It was found also in the camp site of Hassuna IA. But this stage, not earlier than the late seventh millennium BC, has for some time been recognized as by no means the beginning of village life, and as signifying the transmission of influences from outside rather than being their source. This is particularly clear in the Cilician Plain, where the long Neolithic sequence at Mersin, with ten metres of deposits, demonstrates connections with the Konya Plain and the sources of obsidian, contrasting with the

Pl 6. Clay tablet from the site of Jemdet Nasr.

Pl 5. Opposite: Many of the wall-paintings of Çatal Hüyük are not representational but comprise decorative schemes, based largely on triangles, resembling woven rugs: most probably these paintings imitate wall-hangings, not *vice versa*. The evidence for this belief includes representation of stitching along the border of a *kilim*, the red, black, and white weave of a *kilim* on a buff ground and a pattern imitating the spots of a leopard skin. Such *kilims* tend to cover a whole wall: one shrine in Level III was decorated exclusively with textile patterns.

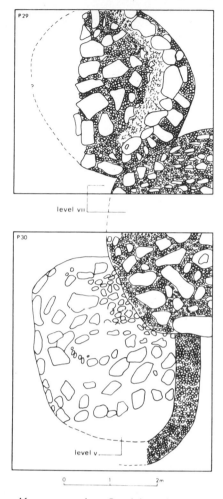

level vII

level v

0   1   2m

27. Above, opposite: Overlying the Natufian settlement of Mureybet I are five levels with round houses, comparable with the eight levels (I–VIII) found in the excavations of the main site and resting on virgin soil. These round houses had stone foundations, open working areas and roasting pits, and represent a period when the earlier Natufian economy was still largely continuing, but when there is clear evidence of cultivation of grain, from the size of the settlement, with some two hundred round houses.

eastern influences later apparent; and where the steady development of agriculture at the expense of hunting is exemplified by the decline of the obsidian lanceheads. Shell-impressed 'rocker' decoration and hole-mouth jars characterize the pottery of these Neolithic communities.

Recent discoveries, however, have carried the record of settled life in this region, at least in the middle valley of the Euphrates, and of semi-sedentary hunting groups back into the ninth millennium BC. One excavation indeed could even indicate that the main centre of the Natufian culture lay not in Palestine but far to the north, on the banks of the middle Euphrates. More probably the Natufian homeland embraced both these areas equally. The significant excavation is that of a Natufian settlement of hunters and fishermen, Mureybet I, with four levels, in the earliest of which was a round hut, on virgin soil, of flimsy posts and clay; in the overlying levels were stamped clay floors with hearths and roasting pits. In the first level a clay bench had been deliberately built encasing an aurochs' skull and two shoulder blades of equids, a hint of the ancient origins of the cult of Çatal Hüyük and elsewhere. The chipped-stone industry was of flint, with no obsidian: picks and adzes were typical, with a few arrowheads also occurring throughout the four levels and a proportion of microliths, mainly lunates. Sickle-blades are very rare. The bone industry includes awls and cylindrical beads. Animal bones are principally those of the Palestinian wild ass, with aurochs and gazelle; birds, fish and fresh-water mussels were also eaten in large quantities; plant remains include wild barley. A radio-carbon determination of 8640 ± 140 BC for the final burning of this Natufian settlement is fully consistent with the dating of the subsequent phases, and suggests a date of approximately 9000 BC for the first occupation. A small Natufian settlement on virgin soil was also uncovered in the rescue excavations at Tell Abu Hureyra, twenty-five miles downstream from Mureybet and on the opposite (west) bank of the Euphrates.

Three sites—Tell Mureybet II–IV, Tell Abu Hureyra and Bouqras—together indicate beyond serious doubt that the middle Euphrates valley, as far downstream as the confluence of the Khabur, near to which Bouqras is situated, was a major area of settlement from the first phases of the Neolithic Revolution. To hunting and fishing were gradually added experiments in food collection and agriculture, brought to an end at much the same time, perhaps by long-term failure of crops and attributable to a climatic change bringing desiccation around 6000 BC. Such a change would have affected Palestine, bringing the PPNB culture to an end. Almost certainly the wild einkorn and wild barley in this region, though morphologically undomesticated, cannot have been merely collected: if so, Mureybet II has a good claim to be the site with the first known traces of agriculture. Animals were not, however, domesticated. Few sickle-blades have been found.

In Mureybet III (Levels X–XVII) the village covered an area of three hectares, with more developed architecture of rectangular houses built of blocks of the soft local limestone, which would have been easily cut with the available flint tools. Round houses still, however, continued to be built. These two phases (Mureybet II–III) may be reckoned approximately contemporary with the PPNA of Jericho, ending c. 7350 BC, though the rectangular plan of most of the houses points forward to the next period [27].

The cultural traditions associated first with the PPNB of Jericho and elsewhere in the Levant are widely represented in the middle Euphrates valley and to the north and west, or at least are echoed. The site of Çayönü lies north-

north-west of Diyarbakir and just south of the Taurus range, has five levels and seems from radio-carbon determinations to date to *c.* 7500–6800 (?) BC, contemporary with the early PPNB culture of the Levant. The architecture is remarkably sophisticated in plan and construction, with stone used in the second earliest level (II) for rectangular buildings up to 5 × 10 m. in area, with plaster floors and internal partitions. In some buildings the floor may have been raised above the ground on a grid of foundation walls. In Çayönü III is a structure possibly serving as a shrine, with internal buttresses, a bench at the rear and a finely patterned mosaic floor of pink stones set in red mortar with two thin strips of white marble pebbles, this whole floor being ground and polished. In Çayönü IV–V mud-bricks were used: a model from Çayönü IV represents a flat-roofed house, having a doorway with curved jambs and sunken hearths and clay bins inside. In the same Level IV a workshop with six or seven small rooms yielded two sickle-hafts of deer antler and many implements of bone and ground-stone. There was evidence of tentative pot-making. Most remarkable however, was the appearance of native copper, hammered to make pins with ground point and drilled to make beads; malachite also occurs in the later levels. Both were obtainable from Ergani Maden, only twelve miles away. The progression from wild to domestic emmer and einkorn wheat is apparent through the five levels; the dog was the first animal to be domesticated, followed later by sheep, goat and perhaps pig.

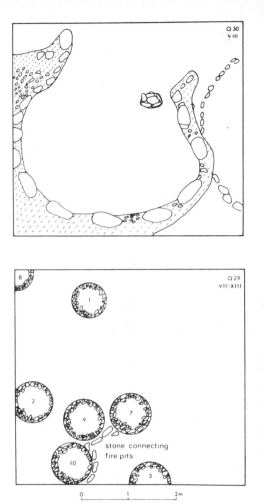

Tell Abu Hureyra is the largest known site of this period, covering twelve hectares, and now submerged beneath the waters of a dam. Rectangular houses were built of *pisé* (*tauf*) and later of mud-brick; floors were of stamped earth or of burnished red or black plaster; wall-paintings are indicated by fragments of white plaster with red lines. Burials were beneath the rooms or courtyards, mostly contracted and often with red ochre. Pits were filled with bones and skulls, and the skull cult was evidently practised. This aceramic Neolithic culture was based on a mixed economy, with fish-bones, wheat and barley, but few sickle-blades, these last also rare at Bouqras. The chipped-stone industry includes tanged arrowheads, spearheads and many flake- and core-scrapers, all stressing the continued importance of hunting. Woodworking is also indicated. Pebbles stained with bitumen were presumably used for hafting tools.

At Bouqras seven levels have been distinguished, comprising an early phase with two levels of *pisé* houses, followed by a phase of four levels with mud-brick houses with plastered floors, benches and pillars, clearly comparable with the aceramic Neolithic of Tell Abu Hureyra. Both sites have yielded many stone bowls, at the latter only in the later aceramic levels. A white chalky stone ware, of lime and ashes, at Tell Abu Hureyra suggests a date in the mid- or late seventh millennium BC, since this distinctive ware is widespread in the Levant, occurring at Hama-on-the-Orontes, at sites along the Mediterranean coast (Ras Shamra VB, Tell Sukas, Byblos Early Neolithic), at Tell Ramad II and at Munhata in north Palestine. Trading contacts are especially apparent from the obsidian at Bouqras, some from central Anatolian sources and some from the Van region, suggesting that not later than the early eighth millennium BC the settlers of the middle Euphrates valley were in touch with widely separated regions. Cowrie-shells and greenstone at Tell Abu Hureyra likewise indicate trade. This may have played a prominent part in the very survival of these communities, seeing that at Bouqras pounders, querns and sickle-blades appear to have vanished after the first phase, suggesting the abandonment of agriculture. By the third and final phase at Bouqras, with one level, some sheep and cattle

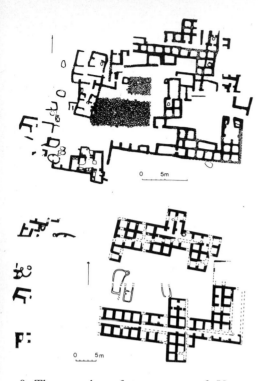

28. The complex of store-rooms of Umm Dabaghiyah III was very carefully laid out, but for the most part found empty, though one arsenal contained over 2,400 baked clay sling missiles and other heavy clay balls.

may have been domesticated. It is hard not to suspect that all three settlements along the Euphrates, with many others elsewhere, were more advanced in their control of local resources than the published evidence demonstrates. El Kowm, a settlement of PPNB affinities in the winter grasslands south of Tell Abu Hureyra, had the characteristic rectangular rooms, with a plastered staircase winding round a central pier. It could be said that these sites were the easternmost of the PPNB culture, whose main homeland lay in Syria.

Both Bouqras and Tell Abu Hureyra, like Tell Ramad and other sites in the Levant, came to an end at a date which can be determined by the occurrence in their final phase of 'dark-faced burnished ware', which originated in the Syro-Cilician region in the late seventh millennium BC and thus probably reached these sites soon after c. 6000 BC. A radio-carbon determination of c. 5900 BC for Bouqras III supports this.

NORTH SYRIA AND MESOPOTAMIA

The cultural sequence of north Syria and Mesopotamia during the sixth millennium BC has been extended, clarified and indeed in some degree modified by excavations at several sites. No longer is it enough to rely on the well known discoveries at Tell Hassuna and Samarra. Radio-carbon determinations add weight to the new evidence, which makes it almost certain that there were three cultural provinces largely contemporary—Early Halaf, Hassuna and Samarra—rather than in sequence. Tribal groupings led naturally to preservation of tribal traditions, some more advanced in terms of technology and social organization than others.

The excavations at Umm Dabaghiyah, at the southernmost edge of the cultivable land south of the Jebel Sinjar, in the Jezireh steppe, resulted from a survey revealing seven pre-Hassuna sites, with little evidence of any occupation after Hassuna IA, described below. In a hostile environment, where dry farming was marginal, as it is today, the economy of Umm Dabaghiyah was unusual in some respects. Evidence for agriculture is limited; and the gypsum subsoil made irrigation impracticable. Hunting played a major role, with onager accounting for no less than 68.4% of all animal bones, the highest percentage for any known Near Eastern site. Twelve phases have been distinguished, belonging to four main building periods, of which the earliest (IV) is the most impressive, for buildings and pottery alike. The neatness of the buildings would be consistent with derivation from an aceramic culture related to PPNB in the Middle Euphrates valley. In Umm Dabaghiyah IV store-rooms were ranged around a rectangular court, entered by trap-doors in the roof, and were used for preserving onager hides and meat, after the hides had been dried on low parallel walls. Entry to the houses was either from the roof or by a door, one room having an arch across its whole width, dividing it in two. This is the first known example of an arch, proving the great antiquity of Mesopotamian versatility in the use of mud-brick. One oven had a plastered kerb and chimney hood. The east wall of one kitchen was decorated with a painting of five running onagers in red ochre, being stampeded into a net by hunters waving weapons or torches. Some mural patterns resemble those on the painted pottery; and pregnant onagers appear on relief-decorated pots [28].

Pottery was abundant, for the most part locally made, coil-built, straw-tempered and undecorated. Burnishing, paint and relief occur, with incision appearing in the latest levels. Some burnished ware of Amuq A dark-faced type was imported. The difficulties created by the environment are perhaps stressed

by the progressive shrinkage of the area of the village from one period to the next. The absence of any overlap with Hassuna IA would be more readily acceptable if the Jezireh had been, however briefly, abandoned by village communities, since there are over sixty Hassuna-Samarra sites in this area. The most probable dating for the whole time-span of the Umm Dabaghiyah culture is *c.* 6000–5600 BC, though the initial chronology placed Umm Dabaghiyah II–I, when the settlement was in decline, contemporary with Hassuna IA (*c.* 5600–5500 BC).

In a belt extending from Cilicia to Khuzistan the presence, perhaps rather fleeting, of semi-sedentary farmers is discernible. Artefacts including querns, pounders, flint sickle-blades and sandstone and quartzite hoes fixed with bitumen to wooden handles demonstrate agriculture. One such group set up camp at the spot, Tell Hassuna, destined to be chosen by villagers, and left the remains of three phases of camp (Hassuna IA). The pottery includes fine burnished bowls and coarse, straw-tempered hole-mouth jars with sharp carination, but no painted or incised decoration.

The successors of these camp-dwellers at Tell Hassuna, near Mosul, were wholly sedentary farmers, whose culture, named after this site, endured through seven levels (IB–VI). Elsewhere this is exemplified by Yarim Tepe I, in the Jebel Sinjar area west of Hassuna, with ten levels (X–I); at Tell es-Sawwan I–V, farther down the Tigris near Samarra; at Matarrah; and at Tell Shemshara

Pl 7. Above left: In the Jemdet Nasr period, in addition to relief decoration, there appears a new and highly distinctive form of ornament, comprising inlaid bands—horizontal, vertical or as circles—the inlay giving the effect of a mosaic, consisting of little pieces of stone and shell set in bitumen. This fashion is paralleled in Eanna IIIB at Warka by flat plaques used as architectural ornament, supplementing the older fashion of cone mosaics.

Pl 8. Above right: Scarlet ware, which had a wide distribution, being found as far apart as Mari and Susa D. Unlike the Jemdet Nasr painted jars, painting was not confined to the shoulder but spread over most of the exterior of the vessel. Both representational designs, such as a funerary wagon, and geometric patterns occur, the brightness of the red paint accentuated by its being bordered with black, on a buff surface. The red paint was, however, poorly fixed. Incision was also popular on E.D.I. pottery, sometimes applied all over the vessel.

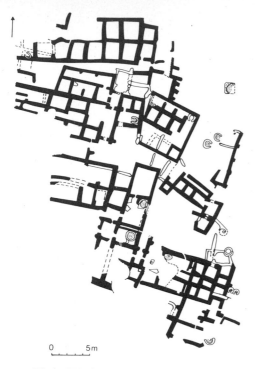

29. Plan of Yarim Tepe 1, Level 5.

30. Head of a lizard figurine from Chogha Mami; this resembles some from Sawwan, of strangely Sumerian appearance, most closely comparable with the late Ubaid lizard figurines.

in the hills of Iraqi Kurdistan, now submerged by a dam. At this last site an aceramic phase (Shemshara 16–14), contemporary with the earlier Hassuna levels, was followed by a ceramic phase (Shemshara 13–9), contemporary with the full flowering of this culture at the type site (Hassuna III–VI). Both Tell es-Sawwan and Shemshara exhibit features, especially in their stone industries, showing that there was no complete break in continuity between ceramic Jarmo and the Hassuna culture of the north Mesopotamian plain, and that influences from the Zagros highlands penetrated northern Mesopotamia as well as Khuzistan. At Tell Hassuma itself, however, this is not apparent.

The variety and development of decorated pottery at Tell Hassuna, with the burnished Archaic painted ware in Levels IB–III and the matt painted (Standard) ware evolving out of it, having a rather limited range of patterns using chevrons and cross-hatching, yields evidence of change through successive levels. There was also incised and the rarer painted-and-incised ware. A late arrival at Tell Hassuna was a wholly different and more sophisticated painted pottery, Samarra ware, persisting into the following period, when Halaf pottery had arrived (Hassuna III–VIII), and found from the first in ceramic Shemshara.

The architecture of Tell Hassuna was typical of an open village in the plain, without public buildings but with an improvement in the design of houses, which, by Hassuna III–VI, were rectangular, probably gabled and having several rooms with internal buttresses, benches and screens, in addition to the predictable fireplaces and ovens. Storage was as important as in every village, and provided by grain-bins made as large pots, normally damp-proofed outside with a heavy coat of bitumen, some being lined inside with gypsum. The architecture of Tell Hassuna marks it as a village in no way ahead of its time, indeed as less sophisticated than the earlier Umm Dabaghiyah. Yarim Tepe I, with a layout of gypsum-plastered passages, courtyards and buildings in Level V and a storage complex similar to that of Umm Dabaghiyah III, seems to represent the highest achievements of this culture [29].

From Hassuna II onwards appear oval, flat-bottomed dishes corrugated inside with a stick applied to the wet clay and evidently used as husking trays, for separating the grain. Their wide, if spasmodic, distribution from Ras Shamra to Eridu gives a hint of far-flung cultural connections made the more explicit in western regions by the distribution of painted pottery in general terms comparable with Hassuna Archaic ware and classified as Early Chalcolithic. This occurs especially in north Syria (Amuq B) and in the Cilician Plain (Mersin XXIV–XX), with a southward extension as far as Tell Ghrubba in the lower Jordan valley. The 'pottery Neolithic' of Jericho, with its two phases A and B, or Jericho IX–VIII, may be better understood in the context of connections with this widespread Early Chalcolithic cultural tradition, marking the first diffusion of painted pottery. It would of course be mistaken to see the Mosul region as necessarily the main focus of the culture to which Tell Hassuna has given its name.

Tell es-Sawwan, on a bluff on the east bank of the Tigris near Samarra and thus some distance downstream from Hassuna, stood just outside the limits of the zone where rainfall was enough to permit dry farming. Hybrid cereals (six-row barley and bread-wheat) and large-seeded flax are interpreted as reflecting early irrigation, the techniques of which may have been introduced from the foothills east of the Tigris as early as the first occupation (Sawwan I), which was contemporary with Hassuna IB. This amounted to no less than a revolutionary innovation, with far-reaching implications for crop yields and social stratification. Such a concentration of wealth, modest as it may have been, could explain the need for security apparent in the V-shaped defensive ditch around the perimeter of Sawwan I, though only 2.5 m. wide and soon filled in. Later, in Sawwan IIIA, a buttressed enclosure wall fulfilled a similar function, again briefly. Even in Sawwan I a developed mud-brick architecture is evident, with large, rather flimsily constructed buildings of mud-bricks made in a mould, an innovation in Mesopotamia. One of these three buildings, with a niche, may have been a shrine: domestic features such as hearths are absent. Inside were found stone vessels, unfinished alabaster figures and clay statuettes of mother goddess type [31, 32].

Pottery is rare in Sawwan I, such as was found indicating correlations with Hassuna IB: Tell es-Sawwan I has yielded a radio-carbon determination of *c.* 5506 BC. Not till Sawwan IIIA does painted pottery appear, by IV being predominantly in the Samarra style, previously known only from cemeteries or associated, as in Hassuna III–VIII, with other ceramic styles.

Samarra ware was the hallmark of a distinctive culture, perhaps centred around the type site, where a cemetery of the period was found, with settlements at Baghuz and Tell es-Sawwan and with influence extending as far south-east as the Susiana A (Jaffarabad) culture of Khuzistan and as far west as the Amuq, at a time coinciding with the Early Halaf phase (Amuq B–C). Another criterion of the Samarra culture, on the evidence of Tell es-Sawwan, must be the stone vessels and statuettes, utterly alien to the Hassuna culture, and representing a tradition probably far older than the Samarra painted pottery. But for the discoveries at Tell es-Sawwan, this would still be unknown.

To the east of Tell es-Sawwan and close to the Iranian frontier, on the Iraqi side, is situated Chogha Mami, geographically and chronologically between the dry-farming Hassuna culture of the northern plains and the Ubaid culture of the south. This was a small town, dependent on irrigation, which has left vestiges in the form of small ditches on the edge of the settlement in successive levels. This has added a new dimension to the role of the Samarra culture, whose late phase is at present known only at Chogha Mami. The scarcity of charcoal from prehistoric Mesopotamian sites gives added importance to the radio-carbon determination of *c.* 5101 BC for the earliest phase of Chogha Mami 9, transitional between the Samarra and Hajji Mohammad (see p. 54) cultures, contemporary with Hassuna V (with radio-carbon determination of 5090 ± 200 BC) and Eridu XVIII–XVII ('Ubaid I'). The economy of Chogha Mami was based on mixed farming, with domesticated goat, sheep, pig, cattle and dog. As at Tell es-Sawwan, but unlike Hassuna and Matarrah, mud-brick was used. Tradition and the preservation of family property are suggested by the continuity of houses on the same site, as in so many Near Eastern communities, and by stamp seals, often handed down as heirlooms. Buttressed compound walls may indicate a community of extended households.

During the sixth millennium BC in Mesopotamia the first beginnings of towns can be detected at Tell es-Sawwan and Chogha Mami, within the Samarra cultural province. The Early Halaf phase in the north and the more conservative Hassuna villages in the intervening region were contemporary. Except for evidence for irrigation and defences, no specific advance on earlier settlements can be pinpointed as decisive. Yet in the context of Halaf-Hassuna-Samarra lay the seeds of later changes. With its long duration into the mid-fifth millennium BC, the Halaf culture still forms a fitting prelude to the next chapter, though there is no break in the story.

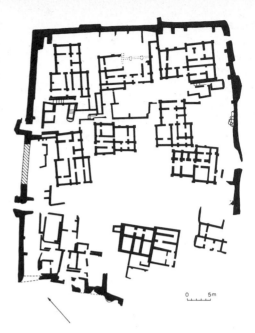

31. Sawwan IIIA, when architecture reached its most impressive stage, with T-shaped buildings inside the enclosure wall.

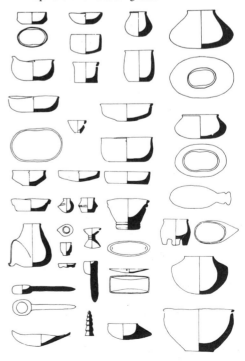

32. Alabaster vessels from the cemetery of Sawwan I, where copper beads and phalli also accompany the burials; but most distinctive are the alabaster statuettes, from 5 to 15 cm. high, with up to three in each grave.

49

The Rise of the First Cities:
Sumerian Civilization in Mesopotamia

The origins and development of towns and cities can no longer be attributed without much discussion to a few factors peculiar to the environment of the first settlements in the Mesopotamian Plain. The sequence of cultures named after a type-site and most clearly distinguished by styles of pottery should not be given exaggerated significance. From Halaf to Jemdet Nasr and on through the Early Dynastic period these changes are traced in Mesopotamia. Provided that the archaeologist does not become mesmerized by typologies and schemes of comparative stratigraphy, and is aware that economic and social changes cannot be directly related to fashions in pottery or other artefacts, the classification of excavated and other material must be of help.

Field surveys have done much to elucidate shifts in patterns of settlement in certain areas. While the story in central Mesopotamia seems to be one of a steady progression from villages to a balance between towns and rural settlements, developments in the far south, the heart of the Sumerian homeland, were far more complex. Limited local resources had to be protected. Irrigation followed, rather than preceded, urban growth. Trade must not be given an exaggerated role in the formation of towns and cities. Gathering of rural population into major centres, a phenomenon of the later prehistoric centuries in southern Mesopotamia, may well have been stimulated by the need for greater security, possibly against nomadic intruders.

Rivalries between the city temple and its secular ruler, whether governor or king, probably date back earlier than formerly supposed. Political overtones appear in the epic of Gilgamesh, with the role of the assembly and the threat from an ambitious leader. Written sources bring the closing phases of the Early Dynastic period into much clearer light than the preceding centuries. By then, Sumerian society was in some respects on the brink of dissolution. By then, too, the 'urban revolution' had spread well beyond the Tigris-Euphrates plains. Nowhere else, however, did the urban population exceed that of the countryside: in this respect at least the emergence of cities was a Sumerian phenomenon, one of the achievements of a remarkable people, also the first to perfect and persist with a system of writing.

THE HALAF CULTURE

Leonard Woolley's excavations at Carchemish included work in the Yunus area, where he discovered a number of kilns, with which were associated wasters from misfired vessels. The ware, distinctively painted, he termed 'Neolithic'. The appearance of a new class of painted pottery in northern Mesopotamia in the mid-sixth millennium BC might seem to deserve scant attention. Indeed archaeologists are apt to enmesh themselves in the details of the wares, shapes and decoration of pottery. But this development had a wider significance.

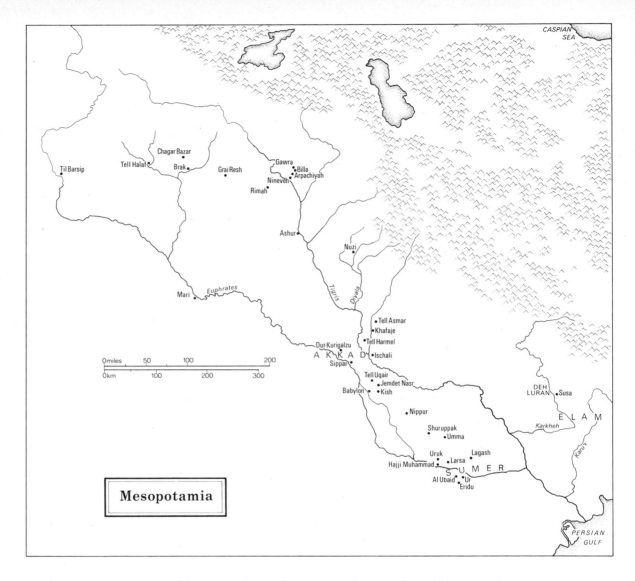

Mesopotamia

33. Map of Mesopotamia.

The same pottery has since been found at Tell Halaf, in the Khabur valley, the site which has given its name to the Halaf culture. The most important settlement of this culture is Tell Arpachiyah, near Mosul.

The stratigraphy of Tell Arpachiyah alone must indicate a long time-span for the Halaf period, since there are ten levels, divided into three phases, Early Halaf (Arpachiyah TT15–TT11), Middle Halaf (TT10–TT7) and Late Halaf (TT6). A more westerly site, Tell Chagar Bazar in the Khabur valley, also has ten Halaf levels (15–6), though the last three (8–6) are transitional to the succeeding Ubaid culture. An eastern and a western style of Halaf pottery, centred in the Mosul region and the Khabur valley and westwards respectively, can be distinguished. But there is no doubt that the homeland of the Halaf culture, from whatever direction the newcomers may have arrived, was in the upper Tigris valley around Mosul: indeed the culture may well have evolved here. Farther west the sequence of phases is less clear and less complete, nor is the culmination of Halaf painted pottery, in Arpachiyah TT6, paralleled at western sites.

34. Halaf pottery, attractive as it is in its shapes and painted decoration, is even more significant for its high firing temperatures. This firing, together with shapes such as the 'cream bowl' with its sharp carination, suggests the practice of true metallurgy, the knowledge of smelting ores to remove impurities.

Clearly these people were no city-dwellers, for they lived in small unfortified villages in the open plain. The economy was primarily agricultural, though hunting, with the aid of the sling rather than the bow, persisted as a significant source of food. Trade, indicated by obsidian from the Van region, copper perhaps from the Ergani district near Diyarbakir and shells from the Persian Gulf, is significant more for its evidence of distant contacts than for its scale. Nevertheless, without trade neither the chipped-stone industry nor copper-working would have been possible.

The absence of many metal artefacts in wholly reliable context is scarcely surprising, since copper was then much too valuable not to be melted down for reuse. The social implications of this advance on the technology of the Hassuna culture are profound, for now clearly there had come into being a class of professional craftsmen, among them the potters who produced the polychrome plates of Arpachiyah TT6, the coppersmiths and the makers of flint and obsidian tools. The house in the middle of the Late Halaf village of Arpachiyah was a workshop, showing that these products were not imported by itinerant traders from elsewhere but were manufactured on the spot. Here, on a small scale, was the modest beginning of that dependence on industry which was to become a major element in the urban economy of the Sumerian south.

The pottery shows an improvement in quality of clay, firing and decoration throughout the Halaf period. The so-called 'cream bowl', appearing so characteristic of the Middle Halaf phase, may imply from its profile that not till then was metallurgy significantly developed [34].

Though lacking any large public buildings or defences, the village of Tell Arpachiyah contained a number of structures termed *tholoi*, from their superficial resemblance to the beehive tombs of Mycenae. A small amulet representing a gabled house with a bending roof-pole has been cited as evidence that the anteroom attached to the round chamber of these *tholoi* was similarly gabled. The use of the dome, made of *terre pisé* on foundations of boulders and stones set in mud, is a remarkably precocious feat of engineering. Argument has centred around the function of the *tholoi*, whether they were shrines or houses or store-rooms. This last seems improbable. The preservation of the stone foundations of disused *tholoi*, in spite of the great effort involved in their transportation to the village, must surely lend weight to their identification as shrines, with the characteristic Mesopotamian respect for the sites of sanctuaries; and the presence of burials against one *tholos* adds support to this theory, as do the burials associated with the two *tholoi* of slightly later date at Tepe Gawra (Level XVII), not far from Tell Arpachiyah.

Figurines include some of the familiar 'mother goddess' type, of Neolithic derivation; but suggestions of connections with the Minoan civilization of Crete, through the amulets of double axe and dove forms found at Tell Arpachiyah, ignore the great gulf in time and space.

The westward expansion of the Halaf culture extended as far as Tell Judeideh XIII (Amuq C) and beyond to Mersin XIX–XVII and Ugarit IV on the Mediterranean coast. The imported Halaf pottery was soon being imitated in local products. Northward the culture extended its influence into the Malatya region, as at Arslantepe, and through the obsidian trade to Lake Van, where true Halaf pottery, burnished and painted, has been found at the small mound of Tilkitepe, with large obsidian cores.

The radio-carbon dates may be used tentatively to suggest a maximum time-span for the Halaf culture in its homeland from *c*. 5400 BC until *c*. 4500 BC.

THE UBAID PERIOD

Although the Halaf villagers had achieved certain advances, in pottery, metallurgy and architecture, well before the end of their long history, changes were coming about in the far south, in the lowermost reaches of the Tigris-Euphrates alluvial plain, the land later known as Sumer. Precisely who were the first inhabitants of this inhospitable region, or when, whence or how they arrived are questions which may never be answered to the satisfaction of every specialist. The balance of evidence seems to favour the identification of these first settlers as Sumerians: at no subsequent stage was there any break in cultural continuity decisive enough to indicate the arrival of newcomers in very large numbers. Written records alone, however, can provide proof of the identity of any population in ethnic or linguistic terms. The Sumerians themselves held that they had arrived from the sea, that is, from the Persian Gulf. The only alternative direction would be from the highlands of western Iran. The vast geographical extent of the culture named after the relatively minor site of Al 'Ubaid, four miles west of Ur, from western Iran to the Mediterranean coast, could suggest an early expansion of the people who made their first and most enduring home in the land to which they gave their name, around the marshes and lagoons at the head of the Persian Gulf.

The story of the cultural succession in Sumer begins, however, before the stage strictly represented by the pottery named after Al 'Ubaid, the most widespread feature of this culture. Significantly it is at Eridu that the earliest remains of occupation have been excavated, for, according to Sumerian tradition, it was the first of five cities to hold the kingship over the land before the Flood. Situated between desert dunes and steaming swamps, the people of Eridu must always have had a struggle to exist. This very struggle may well have been the reason for the achievements of these early settlers. It seems improbable that any very large settlements will ever be found in this region dating back earlier than Eridu.

The dominant feature of Eridu was its succession of shrines, built in the same area, each one immediately or closely overlying its predecessor. The first was in Eridu XVIII, built on a sand dune beneath which could lie yet earlier remains awaiting excavation. The earliest complete plan was exposed in Eridu XVI, where a small building, only 4 m. square, was constructed of a distinctive variety of mud-brick, long and with thumb impressions on the upper side, with a roughly contemporary parallel only at Tepe Sialk in central Iran. The door was slightly off centre; inside were two podia, one of which, in a bay on the north-west side, probably served as the main altar. The institution of sacrifices is suggested by round tables, apparently for offerings, and traces of burning. Comparable evidence was obtained at Warka, where clay-plastered troughs were filled with offerings, in a succession lasting a thousand years from the Ubaid period till the end of the Jemdet Nasr period. In Eridu XIV–XII the temples were overlaid by the ziggurat of the Third Dynasty of Ur. Thereafter came a succession of temples, dating to the Ubaid period and culminating in Eridu VI [35].

It seems certain that fishing was the principal livelihood of many of the earliest settlers at Eridu, Ur and elsewhere in Sumer, and is illustrated by the occurrences of baked clay net-sinkers. The juxtaposition of reed huts of wattle-and-daub construction and mud-brick buildings was a widespread feature of the Ubaid culture in southern Mesopotamia, attested at Eridu, Ur and Warka. This could indicate that the first settlers arrived with a tradition of building in mud-

35. Characteristic of the Eridu temples, including this example from Level VII, was their tripartite plan, comprising the central nave or cella, with smaller rooms ranged along either side, presumably for the priests and temple equipment. The temples were orientated with their corners to the cardinal points, as in later centuries in Mesopotamia. In Eridu VIII the temple had a cruciform buttress in the centre of a large external niche behind the altar. Between pavement surfaces surrounding temples VII and VI were found deposits of fish bones which can surely be associated with Enki, the Sumerian god of fresh waters, of craftsmanship and learning, who lived in the *apsu*, the watery deep, and who was the patron god of Eridu.

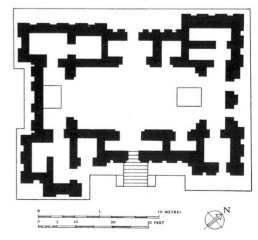

36. The finest products of the Ubaid potters were these bowls of fine 'egg-shell ware'. Ubaid pottery in general is aesthetically inferior to Halaf pottery but technically its equal: it is of one ware, with a tendency to over-firing causing the greenish colour. Deep bowls and beakers are normally of fine ware, plates and large jars of coarse ware. Most of the pottery is hand-made, though the slow wheel seems to have been in use. Patterns are not normally representational, except for some sherds from Lagash and Tell Uqair depicting birds and horned animals and showing inspiration from Iran.

brick, which they subsequently continued as best they could in the different environment of their new homeland.

Details of pottery are no part of this necessarily cursory discussion; but some reference is unavoidable, since it is the ceramic evidence alone which makes any attempt at precision in comparative stratigraphy at all practicable. The earliest phase at Eridu (XIX–XV) is characterized by a distinctive style of painted pottery, locally made but with geometric designs owing much to Halaf inspiration from the north, and doubtless contemporary with the later stages of that culture. Side by side with this pottery was a proportion of greenish ware of Ubaid type, suggesting that the Ubaid culture may already have taken root. Then came a phase (Eridu XIV–XIII) when another type of painted pottery with characteristic shapes and decoration, and named after a site near Warka, Hajji Muhammad, came into fashion. Overcrowded painting, often purplish-black, and miniature reserve patterns are prominent features.

With the advent of the next phase (Eridu XII–VIII), the Ubaid culture had come to maturity. No longer is Eridu the sole significant source of evidence, probably to be supplemented by recent discoveries at Warka, where excavations continue, pottery providing hints of occupation dating back to the earliest two phases at Eridu. The earliest settlement at Ur (Woolley's Ur-Ubaid I), on the bank of the Euphrates twelve miles from Eridu, was contemporary with this phase at Eridu, while Ur-Ubaid II is equivalent to the late Ubaid phase (Eridu VII–VI). The pitfalls of taking one site alone as giving the complete sequence of any cultural period may be exemplified by the deep sounding in the Eanna precinct at Warka, where the Ubaid levels (Eanna XVIII–XIV) extend for a depth of about ten metres, representing a considerable time-span, yet by their pottery contemporary only with Eridu VIII–VI. Of course the number of levels is a far surer guide to time-span than depth of deposit, particularly where rubbish may have accumulated rapidly.

The pottery of Eridu XII–VIII, classifiable in two sub-phases, includes a hole-mouth jar with long spout, a highly distinctive form first appearing in Eridu XIII: bones found inside one such jar show that they functioned as fish-kettles. Their occurrence in northern Mesopotamia soon after the end of the Halaf period (Tepe Gawra XIX and XVII) gives a valuable cross reference. In the second sub-phase (Eridu IX–VIII) a very fine, eggshell thin ware appears, in small hemispherical bowls with painted geometric patterns including rosettes and stylized foliage [36, 37].

Outside the city of Eridu and contemporary with temples VII and VI was a late Ubaid cemetery, containing originally at least one thousand graves. But the number of actual burials was greater, since some graves were used through several successive generations, with earlier burials carelessly pushed to one side. All the graves seem to be sunk from roughly the same surface, seldom overlap and therefore probably represent a fairly brief period: they are rectangular boxes of mud-brick, sunk in the drift sand, and after the burial filled with earth and sealed with a lid of the same bricks. Like the buildings they are orientated to the north-west. The bodies are all extended, probably a tribal custom, not invariable at Ur or elsewhere. Children were usually given smaller graves, with miniature pottery; one boy had his dog buried beside him, with a meat bone. A cup and a plate were essential, put near the feet; with secondary burials the pottery was put near the head. Meat offerings for the dead are shown by animal bones on the lid of a grave. The contemporary Ur–Ubaid II graves are pits, sometimes paved with sherds, the bodies extended and the hands crossed over the pelvis.

Plates, bowls, goblets, cups and other forms characterize the pottery of the Eridu cemetery and elsewhere in this final phase of the Ubaid period (Eridu VII–VI). The general quality of the potters' products declined, the fine eggshell ware vanished and painted decoration became perfunctory. The one advance was the use of the wheel, though this did not become common until the following Uruk period.

In some sense the chronological terms employed by archaeologists are merely labels of convenience. If pottery alone is studied, the successive periods in Mesopotamia, from Hassuna to Jemdet Nasr, may be looked upon as clearly defined stages in a cultural advance marked by a sequence of more or less fundamental changes, often brought about by the arrival of newcomers. Yet even the ceramic evidence now suggests gradual transitions, almost as much the outcome of changes in fashion as of more radical causes. Thus the northern ceramic influences apparent in Eridu XIX–XIII finally gave way completely to the Ubaid tradition, which by the time of Eridu VII–VI was in turn beginning to give place to Uruk types. Likewise the Eanna sounding at Warka revealed monochrome red and grey wares of Uruk type already occurring in the Ubaid levels; and polychrome red and black pottery of Jemdet Nasr type seems to have first appeared well before that period. Moreover, in Eanna VI some spouted pots akin to Early Dynastic forms occur.

Thus the Ubaid period must be seen as one stretch of time in a more or less uninterrupted progression from the first settlements to the full maturity of Sumerian civilization in Early Dynastic times. This makes it all the more plausible to identify the first settlers as Sumerians. The Ubaid settlements can no longer be regarded as restricted to a village economy, with the true Urban Revolution not occurring till the Uruk period. Population must have increased considerably, both in Sumer and in neighbouring areas, such as the Deh Luran Plain of Khuzistan: Eridu may have had a population of 4,000 or more in the Ubaid period, the town covering an area of up to ten hectares. Ur was little smaller. By the Uruk period, Warka extended over not less than eighty-one hectares, with perhaps at least 25,000 inhabitants.

There is good reason to believe, from evidence including the size of linseed found in the Ubaid levels at Ur, that irrigation must have been practised in this period. The great expansion of the Ubaid culture, with a proliferation of new sites upstream from the lowermost stretches of the alluvial Tigris–Euphrates Plain, suggests the successful exploitation of the available water supplies through control of destructive floods and conservation of water for irrigation in the dry summer months. Canals attributable to this period have not been identified, and would anyhow be very hard to distinguish from later remains, although traces near Eridu may be as early as the Ubaid period.

The rivers and larger canals were already in use as highways for transport and trade: this is illustrated by the model boat of baked clay from the late Ubaid cemetery at Eridu. Its design, with mast-socket amidships and hooks for stays, as well as a hooked ornament at bow and stern, resembles that of the simple craft which still sail the lower Euphrates. The very distribution of several of the chief cities—Ur, Warka, Shuruppak and Nippur along the Euphrates, with others, including Lagash and Umma, along the Iturungal–Sirara watercourse to the east—shows that by the Uruk period, if not earlier, the cities of Sumer were linked by these natural highways.

Cattle may not have played a major role in the economy until later periods, though painted models could suggest otherwise. Barley and sheep have been

37. The practice of a cult peculiar to the Ubaid people in their homeland is suggested by the discovery in Ur-Ubaid I and II of numerous baked clay figurines, all female, with slender, well modelled human bodies but with the head of a reptile, evidently a lizard, often with a high bitumen cone as headdress. Ornaments are depicted by painted bands and stripes. A male counterpart occurs in the late Ubaid cemetery at Eridu.

discerned as the main sources of food supply for the south Mesopotamian communities from the Ubaid period onwards, and similarly in Khuzistan. Agriculture was the mainstay of the industrial economy which evolved in the Sumerian cities, each separated from its neighbours by stretches of desert and swamp.

The lack of raw materials in the alluvial plain is clearly demonstrated by the range of artefacts produced in baked clay, especially typical being the Ubaid curved sickles, first found numerously in Eridu XII and fired almost to vitrification. Flint was imported and also used for sickle blades and for roughly chipped hoes. Fishing is illustrated by clay bent nails, probably used for hanging up nets, and clay net-sinkers. Flax seeds and clay loom-weights suggest the weaving of linen. Thus the implements required for agriculture, fishing and the textile industry were for the most part made of clay, the one local material.

Among imported materials, apart from obsidian and a variety of stones including amazonite, was copper, perhaps brought from Oman. Though few artefacts have been found in Ubaid levels, baked clay socketed axe-heads and painted models of similar implements strongly suggest not merely the existence of a copper industry but also the appearance, even at this early period, of a type which was to continue as typically Sumerian till the end of the Early Dynastic period and beyond. This evidence is reinforced by the reference in later tradition to Bad-tibira, 'the fortress of the metalsmiths', among the cities which existed before the Flood.

From its homeland in southern Mesopotamia the Ubaid culture spread abroad, both eastwards into southern Iran and northwards into upper Mesopotamia, later Assyria. Thence it expanded farther west to the Mediterranean coast and Cilicia, being manifest in Amuq phase E, in the Antioch Plain, where pottery imitating Ubaid wares was characteristic of Tell esh Sheikh. It also expanded into the Urmia region of north-west Iran. Thus came about an unprecedented expansion of one culture, in Mesopotamia at least marked by the incipient growth of towns, but with adaptation to the ecological differences between one region and the next, the pottery being a common factor. Irrigation, through the need for communal organization the strongest factor promoting the rise of cities in southern Mesopotamia, was not so much required, if at all, in more favoured areas to the north. There rainfall sufficed to permit dry farming in the eastern foothills, down to the 200-m. contour. This alone explains the tardiness of the Urban Revolution in northern Mesopotamia and still more so in regions farther away from Sumer.

TEPE GAWRA

Tepe Gawra, 22 km. east of Nineveh and near the mountain zone, is a site of unique importance for the Ubaid period in northern Mesopotamia, although hardly typical. Its sequence of levels (XIX–XII), Gawra XX being transitional from the Halaf period, is alone enough to suggest a long time-span. The series of temples, from Gawra XIX onwards, continues well beyond the end of the Ubaid period, reveals some similarities with the temples of Eridu and suggests the early establishment of some form of urban life. The peculiarity of Tepe Gawra is that this urban community was not imitated elsewhere in northern Mesopotamia for many centuries.

From the beginning of the series, the temples of Gawra XIX and XVIII were of tripartite plan: their walls were orientated to the cardinal points, whereas the later temples had their corners thus orientated, as at Eridu. The construction of these earliest temples at Tepe Gawra was remarkably flimsy, their walls being

38. The Northern Temple, Central Temple and Eastern Shrine of Gawra XIII occupied altogether an area little more than 30m. square. Impressive as the whole group must have been, it was of fairly modest scale compared with the great Eanna precinct at Warka.

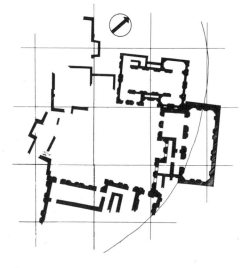

not more than a brick and a half thick, implying that they cannot have stood for very long in the wet winters of the north. Much of the architecture of Tepe Gawra, sacred and secular buildings alike, may thus have been lost. Continuation of Halaf traditions may be discernible in the *tholoi* of Gawra XX and XVII, which, with the temples of Gawra XIX and XVIII, were superimposed on one another, forming a sacred area. Many graves associated with the two *tholoi* of Gawra XVII provide evidence supporting their identification as shrines.

In Gawra XVI a large private house had traces in one room of a wall-painting of a running lozenge pattern in alternate rows of red and black on white plaster. There were also kilns, one subterranean and another domed, with a grating to hold the pots and a fire in the hole beneath. The pattern of settlement over the site as a whole changed considerably from one period to the next: in Gawra XV the 'east peak' was a residential quarter and the 'north peak' an industrial area, with kilns or ovens and store-rooms. In Gawra XIV an innovation occurs: there is a large building with foundations entirely of boulders—the first use of stone for building at this site—and consisting of seventeen rooms, including a large central hall about 12.5 × 3.5 m.; this could as easily have been a temple as a house.

In Gawra XIII the summit of the mound was almost entirely given up to temples, with three such buildings grouped round an open court. With their thin brick walls reinforced by buttresses, each with a niche in the centre, and brightly painted red, black, ochre and vermilion, these temples must have been of striking appearance. Only the Northern Temple has its whole plan preserved: though slightly similar to the temple of Eridu VIII, its two buttressed internal partition walls are unusual. Each of the three temples of Gawra XIII was reached by a side entrance, the Central Temple having a deep niche framing a double doorway into an antechamber to the cella. A special size of mud-brick was used for each temple; and something of the significance attached to the art of building may be guessed from the occurrence in the Eastern Shrine, probably the eldest of the three, of ninety-nine model bricks, agreeing in their measurements with those used in the Northern and Central Temples but not with those used in the Eastern Shrine. Whatever the differences in their plans, there can be no doubt of the general affinity to the architectural traditions of southern Mesopotamia [38].

True stamp-seals appear from the earliest Ubaid levels of Tepe Gawra, side by side with the engraved seal-pendants of Halaf type: rarer in the south of Mesopotamia, these may well have been a northern invention. Most of these stamp-seals are shaped like a round button, with a loop on the back for hanging [39].

Beads illustrate the taste for jewellery of the people of Tepe Gawra and the trade stimulated by the demand for different stones. The commonest materials used were obsidian, white frit, carnelian, limestone, marble and clay. Some burials contained thousands of beads, worn as necklaces, bracelets, armlets, anklets and girdles. In Gawra XIII amethyst and lapis lazuli, the latter imported from Afghanistan, were used for beads. Stoneworking in general reached a climax in Gawra XII, with more stone implements than at any other time.

The old fertility cult persisted, in the form of female figurines of baked or unbaked clay, the head being peg-shaped, with some apparently veiled.

The very few metal artefacts from the Ubaid levels, all of cold-hammered copper, may suggest a slight priority over the south in the earliest phase of metalworking, with a marked increase in the number of metal objects found at

39. Stamp-seals are among the most characteristic finds from Tepe Gawra, mostly made of steatite but also of other stones, bone, frit or clay. Nearly 600 varieties altogether were found, both seals and impressions, most from Gawra XIII and later levels.

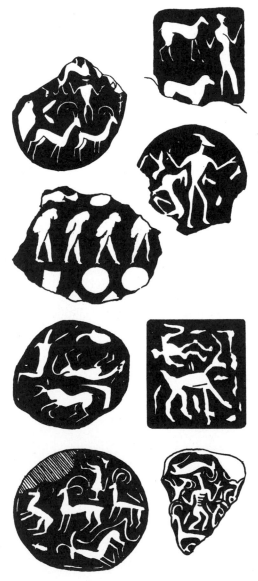

57

Tepe Gawra in the levels of the Uruk and Early Dynastic periods.

In addition to jewellery, the dead were provided with offerings of wheat, barley and mutton, other offerings including pottery, marble bowls and gaming pieces. The bodies were normally laid in the flexed or contracted position.

THE URUK PERIOD

The general appearance of distinctive types of pottery, wheelmade and especially comprising grey burnished wares, has for some years been taken as the ubiquitous evidence in southern Mesopotamia for the advent of the Uruk period, named after the site of Warka. The sequence at Ur now suggests that the plumred and polychrome painted wares hitherto associated with the following Jemdet Nasr period may occur likewise from the beginning of the Uruk period. Although firm data for an absolute chronology are still lamentably meagre, it seems that this may have begun by *c.* 3800 BC. Eight centuries would give a time span by no means too long for the Uruk and Jemdet Nasr periods. The earlier Uruk phases in southern Mesopotamia require much further investigation; but the most important innovations did not occur until towards the end of the period, in Uruk IV. The advent of newcomers, possibly Semites from north Syria, remains an attractive theory, and, considering the nature of the evidence, unlikely ever to be conclusively proved or disproved. Certainly the general tradition of burnished pottery was indigenous to Anatolia, Cilicia and the northern parts of Syria, as it never was to Mesopotamia; but attempts to identify 'Uruk grey' ware in Anatolia have surely been misguided.

The Ubaid period in northern Mesopotamia came to a violent end in fire and massacre, with the destruction of Gawra XII. Thereafter the surviving inhabitants sought greater security by building their houses on the top of the mound, the area previously occupied by the sacred precinct, and by fortifying the town. Grai Resh III in the Jebel Sinjar was likewise fortified. To the west, the Ubaid phase in the Antioch Plain (Amuq E) was followed by a long period of change very probably brought about by migrations and newcomers.

The incompleteness of the record as at present known should not obscure the achievements of the Sumerian population of the cities of southern Mesopotamia, of which Warka and Ur were now the most important, Eridu relatively less so than before. Much discussion has revolved around the most appropriate terminology for the later prehistoric phases in southern Mesopotamia, American specialists preferring to restrict the term 'Uruk period' to levels XIV–IX of the Eanna precinct at Warka and to use the term 'Protoliterate' to describe the ensuing phases (A–D) until Early Dynastic I. In terms of the Warka sequence, Protoliterate A is equivalent to Eanna VIII–VI, Protoliterate B to Eanna V–IVA and Protoliterate C–D to Eanna IIIC–IIIA. In this book the terminology favoured by British archaeologists from Woolley onwards will be adhered to, whereby Eanna XIV–IVA comprise the Uruk period and Eanna IIIC–IIIA the Jemdet Nasr period, so named after the style of painted pottery first associated with that small mound situated fifty miles south of Baghdad and now totally destroyed. Whatever the complexities of these periods, particularly of the sequences of temples at Warka, there can be little doubt that the Uruk period was of considerable length, and that the Jemdet Nasr period was longer than the evidence of Warka itself might suggest.

A ceramic sequence based on the pottery from Eridu V–I comprises an Early Uruk phase, equivalent to Eanna XIV–VII, and a Late Uruk phase, contemporary with Eanna VI–III. The earlier phase is distinguished by 'Uruk grey' and 'Uruk red' wares, the former being commoner in northern than in southern Mesopotamia and the latter comprising varieties of bowls and jars. At the end of the Early Uruk phase appear jars with pierced lugs on the shoulder; the Late Uruk phase is most clearly distinguished by the roughly made bowls with bevelled rim, very numerous at Eridu and at Warka, and produced in kilns at Ur. These bowls are often found upside down and containing food offerings. Their continuation in the Jemdet Nasr period at Warka illustrates the unreality of any attempt to classify every aspect of material civilization in successive and mutually exclusive periods.

By far the largest and most important site is Warka (Uruk), the biblical Erech, which gives its name to this period. The Sumerian tradition of its having long been a great city is borne out by the archaeological evidence obtained over many seasons by the painstaking work of the German excavators. The nature of the remains makes it hardly remarkable that the architecture, though not always well preserved, has received the most attention. By the Early Dynastic period the city wall had a perimeter of six miles, thus enclosing a truly vast area. Although probably not so large in the Uruk period, the size and wealth of Warka must even then have been unrivalled. It seems likely that about one third of the area enclosed within the perimeter was occupied by public buildings and the houses of the rich, one third by the houses of the poor and the remainder by gardens, cemeteries and open spaces. A city of the Near East might well have its territory comparably divided today.

The Eanna precinct, originally dedicated to the sky god Anu but later to Innin (alias Ishtar), goddess of love, formed the very heart of the city of Warka in the great period of Eanna V–III. Before the time of Eanna VII the so-called Anu 'ziggurat', discussed below, may have been more important. Two architectural innovations in Eanna VI are the distinctive form of mud-brick termed by the excavators *Riemchen*, flat and square in section, and cone mosaics used in mural decoration, almost certainly originating in the Ubaid period. The Limestone Temple of Eanna V, so named from its foundations of irregular slabs laid over a layer of *terre pisé*, was of tripartite plan, at least 76 × 30 m. in area. The Mosaic Temple at Warka had limestone walls, with floors of gypsum paving elaborately laid over a course of limestone slabs set in bitumen. Stone was used on an even more lavish scale at Eridu, where the final temple (Eridu I) was built upon a massive stone-faced platform. For the stone thus required rafts or large boats down the Euphrates must have been used, or, less probably, up from the Persian Gulf.

With the great temples of Eanna IV, constituting what has aptly been termed a cathedral city, the civilization of the Uruk period attained its climax. There were three phases of this level, of which IVB was perhaps the most important of all the prehistoric Eanna levels, with three buildings (Temple A, Temple B and the Pillar Hall). The whole precinct seems to have centred on the Court Terrace, overlooked by the Pillar Hall and by Temple A [40].

Eanna IVA, the last building level of the Uruk period, has a very different plan from IVB. Temple B was demolished, to make way for a new and very large building, Temple C, 54 × 22 m. in area, like most of the temples being orientated from north-west to south-east. The precise sequence of repairs, alterations and rebuildings is, however, not always altogether clear, making it difficult to distinguish late Uruk (Eanna IV) from Jemdet Nasr (Eanna III) building remains, the exact date of some of the finds consequently being problematical. In contrast to most prehistoric temples in Mesopotamia, the

40. The approach to the Pillar Hall of Eanna IV was flanked by these engaged columns. The facade of the Pillar Hall had two rows of four very stout columns, 2.62 m. in diameter, the earliest known example of the use of free-standing columns. Their girth and primitive method of construction, with bricks laid radially to form an approximate circle, suggests a hesitant and experimental approach. Over the surface of the columns thick mud plaster was daubed; and, when it was still wet, cones of baked clay were inserted to make mosaic patterns, appearing to imitate the bark of a palm trunk or alternatively basketry or reed matting. On the columns black and white cones were used, while red cones occur in the mosaics elsewhere in the Pillar Hall and its surroundings.

sanctuary (or cella) of the Eanna temples is not readily distinguishable by altars, hearths or statue-bases. Temple C is unusual in having a plain façade, with internal niches only.

The oldest area of Warka, dating back further into the Ubaid period than the Eanna precinct, was probably that dominated by the Anu 'ziggurat'. This structure was not strictly a ziggurat but a series of temples, built one on top of another, each on a high platform, of which the White Temple is the best preserved. This temple, built on the normal tripartite plan, contained an offering table and a statue base; there were five doors. The roof must have been flat, and was accessible by stairs from two small rooms. Small *Riemchen* were used, laid mostly as headers, in the bonding called by the excavators *Riemchenverband*. This is a curious method, since the lateral joints are usually above one another, though lengthwise each course overlaps the course beneath by half a brick. Even at this relatively late date, therefore, it seems that there was no fixed tradition of building in mud-brick. At the east corner a space in the lowest course was left for a foundation sacrifice, where two animals, a leopard and probably a young lion, were deposited, obviously not as a food offering. This is an early example of a long tradition of foundation deposits in Mesopotamia. The platform whereon the White Temple stood had a pronounced batter, with shallow niches, very narrow and close together in proportion to the height of the platform; and this had been faced perhaps annually with many successive coats of plaster. Above the niches was a band of pottery jars driven into the brickwork, serving as both decoration and reinforcement. The Anu precinct at Warka demonstrates the sanctity attached over many generations to the precise site and ruins of successive temples; the White Temple also shows how such a building could be levelled while still in good condition, its rebuilding probably being dictated by ritual as much as by structural demands [41].

Thus in the Uruk period the cities of Sumer came to be dominated by temples, usually set on a platform, the Anu temples at Warka being far more typical than those of the Eanna precinct. Eridu had its temple platform extended five times, the latest temple (Eridu I) being faced with engaged columns and two types of mosaic, using baked clay and stone cones, some with copper-plated heads, and also coloured stone tesserae. The use of the corbelled arch is attested at Eridu in this period. To the north, at Tell Uqair, was a temple with remarkable internal painted decoration.

The development of technology in the Uruk period has to be inferred rather than deduced from direct evidence. Metallurgy is not exemplified by many stratified artefacts, though from Uruk XII onwards, when the first bowl with bevelled rim and the first plum-red wares appear, the ceramic forms increasingly suggest metal prototypes. With the use of the wheel, not so much for pottery as for four-wheeled carts, among the earliest pictograms of Uruk IVB, it can be assumed that wheeled transport had come into general use, though it may have appeared already in the Ubaid period. Water-borne trade must have expanded. Irrigation works were extended, new settlements were founded and population increased.

The wealth of the Sumerian world in the Uruk period is scarcely hinted at by discoveries in southern Mesopotamia. Gold foil was evidently used in the Anu temples of Warka. The graves of Ur-Ubaid III, dating to the very beginning of the Uruk period, had fairly modest equipment, largely of pottery, the burials being slightly flexed. A contrast is provided by the eighty Uruk and Jemdet Nasr tombs excavated in Gawra XIA–VIIIB. The wealth and individuality of Tepe Gawra may be partly attributable to its proximity to the mountains, with the advantage which this gave in access to the eastern trade through Iran. The use of a gabled roof for some tombs, with a ridge pole and supported by vertical posts, gives a hint of construction on a larger scale in the temples of Tepe Gawra. Social stratification is suggested by varying burial equipment, the more lavish including garments dyed blue, green and red. Beads were very popular, one tomb in Gawra XA containing over 25,000; a collection of over 750 cowrie shells must have come from the Indian Ocean. One tomb in Gawra X yielded 450 lapis lazuli beads, and illustrates the great growth in this trade from Afghanistan through Iran at this time, equivalent to Uruk VI–IV, when lapis lazuli may have reached Tepe Gawra sooner than southern Mesopotamia. Beads and amulets of many other materials were also found, including ivory, turquoise, jadeite, carnelian, haematite, obsidian, quartz, diorite and faience. Thus trade must have flourished. Gold, too, was imported and much in evidence in the tombs of Tepe Gawra, being especially popular for headgear, with rosettes, ribbons or tabs, beads, buttons and studs. There was a general improvement in stoneworking, exemplified by stone vessels from tombs of Gawra X.

Nineveh, only fourteen miles west of Tepe Gawra, was more closely connected with lands to the west, including the Jebel Sinjar. There the site of Grai Resh has yielded a succession of levels from the Ubaid period (IX–VI) through two transitional levels (V–IV), to the Uruk–Jemdet Nasr period (III–II). Grai Resh III was fortified with a very massive town wall, adding to the evidence from Gawra XIA of the unsettled conditions of the early Uruk period. Grai Resh II included a building of tripartite plan, probably a temple. The settlements in the Jebel Sinjar were characterized by grey burnished Uruk pottery and by the very crudely made bowls with bevelled rim, typical of the periods termed Ninevite 3 and 4 respectively at the great site of Nineveh itself, the largest in the whole region in the Uruk and Jemdet Nasr periods. In the Ninevite

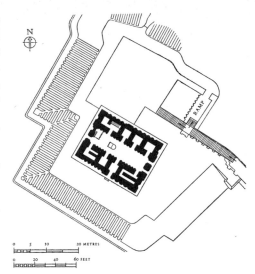

41. The eight successive buildings of the Anu Ziggurat were generally similar in plan, the temple platform being raised from 9 m. high (Level X) to 13 m. (Level B); this, the White Temple, perhaps of the Jemdet Nasr period, is the best preserved, standing on the south-west section of the platform; to the northeast an area was left open, probably for burnt offerings; the corners of the platform were orientated to the cardinal points.

3 period, northern Mesopotamia was culturally independent of the south, whereas by the time of Ninevite 4, approximately contemporary with Uruk IV–III, connections with the south were close, and Nineveh had grown into a very large town. The first of the temples at Tell Brak on the Khabur River, the Red Temple, was roughly contemporary with Uruk IV; Tell Brak shows links with the sites in the Jebel Sinjar.

It is difficult to avoid the conclusion that the major cities of Sumer have hitherto yielded a very inadequate record of their material civilization in the Uruk period, and likewise in the centuries following until the advent of the Third Dynasty of Ur, largely owing to the superimposition of massive buildings on top of the earlier levels. Moreover, the generally peaceful development militated against the survival of large quantities of metalwork and jewellery, with some obvious exceptions. The sheer size and concentration of cities in the south can leave no doubt of its being the most advanced region of its time.

In Uruk V there appear the first cylinder-seals, a Mesopotamian invention more extensively used there than anywhere else. Even when found securely stratified, their date of manufacture cannot be quite certain, for they were valued enough to be handed down as heirlooms. Much research has been devoted to the diversity of forms and materials and to the evolution of subject matter and style in the seal-cutter's craft, commonly called glyptic art. Although there are pitfalls in any such classification, necessarily as much typological as strati-graphic, the glyptic art of Mesopotamia may justly be said to reveal more of the artistry, religion and outlook on life of the Sumerians and their successors than any other single class of product. In a book of this scope attention must be confined to a selected range of seals, with the reminder that there is much that defies comprehension.

There was no abrupt change to the use of cylinder-seals, for the older stamp-seal, now with animal designs, was used in early Uruk levels, only gradually being ousted in later levels. As later evidence shows, the symbols of various deities appear on some seals, such as the lion-headed eagle, Imdugud, which in the later Early Dynastic period was the subject of the famous copper panel from the temple at Al 'Ubaid. Heraldic designs also occur. An important theme is the sacred temple herd, indicated as such by streamers hanging from a pole, the symbol of the mother goddess. Such seals suggest the power and wealth of the Sumerian temples in the Uruk period. Another theme is that of a herdsman defending a calving cow against a lion. Limestone and marble alone were used for Uruk cylinder-seals, which are always oblong [43].

Far wider in its significance was an invention which alone would suffice to entitle the Sumerians to a leading place in the story of human development, and without which it could not be recorded: the very art of writing. It appears on hundreds of clay tablets excavated at Warka (Uruk IVB). These were marked with a reed or stylus in a primitive script which can be described, by comparison with later tablets, as the ancestor of cuneiform writing. Though loosely termed pictographic, this script must in fact also be ideographic, each sign representing an idea or even a word. The derivation of this script may have been from property-marks; and some of the tablets from Warka have impressions of cylinder-seals on them, as marks of ownership [42, *Pl 6*].

The details of the evolution of this script into cuneiform, let alone questions of philology, are beyond the scope of this book. Suffice it to say that the demands of daily administration in the temples of Warka, with the need for reliable wage-lists and accounts, led the priests to take this great step forward, the implications

42. In the script of Uruk IVB are included representations of parts of the human body, of animals, plants and inanimate objects, among these a hut, a tent, a four-wheeled cart, a two-prowed boat and varieties of tools, weapons and household vessels.

EARLIEST PICTOGRAPHS 3000 B.C.	DENOTATION OF PICTOGRAPHS	PICTOGRAPHS IN ROTATED POSITION	CUNEIFORM SIGNS CA. 1900 B.C.	BASIC LOGOGRAPHIC VALUES	
				READING	MEANING
	HEAD AND BODY OF A MAN			LÚ	MAN
	HEAD WITH MOUTH INDICATED			KA	MOUTH
	BOWL OF FOOD			NINDA	FOOD, BREAD
	MOUTH + FOOD			KÚ	TO EAT
	STREAM OF WATER			A	WATER
	MOUTH + WATER			NAG	TO DRINK
	FISH			KUA	FISH
	BIRD			MUŠEN	BIRD
	HEAD OF AN ASS			ANŠE	ASS
	EAR OF BARLEY			ŠE	BARLEY

of which they can scarcely have been aware. Once writing came into use the temple priesthoods acquired yet more power over the laity, for they alone possessed this knowledge, and could exercise it for the aggrandizement of their city god or goddess and could train the boys who would continue and improve this skill. Writing meant both the knowledge of communication beyond the limits of direct conversation and storage of facts and figures for future reference, and eventually also the perpetuation of traditional stories. Without writing, civilization, in any true meaning of that word, was impossible. Literacy had the further effect of unifying the Sumerian world and counteracting the divisive jealousies and wars between neighbouring cities.

THE JEMDET NASR PERIOD

The Jemdet Nasr period in southern Mesopotamia was not a time of great innovations such as those which occurred in the Ubaid and Uruk periods. It was rather a time of consolidation, with relatively minor experiments. No such clear chronological division, however, can be distinguished in the north, where the post-Ubaid sequence is marked by a fusion of southern elements with indigenous elements.

Growth of population, whether purely by natural increase or with the help of immigration, is discernible in the number and size of sites. In the Uruk period

43. Uruk cylinder-seals show that this was a typically formative period, with no one formal style. Some cylinders have a suspension-loop, cut in one piece with the seal; others have a metal recumbent ram fastened to the axis. Both these features survive into the Jemdet Nasr period but not later. The subject matter of some Uruk seals is purely decorative; others represent action.

population, and with it the number of small, widely dispersed sites, had greatly increased, especially in the last phase. This trend continued in the Jemdet Nasr period, when, for example, rural settlement reached its maximum around Warka. It has been suggested that there may have been an influx of newcomers into Sumer from the southern littoral of the Persian Gulf, nowadays northern Saudi Arabia, where settlements contemporary with the Ubaid period were abandoned, presumably owing to the extension of desert conditions. This is an attractive theory, with far-reaching implications for the Uruk period and perhaps also for the origins of the Sumerians. The evidence from archaeological surveys, especially in the environs of Warka and Nippur and in Akkad and the Diyala Plain, has clarified the main trends of settlement in Mesopotamia proper, at the same time demonstrating local peculiarities. Accidents of preservation and visibility, with ancient land surfaces exposed by erosion from wind, may account for some of the differences between closely adjacent areas; but political and economic factors surely played the major part. At least one area, south of the city of Umma, was occupied by closely grouped sites first established in the Jemdet Nasr period and, with the presence of a canal where no watercourse had previously existed, suggesting planned settlement or colonization. It seems that in this period the population of the alluvial plain of southern Mesopotamia had so grown that large areas of marginal land had to be brought under cultivation, by extended irrigation and intensive labour. The total cultivated land seems at this time to have reached its maximum, leaving only small scattered areas of steppe. An exception was the district of Nippur, where the territory outside the city was by this time largely abandoned: this was, however, probably attributable to the drying up of a former channel of the Euphrates. A constant threat to the Sumerian farmer was salinity of the soil, causing the poorer land, the last to be cultivated, to be the first abandoned; it was also a reason for the eventual introduction of barley in place of wheat, being more resistant to salt, as the staple crop supporting the cities of Sumer and Akkad, by *c*. 2000 BC.

With the growth of settlement came an expansion of Mesopotamian influence, and thus of Sumerian civilization, far beyond the homeland in the south. It seems that new cities arose at Shuruppak (Fara) and Jemdet Nasr in the territory later to become Akkad, and at Mari on the middle Euphrates, a region perhaps little occupied in the Uruk period. Earlier settlements at Kish in Akkad and at Tutub (Khafaje) in the Diyala valley grew into cities. The cultural expansion which took place to east and west in this period can be illustrated by the adoption of the Sumerian script in Elam, as Proto-Elamite, and by the evidence of Jemdet Nasr influence in Egypt before and after its unification by Menes, probably *c*. 3300 BC. There is no doubt that this influence, most permanently manifest in mud-brick architecture but also in more ephemeral elements, was from Mesopotamia to Egypt, although by what route is uncertain. Excavations at Jawa, in the desert of Trans-Jordan, have revealed a town with sophisticated water supply in the late fourth millennium BC, and could just possibly suggest an overland trade route connecting the Tigris–Euphrates Plain with the valley of the Nile.

The connections with Egypt, where the framework of absolute chronology is surer than in Mesopotamia, reinforce the evidence that the Jemdet Nasr period was no mere brief transition from Uruk to Early Dynastic times.

It would be fair to say that there was a general advance in all arts and crafts in Jemdet Nasr times, if not always in artistic attainment. This advance must be seen against the background of increased efficiency implied by the recent inven-

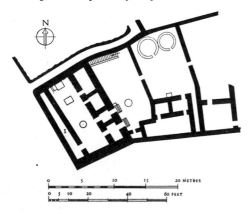

44. Plan of Sin Temple V. At Khafaje five building periods, represented by Sin Temples I–V in the sequence of shrines dedicated to the moon god, belong to the Jemdet Nasr period, for which a dating of *c*. 3400–3000 BC is neither too high nor improbably long.

tion of writing and of the continuing extension of irrigation works, external trade and specialized crafts. The power of the temple in each city seems also to have grown, with enlargement of temple estates. There is slight evidence of warfare.

The pottery, which, together with the cylinder-seals, forms the most readily recognizable criterion of this period, is found throughout Sumer, Akkad and the Diyala region but not farther north. Metals now become relatively plentiful, being most abundantly documented at Warka, where in Eanna IIIA was found the *Kleinfunde* hoard, including a silver spouted jar. Copper, lead, silver and gold were all worked. The complicated process of extracting silver from lead had been mastered; and a small copper bowl from Ur has legs soldered to its sides. Spouted pottery vessels and clay model shaft-hole axes copy metal originals. The skills already implied even in the Ubaid and very early Uruk ('Ur-Ubaid' III) periods were maintained and advanced.

On varying scales in architecture, sculpture, vessels, cylinder-seals, amulets and beads there was a general increase in the use of stone. Small carvings included many amulets of couchant sheep or cows. Beads of limestone, carnelian, rock crystal, gypsum, lapis lazuli, amazonite, agate, amethyst, diorite and aragonite all occur at Warka, as well as shell and bone beads, usually in simple cylindrical, barrel, ring and biconical forms [45, *Pl 7*].

No sudden change is evident in the cylinder-seals, but rather a disintegration of the old repertoire of glyptic designs. But the seals display more variety; and there were experiments with shape, material, size and method of suspension. The drill was extensively used and is very evident in scenes of pigtailed figures. Rows of horned animals, spiders, scorpions and fish occur, as well as decorative patterns perhaps derived from textiles.

The script undoubtedly improved on that of the late Uruk period, some signs being used phonetically, so that words could be spelt out. The characters are still, however, largely pictographic.

Architecture is best represented by the three phases of Eanna III C–A at Warka and by the first five temples at Khafaje (Sin Temples I–V) devoted to the cult of the moon god. The Eanna precinct now had two parts, and was considerably extended and changed. Eanna IIIA was the latest and most important phase, comprising the L-plan temple-terrace enlarged to thrice its original area, its façades having shallow niches decorated with panels of cone mosaic, as well as buildings to the south-west. These were surely the most splendid years of the Eanna temples.

Outside the Sumerian homeland of southern Mesopotamia the cultural sequence of Khuzistan continued through successive phases following the Sabz–Jaffarabad–Susiana A phase. Next in the Deh Luran succession is the Khazineh phase, equivalent to Susiana B and with painted pottery closely paralleled at Hajji Mohammad and Ras el-Amiyah in southern Mesopotamia. The economy of the Deh Luran Plain continued unchanged in the following Mehmeh phase, contemporary with the early Ubaid period, in the later fifth millennium BC. Latest in the Deh Luran Plain comes the Bayat phase, the full flowering of the Ubaid economy, based on barley and sheep, and continuing into the early Uruk period in Mesopotamian terms. By then the Sumerian homeland had for centuries been in the lead compared with Khuzistan. Multiple burials in slab-covered cist-graves at Hakalan in Luristan seem to belong to nomads of the late Mehmeh and Bayat phases, who may have wintered in the Deh Luran Plain. Thus contacts between the Zagros highlands and the lowlands of Khuzistan persisted into the fourth millennium BC.

45. The outstanding piece of sculpture in the round is an almost life-size marble head from Eanna III, of a naturalism unparalleled earlier or later in the known record of Sumerian art. The eyeballs, now lost, may have been of lapis lazuli; and the eyebrows were originally inlaid.

65

THE EARLY DYNASTIC PERIOD

The long duration of the Early Dynastic (E.D.) period in Mesopotamia cannot be fully understood from the excavations in the great cities of the south, the main Sumerian homeland. Here the later remains obscure those of this period. It was the Oriental Institute of Chicago expedition in the Diyala valley in the 1930s which recovered evidence from two of its excavations—at Tell Asmar (ancient Eshnunna) and Khafaje (Tutub)—proving beyond doubt the lengthy time-span of the whole sequence of E.D.I, II, IIIa and IIIb. Six centuries (*c.* 3000–2370 BC) is not excessive, the minimum time-span for E.D.I, II, and III being two centuries, one century and two and a half centuries respectively. Except perhaps for the cylinder-seals, the archaeological evidence does not always emphasize or even confirm these sub-divisions of the Early Dynastic period; but there is some historical support for these three sub-periods, while E.D.III certainly had two phases.

The god of vegetation, Abu, had been worshipped at Tell Asmar in shrines of the Jemdet Nasr period. The Archaic Shrine of E.D.I marks the new period by the introduction of the most tell-tale feature of Early Dynastic Mesopotamia, the plano-convex mud-brick. This temple endured through nine distinct phases of modifications to the plan, all within the E.D.I period, which thus can scarcely have been very brief. Its design comprised an oblong sanctuary, or cella, with podium or altar at the short end, following the 'northern' plan, and with subsidiary rooms and a court at the west end. There was a radical alteration of plan and reorientation in the following E.D.II period, when the Square Temple comprised three sanctuaries grouped round an approximately square court. It lasted through three main phases in the E.D.II period. For some reason the E.D.III temple, the Single Shrine Temple, consisted once more of a single sanctuary [46, 47].

The succession of temples of the moon god Sin at Khafaje endured for nearly one thousand years. Sin Temples I–V fall within the Jemdet Nasr period. But in E.D.I the building was replanned to form Sin Temple VI: the courtyard was enlarged, covering within its area that of the court of the earlier Sin temples. One sanctuary stood above the earlier ones; but a second sanctuary now appears, between the first one and the courtyard. This implies, if not change, at least elaboration of the ritual. Sin Temple VII, with deeper and larger foundations, marks the change to the E.D.II period. Sin Temples IX–X fall in E.D.IIIa–b, the latter having five reoccupations and standing eight metres above the orignal Sin Temple I.

Just south-west of the Sin temples at Khafaje stood one of only two known examples of a distinctively Early Dynastic temple-complex, the other being at Al 'Ubaid, far to the south. This was the Temple Oval, so named from the plan of its two concentric enclosure walls. Some special sanctity attached to this entire area, because it was dug down to virgin soil, through the accumulated depth of earlier building levels, and then filled with clean sand. Foundations of a depth greater than structurally requisite were laid in the sand and clay packed down against the walls [48].

The temple built on a platform, normally encasing the remains of previous structures and emphasizing the Sumerian reverence for the site of a sacred building, was architecturally the prototype of that most typically Mesopotamian monument, the ziggurat. This was never a tomb, any resemblance to the Step Pyramid of Zoser in Egypt being fortuitous. The earliest known representation of a ziggurat is on a cylinder-seal of the Uruk period; Early Dynastic seals also

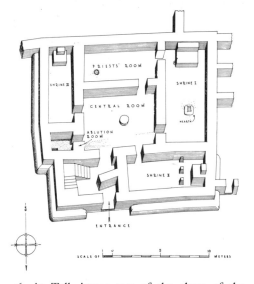

46. At Tell Asmar two of the altars of the Square Temple, shown above, were at the south and one at the west end. This represents the 'southern' plan, perhaps reflecting Sumerian influence, as the Diyala valley became culturally more fully integrated with the south.

show this structure. The first written reference occurs in the time of Gudea of Lagash (see p. 86). At Ur the first ziggurat dates back to the Uruk period, though hidden within the brickwork of later rebuildings, especially of E.D.III, and of the great reconstruction by Ur-Nammu, described in the next chapter. The earliest remains at Warka of the Eanna ziggurat are similarly concealed. The so-called 'Anu Ziggurat' is merely a temple on a platform. As later written references indicate, the purpose of the ziggurat was to reproduce a mountain, as the abode of the god in the flat alluvial plain. In a later period the largest of the three ziggurats at Ashur, originally sacred to Enlil, head of the Sumerian pantheon, but subsequently to the national god Ashur, was called by a title translated as 'House of the Mountain of the Universe'. Astronomical and astrological

47. The Single Shrine Temple, reconstructed above, had four building phases, and lasted into the succeeding Akkadian period with Single Shrine Temple IV. Already, in Single Shrine Temple II, plano-convex bricks were being set on edge, in a bonding which foreshadows the regular, flat bricks of the Akkadian period.

67

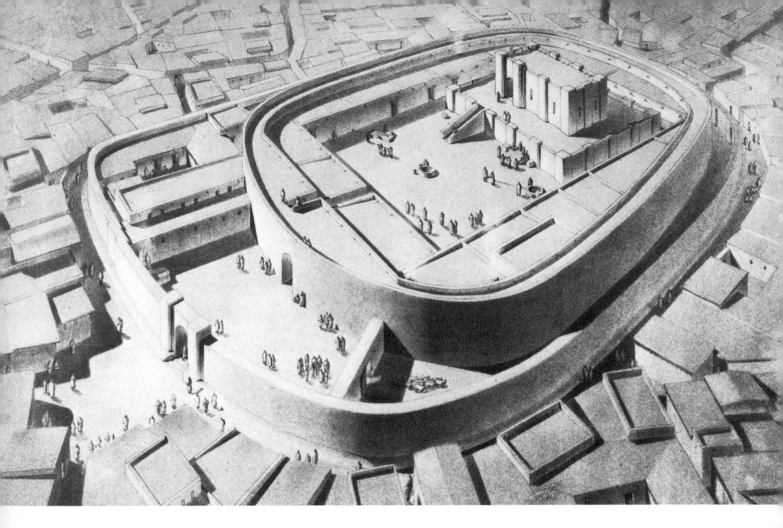

48. The Temple Oval at Khafaje had an area of about 74 × 54 m., the two walls being three metres apart, except on the north-east side, where there was a wider space with a forecourt, entered through a towered gateway. At the north corner stood a building containing a shrine and probably housing the temple staff. The main shrine has vanished, but was built on a buttressed platform and reached by a staircase, off centre but probably in line with its doorway.

significance was not given to the ziggurats until much later, in the Neo-Babylonian period.

Early Dynastic rulers seem to have built themselves imposing palaces, the few yet known being at Eridu, Kish and Mari. Two almost identical buildings at Eridu, 65 × 45 m. in area, had façades with prominent buttresses and deep recesses. Following the general Sumerian custom, the corners were orientated to the cardinal points. Two main gates gave entry through double fortified walls, the outer one being 2.5 m. thick. The largest rooms probably served as audience-halls and were related to the great square court in a manner repeated later in the palace of Zimri–Lim at Mari, where the preceding Early Dynastic palace went up in flames with the rest of the city. At Kish, Palace A very possibly dates to E.D.IIIa–b, though displaying features paralleled in the earlier (E.D.II) Sin Temple VIII at Khafaje. The city of Kish enjoyed great prestige, especially under the dynasty which ruled the whole of Sumer directly after the Flood, in the E.D.II period: the antediluvian rulers can plausibly be equated with E.D.I. Before that time the ruler of each city seems to have lived in the temple, and not in a palace [49].

In ancient Mesopotamia towns were crowded, with no evidence of general planning. Excavations in Early Dynastic levels have revealed relatively little of private houses, the most informative site being Tell Asmar. In Stratum V (E.D.III) was uncovered the so-called 'arch house', with an entrance leading through two small anterooms, perhaps screened from the street and the flies only by matting, into a large central room. This had a bench along one wall, a hearth in the middle and four doors into the side rooms, each spanned by a brick arch built without the use of centring; a small window gave light from the inner anteroom to a larder, and seems to have had a wooden grille of the type still seen in Iraq today. The houses at Tell Asmar had no central court, perhaps explicable by wetter winters than in the south; nor is there evidence of an upper storey. At Khafaje the residential quarters closely surrounded the Temple Oval.

The most distinctive feature of Early Dynastic buildings is a shape of brick, termed plano-convex, peculiar to this period. It was not entirely a practical form, and was commonly laid in herringbone courses; but sometimes three diagonal courses are all laid in one direction, followed by two or three courses laid flat, with the convex sides upwards, acting as an imperfect bonding. In a modern sense bonding was unknown. As at Ur, matting was sometimes used at intervals between the courses of brickwork, an effective reinforcement. Burnt brick was occasionally used behind the limestone blocks used as a footing.for the wall-face, for instance inside the terrace wall surrounding the First Dynasty ziggurat at Ur.

Early Dynastic pottery in Mesopotamia shows that relatively little of the artistic talent of the Sumerians was devoted to this craft. At Kish especially continuity is evident not only in the range of forms persisting from the Jemdet Nasr period but also throughout the Early Dynastic sequence. 'Stone-ware' forms at Kish (E.D.I–II) are very similar to those from the Royal Cemetery at Ur (E.D.IIIa). Spouted jars and large lug-handled jars of Jemdet Nasr types recur at Kish, in the Y Cemetery, Mound A and the A Cemetery. Decoration declined as the Early Dynastic period continued: Jemdet Nasr fashions survived into E.D.II. The outstanding product of the Early Dynastic potter was 'Scarlet Ware', known mostly in E.D.I context. Throughout the Sumerian world in E.D.III—at Mari, Khafaje, Kish, Ur and Susa—a conventionalized nude female figure in relief became a distinctive ceramic feature. By then metal vessels were common enough to relegate pottery largely to the poor people and the cheapest household purposes [*Pl 8*].

Cylinder-seals cover such a wide range of designs, materials and forms that these products of Sumerian craftsmanship, the tradition of glyptic art, have been much stressed as the most informative branch of art in Mesopotamia. There is much truth in this claim, though their importance must not be exaggerated. Being often preserved as heirlooms, their value for dating is unreliable. Nevertheless, each sub-division of the Early Dynastic period produced distinctive cylinder-seals, some types of which are here summarized [**50**].

E.D.II cylinder-seals were often made of semi-translucent white or green serpentine, aragonite and calcite; shell-core also came into use. Texts first appear in E.D.II, but rarely and only with the owner's name. Subject matter, though with no sharp break in style, becomes more varied: the main themes are contests of demons, heroes, animals and monsters, in continuous friezes; banqueting scenes also occur. The animals tend to be in half-erect postures. Bulls are often shown rampant. A two-pointed headdress was fashionable and distinctive of E.D.II. A recurrent theme is the protection of flocks and herds from the attacks of lions: often the hero is joined by a bull-man, now first appearing. This may be Enkidu, friend of Gilgamesh, and at least by E.D.III the friezes and scenes of contest wherein these figures appear are almost certainly based on the *Epic of Gilgamesh*, though not proved to be so by any inscriptions. Among

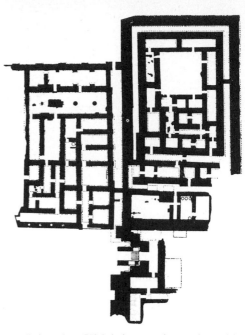

49. Palace A at Kish is large and complex, with steps and columns, recessed facades and fortified towered entrances. Its two wings were built successively. It would have been a fitting home for the greatest of the kings of Kish; and the unsatisfactory character of the report on the Kish excavations makes an E.D.II date not impossible.

51. From the Square Temple at Tell Asmar (E.D.II) comes probably the entire complement of statues dedicated to the worship of Abu, god of vegetation, whose figure stands taller than all the others. Stature, emblems on their bases and the almost terrifyingly large diameter of their staring eyes all distinguish the two divinities, Abu and the mother goddess, from the other statues, representing worshippers. All the men wear the characteristically Sumerian fringed kilt, though that worn by one figure is slightly different: he has a shaven head, and is probably a priest.

E.D.II seals is a distinctive class from Farah (Shuruppak), including contests, boats, snakes and scorpions.

The E.D.III cylinder-seals include many cut from the core of large conch-shells from the Persian Gulf; others were made of lapis lazuli and a few of gold or silver, solid or of foil over a bitumen core. Titles were added to the name, but only officials had their seals inscribed. Modelling in relief became the dominant stylistic feature, contrasting with the linear style of E.D.II seals. Animals and heroes are shown in a more upright posture, the friezes thus being more close-knit, indeed crowded. Another type of frieze has an eagle, often lion-headed, as its central figure, presumably Imdugud, the storm god. Animals walking peacefully in a row often fill the lower registers of seals. A common subject is a ceremonial banquet, with two figures seated facing each other and drinking from tubes through a vessel put between them. A gazelle and plants often symbolize the god of fertility, whose chthonic aspect is frequently depicted by the god Ningiszida in the guise of two entwined vipers, the snake being associated in

50. E.D.I cylinder-seals, which were commonly of black, blue or green limestone or dark serpentine. The 'brocade' style is the most characteristic, so called from the even density of the design, linear and highly stylized with no large masses or empty spaces included in the pattern. Simplified animal and plant forms predominate, in running friezes.

Sumer as, for example, in Minoan Crete, with fertility.

A theme peculiar to Early Dynastic cylinder-seals is the building of a temple-tower, or ziggurat: one such scene shows a plano-convex brick being held up by a priest to be scrutinized by the god. The manner of depicting any type of scene was not yet bound, as in later periods, by rigid conventions. The skill of the glyptic artists is demonstrated by their limited tool kit: for cutting and drilling only copper tools were available, fed with emery powder when hard stones were being worked. In a house of the Akkadian period at Tell Asmar a bow-drill, borer, chisels and gravers were found.

Sumerian sculpture in the round was, frankly, often crude in design and execution. Not till the time of Gudea did the Sumerian sculptor produce masterpieces, though it is important to look at statues from more than one Early Dynastic site: for example, the work from Tell Asmar is provincial compared with that from the wealthier city of Mari. Men's hairstyle in E.D.II was long, but shaven in E.D.III. The E.D.II sculptural style was abstract, the human form being simplified to a series of differentiated planes. Though the cylinder and cone seem to have remained at the back of the sculptor's mind, a more naturalistic style emerged in the late E.D.II and E.D.III periods [51].

52. One of the best known examples of the *cire perdue* technique is the great panel from the temple of Al'Ubaid (E.D.IIIb), depicting the lion-headed eagle Imdugud, the storm god, gripping a stag with each claw.

Large figures were first cast in copper in E.D.II, with sheets of copper hammered over a bitumen core. The *cire perdue* (lost wax) technique was in the same period introduced for human and animal figures and pot-stands [52]. At Al 'Ubaid there is a remarkable inlaid frieze of the temple cattle and a milking scene, the figures in limestone and shell, as well as encrusted columns and stone flower mural ornaments. Copper lions guarded the entrance to this temple of the goddess Ninhursag ('Lady of the Mountain') at Al 'Ubaid. Here may be seen the origin of the device of guardian lions, which were destined to be so popular over so many centuries in the Near East.

THE ROYAL CEMETERY OF UR

Shell, lapis lazuli and carnelian were materials particularly popular with Sumerian society, and therefore much employed by artists and craftsmen anxious to please their clientele. These and other products of the Sumerians, such as goldsmith's work and bronze tools and weapons, had a long tradition stretching back to the prehistoric periods. Nor were they at any time exclusive to one city, even Ur, since Kish and Mari had rich burials at an earlier date (E.D.II) than the better known Royal Cemetery at Ur (E.D.IIIa). Concentrations of economic power, with the skills required to make best use of the whole range of imported raw materials, were both the driving-force and the outcome of the highly organized Sumerian city-states and their far-flung trading connections. These brought in more wealth to Mesopotamia than either before or after the Early Dynastic period. In the Royal Cemetery, however, may be seen by far the largest collection of metalwork and jewellery illustrating Sumerian technology.

Flat plaques cut from the central column of large conch-shells from the Persian Gulf afforded an easily carved medium, with the colour and grain of ivory, for the ornamentation of furniture, sound-boxes of harps and lyres, gaming-boards and cylinder-seals. One method of shell inlay was to engrave the design and then to cut back the ground, leaving slight relief and filling the hollows with bitumen, bituminous and red paste being used for internal detail. Another method was to cut away the background completely, leaving the figure in silhouette with the internal details engraved on its surface: either the figures were set in plain bitumen or, more often, the background was filled in with a mosaic of small, irregular pieces of lapis lazuli set in bitumen. An outstanding example of this use of lapis lazuli is the unique 'Standard'. The origins of shell inlay may lie in the mosaic ornament so typical of Uruk and Jemdet Nasr architecture. In the E.D.IIIb period, mother-of-pearl was used for some of the tesserae, together with red and black stone, covering the columns of the temple at Al 'Ubaid. On the same building are friezes with figures in shell or limestone inlaid against a background of black mosaic [*Pl 9*].

Lapis lazuli was much used in the Early Dynastic period, especially in E.D.III, that from the Royal Cemetery at Ur being of a distinctive and recognizable shade of blue. It was certainly worked on the spot, for unworked lumps were found at Ur: moreover, beads of identical shapes were made of materials imported from different regions. Ring-beads of carnelian, as shown by unfinished specimens, were first roughly chipped into shape; then had the hole pierced with a very fine drill used from both ends; finally they were polished. Long biconical carnelian and gold beads were a favourite type. Lapis lazuli was very popular for beads, usually in combination with carnelian, and sometimes a skull-cap of lapis beads was worn. At Lagash was found a bull's head, with eyes encrusted with lapis and mother-of-pearl. Etched carnelian beads, their patterns in white, indicate cultural contacts with the Indus valley, though precisely where these beads originated remains uncertain: at Ur they continued in use until the Akkadian period, when they occur also at Kish. For the headdress and trimmings of garments the combination of carnelian with lapis was fashionable; but lapis with either silver or gold was more in favour for necklaces. Gaudy as much of the jewellery of Ur may appear to the modern eye, display of wealth was not necessarily the chief motive behind the fashions popular with Sumerian women of the royal court. An innate love of the aesthetic effect of bright colours is apparent.

The goldsmiths of Ur have rightly become famous through the recovery of their work by the expedition of 1923–34. Their skills are manifest in jewellery, vessels and ornamentation of daggers, chariots, harps, lyres and statuettes. To make sheet gold, it was probably beaten on flat, hard stones: a small haematite hammer or burnisher from Ur, slightly bulbous at one end, shows traces of having been used as a rubber. Gold naturally survives best of all metals; silver at Ur was found in fair condition, though normally very brittle. The quality of the gold used at Ur varies very considerably, one spearhead on analysis being found to contain only 30% gold, 60% silver and 10% copper. The best gold was used for ornamental and ceremonial objects; but small ornaments were sometimes made of a base alloy. Silver was usually of good quality, though often with traces of gold. The goldsmiths of Ur deliberately avoided using gold and silver in direct juxtaposition, preferring electrum, the alloy of silver and gold, which added to the range of colours at their disposal. Often, however, it closely resembled pure gold. The famous helmet of Meska-lamdug was found, on cleaning, to contain a considerable proportion of silver, and is estimated to be of only fifteen-carat gold. This helmet suggests the possibility that the Sumerians had learned the modern technique of dissolving silver from the surface of a silver-gold alloy, thus making it appear to be pure gold. But they could not extract silver from gold when the two were alloyed together [*Pl 10*].

Chasing, engraving, repoussé work, filigree, cloisonné, soldering, sweating, granulation and riveting were techniques all known to the Sumerian goldsmiths. For the fine detail chasing was normally used; engraving, which results in some small removal of metal, was rare, though one fluted gold bowl from the tomb of Meskalamdug shows both techniques on one vessel: chasing for the decoration round the rim and base and engraving to touch up the vertical fluting. Cloisonné work is less frequent: examples are a gold finger-ring from Ur with lapis lazuli set in the cloisons and a four-petalled carnelian and lapis flower on a gold ring from Lagash. This technique is suitable for setting stones, each secured by its frame, or cloison, and was common in later periods for enamel inlay. Joins and attachments by soldering and sweating were much used by the Sumerians: 'hard' soldering, using an alloy of silver with gold or copper, was the process employed in filigree work and, among other things, for the longitudinal seam of barrel and biconical forms of gold bead. Sweating made it possible, by control of the heat directed by a blow-pipe on to the flame from an oil lamp, to attach granulations or filigree to the background without the use of solder. Seams could be joined by soldering or by sweating. Granulation was rather coarse. Riveting was used for attaching handles to vessels, whatever the metal, and the hilt to the blade of a dagger. Wire-drawing, however, was one technique not mastered: wire was fashioned instead from strips cut from thin sheets of metal, thus being square

53. Raising is especially suitable for beakers and tumblers; and it must have been used for this silver vase from Lagash, inscribed on the neck with the name of Entemena, king of Lagash, the design being engraved and centred round the lion-headed eagle Imdugud.

in section. These could be twisted round to form wide gold rings, with gold solder applied inside [*Pl 11*].

Metal vessels were normally beaten out of one sheet. The earliest technique, suitable for wide, open dishes and bowls, was hollowing or sinking, used in fashioning copper, gold or silver vessels. Far more complex vessels could be made by the more difficult technique, also mastered by the Early Dynastic metalworkers, of raising. From the Royal Cemetery at Ur no less than 118 types of metal vessel are recorded, from simple bowls and dishes to jars, cauldrons, buckets and fine fluted vessels [53].

The Sumerians imported their copper from Oman, from parts of Anatolia (including the rich deposits at Ergani Maden in south-eastern Turkey) and from the plateau of Iran, each region yielding an ore which contained different impurities. The sources of tin are still uncertain, but may have included the Hamadan region of western Iran, Trans-Caucasia and alluvial deposits in north-eastern Anatolia. To the Sumerians must go the credit for the first extensive use of tin-bronze, whose great advantage over copper is for casting, and thus for a degree of mass production. A higher proportion of tin, over ten per cent, gives a harder but more brittle alloy. Copper can be 'work-hardened' by hammering, as was done in the Egyptian Old Kingdom: the resulting temper, however, does not last long. Bronze was therefore particularly suitable for tools and weapons, of which a great variety was found at Ur.

Sumerian tools and weapons came to be diffused over much of the ancient Near East. Such types as the shaft-hole and transverse axeheads were more sophisticated than the contemporary flat axeheads, with or without lugs, made in Egypt. North Syria, with Til Barsib, was a major centre of the metalworking industry, a meeting-place of influences from Sumer and from Anatolia. Shaft-hole and transverse axes, as well as spearheads, occur as far north as the Kuban valley, and were undoubtedly imported. Thereafter came the inevitable imitation of these imports by local craftsmen. Closed moulds were necessary for the casting of shaft-hole axes and other types, the mould being made in two parts and the molten metal introduced by means of a pouring-cup and one or more runners cut through the mould and the core. The *cire perdue* method was used for statues, such as three from Tell Asmar and the lions' heads from the temple of A-annipadda at Al 'Ubaid. For large statues a core was used, to save metal, only small figures being solid. The *cire perdue* method makes any shape of casting practicable; and fine detail can easily be carved on the wax [54, 55].

The funerary customs demonstrated by the burials of the Royal Cemetery at Ur are not documented in the surviving written sources; and comparisons with the First Dynasty in Egypt are impeded by the lack of evidence from the E.D.I period. Similar practices at Kish appear in E.D.II, and a number of the finds from Ur suggest this period. The cemetery lies on top of two rubbish levels with Jemdet Nasr pottery and seal-impressions and some impressions possibly of E.D.I date. The debris overlying the Royal Cemetery, from the robbed tombs of Mesannipada and his family of the First Dynasty of Ur (E.D.IIIb), provides a *terminus ante quem* for the burials. Some architectural development is discernible in the Royal Cemetery: Tomb 779, plundered but yielding the Standard (see p. 72), was probably the earliest, roofed in stone with a corbel vault. Later in the series was Tomb 1054, with domed roof and courtyard. In one tomb remains of wooden centring used in construction of the roof were recovered. Some tombs had vaults built without centring; and two had an apse and barrel vault. Both the true arch and the pendentive, to achieve the transition from the square plan of the walls to the circular dome, are manifested in the Royal Cemetery. Doors between rooms within one tomb were either arched or spanned by a wooden lintel. Thus these tombs reveal much of the skill of the Sumerian builders in the use of rubble limestone masonry, mud-brick and kiln-fired brick and timber.

Sixteen tombs stand out in the total of over 2,500 graves, as the only ones where the burial was accompanied by the ritual of human sacrifice. Moreover, their design is distinctive, differing from even the richest of the private graves, such as that of Meskalamdug with the gold helmet, which are simply deep shafts with the coffin at the bottom. The royal tombs have a shaft with slightly sloping sides dug down through the earlier levels for ten metres or more, being of rectangular plan, up to 13 × 9 m.; access was by a sloping or stepped ramp. At the bottom of the pit the tomb chamber was usually built. The great majority of human victims in the royal tombs were in the pit outside the tomb chamber.

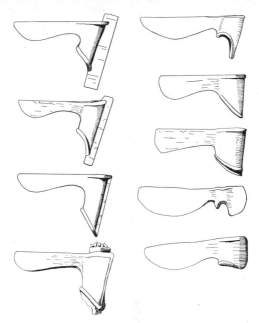

54. Shaft-hole axes of bronze were cast in large numbers in Mesopotamia, being characteristic of the Royal Cemetery of Ur. Hammered copper axeheads, imitating the cast shaft-hole type, also occur at Ur. Daggers from Ur commonly have three rivets, one in the tang and one in each shoulder, appearing some three centuries later (*c*. 2200 BC) in north Syria, Cilicia and Cyprus.

55. Poker-butted spearheads were characteristic of Early Dynastic Mesopotamia, and inspired the metalworkers of north Syria to produce spearheads modelled on this type, though usually with a bent tang of Anatolian derivation.

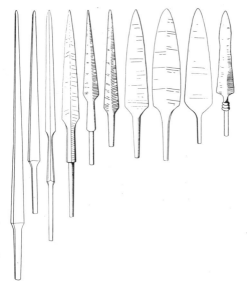

56. The death pit at Ur during excavation by Sir Leonard Woolley 1922–9.

The Great Death Pit contained seventy-four bodies, sixty-eight of them women; but no principal burial was recovered, perhaps suggesting another plundered chamber just outside the pit. The tomb chamber which was discovered is unusual in being outside the pit, at a higher level. Chariots accompanied this holocaust, and cups beside the victims suggest a peaceful death by poisonous drug. It was common practice to fill the tomb shaft by stages, with successive offerings of food and sometimes human sacrifices [56, 57].

What explanation can be given of the funerary customs evident at Ur in the Royal Cemetery? Unfortunately very little with any certainty. The suggestion of a fertility cult is undermined by the age of Shubad—she was about forty years old. Nor is there any evidence that human sacrifice accompanied or followed the annual sacred marriage in later times. Texts mention human sacrifice only in connection with substitute-kings. Propitiation of the gods in times of ill omen is a possible interpretation. The significance of the funeral feast may be underlined by the scene on one side of the Standard.

The ordinary people continued to be buried in graves showing continuity from prehistoric times: the body was normally laid on its side, as in sleep, wrapped in matting or sometimes in a wooden, wickerwork or clay coffin. A cup, jar or bottle and a plate constituted the usual grave-goods, to which was often added a bitumen model boat, frequently containing gifts of food in vessels. This was perhaps intended for some ritual to get rid of the dreaded monster Lamashtu; or it might have served to help the owner to reach the gloomy underworld of the Sumerians unharmed by the perils on the way.

SOCIAL STRUCTURE AND ADMINISTRATION

Much discussion has centred around the origins and growth of cities in Mesopotamia. At the greatest of all these cities, Warka, the most rapid increase of population appears to have come with the beginning of the Early Dynastic period, when the city was first enclosed by a defensive perimeter wall.

The achievements of Sumerian architects, artists and craftsmen and the economic resources which made these possible have long been credited largely, if not predominantly, to the role of the temple as the focus of political and economic power in each city. There is evidence demonstrating the organization of the temples, the obligatory offerings and voluntary gifts which they received and their exploitation of client labour and slaves. Yet this evidence has perhaps been used to overstate the argument for theocratic government. A major contemporary source, dating to the E.D.IIIb period (*c.* 2400 BC), is the archive from the temple of the goddess Bau, consort of the city god Ningirsu, in the city of Girsu, centre of the state of Lagash. Certainly the temples had great power and prestige, and the chief temple of each city occupied a commanding position. The estates of the temple of Bau, however, may have occupied only one tenth of the total area of the city-state. The temptation to press comparisons with feudalism in medieval Europe should be restrained. Like associations in other historical contexts, temples may well have been founded in an age of missionary fervour, such as that of the Gothic cathedral builders; but they seem also to have been destined to a gradually less uncritical loyalty as the centuries passed, and as other elements in society claimed a growing share of the spoils. It seems most probable that the temple formed the centre of many prehistoric communities in Mesopotamia, and continued thus in smaller towns through the Early Dynastic period. In the larger cities, however, each temple formed one among several dominant landowning fraternities, among which were the governor (*patesi*) or king (*lugal*) and his family, as well as other clans or extended families. Wealth depended largely on land, and it seems that most of the estates owned by temples had been acquired by *c.* 3000 BC, the onset of the E.D.I period. But more than agricultural produce was required to secure a lasting position of power in Sumerian society, so that it is hardly remarkable that in the third millennium BC both temples and secular rulers were active in promoting and organizing trade at home and abroad, an activity later to fall mainly into the hands of mercantile families. Workshops were also run by the temples in Sumerian cities.

Perhaps it would be more realistic to see the temple in its most obvious role, as the religious centre of its city. Herein, more than in any secular activity, surely lay its abiding prestige and thus in large measure its hold on the respect and affections of the populace. Each city looked to the *Ekur* at Nippur as the chief shrine of the whole Sumerian world. This may be an echo of a time, before written records, when the city of the god Enlil had led a united Sumer. At least there survived the tacit acknowledgment of an underlying unity, in spite of internecine quarrels.

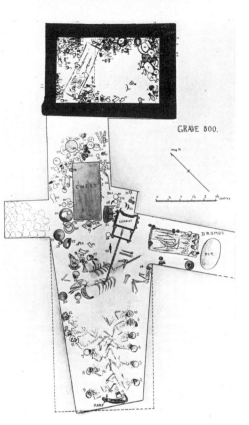

57. No two tombs at Ur are identical: in some the whole pit was occupied by a structure comprising two to four rooms, with a door facing the ramp and the rooms opening off one another. In these tombs the owner was buried in the inner chamber, with a few of his or her retainers in the outer chamber or chambers. A coffin was perhaps often used, though Shubad (Pu-abi) was found lying on a wooden bier, in a tomb of the most usual plan, shown above, with a single chamber built at one corner or end, occupying only part of the bottom of the pit; but a peculiarity of this grave was the construction of the vault after the burial and flush with the floor of the pit. The 'queen' was accompanied by two women at her bedside.

The unity of Sumerian society and the influence of the temples were alike reinforced by the emergence of a trained élite of scribes, already in the Early Dynastic period organized as a privileged group, recruited entirely from the wealthier families. Knowledge of the schools where these young men were trained is partly derived from Shuruppak, one of the oldest cities of Sumer, where school texts were written on tablets. From a later period come practice exercises by pupils. In these schools Sumerian literary compositions, usually more or less religious in character, were written and frequently recopied: without such recopying, then and in later centuries, most texts would have utterly perished. The primary purpose of these schools, however, was to produce bureaucrats for the administration of temples, palaces and estates. Sumerian bureaucracy was no exception: it was self-perpetuating.

KHUZISTAN AND THE NORTH

In Khuzistan, the Susa D culture lasted throughout the Early Dynastic period, is characterized by Scarlet Ware and may prove to have been the formative period of Elamite political power and civilization.

The spread of the urban economy and of Sumerian civilization to the north was a slow process, perhaps retarded in E.D.I–II but rapidly accelerated in E.D.III. Local idiosyncrasies persisted, however, in the material culture of northern Mesopotamia, from the middle Euphrates eastwards to the upper Tigris valley.

Six successive temples, said to be dedicated to the goddess Ishtar, have been excavated at Mari (F–A), the latest (A) being attributable to the E.D.IIIb period. Large stone tombs, built in pairs of gypsum blocks and corbel-vaulted, were associated with the third temple (D), and probably date to the E.D.II period. A feature of the next temple (C), larger in size, was a court with a peristyle of five mud-brick columns, 1.2 m. in diameter.

At Ashur, Temple H was founded on virgin soil, in E.D.I or II; and Temple G, founded later, was destroyed in the Akkadian period. Here were the earliest public buildings of the city destined to become the tribal and political capital of Assyria, until supplanted by Nimrud and Nineveh, and to remain the religious centre of that militaristic state throughout its long history until its destruction (614 BC). Its prestige was enduring, even though the power of the priests in Assyria and the wealth of the temples did not rival that of the priesthoods of the cities to the south.

At Nineveh, following the Ninevite 3 and 4 phases, the Ninevite 5 phase lasted throughout the Early Dynastic period in southern Mesopotamia and the Diyala region, or at least throughout E.D.I–II in Assyria. An incised ware of this period is best known from Tell Billa, and includes rather deep carinated bowls with pointed base and chalices. Incision appears either by itself or combined with relief decoration [58].

THE DECLINE OF SUMER

From the time of Gilgamesh the land of Sumer had been riven by intermittent conflicts between neighbouring cities, often fermented by quarrels over water for irrigation. Such unrest led to areas of sparse population and concentration around the protective walls of the chief city or of its satellites. The flat alluvial plain was unsuited to the survival of the unprotected settlement [Pl 12].

Towards the end of the Early Dynastic period two neighbouring cities, Lagash and Umma, were constantly at loggerheads. Eannatum, king of Lagash,

58. An example of the distinctive wheel-made painted pottery of Ninevite 5, which seems to have been derived from E.D.I types in the Diyala region and Iran: it was not found earlier at Nineveh. There are five main forms: two types of chalice, deep bowls, small jars with a sharp profile, and larger stemmed jars, all wheel-made. The ware is light in colour, the decoration of heavy zones and panels, always in dark purplish matt paint. Long-necked goats, fish and ducks are common motifs.

celebrated his triumph over Umma in the reliefs carved on a victory stele, commonly called the Stele of Vultures [59].

Eannatum was later slain in battle against Umma, and the fortunes of Lagash went into decline. During the reign of his nephew Entemena the men of Umma again stopped the water supply for the ditches cut as a boundary between the territories of the two cities. There were considerable problems of engineering involved in irrigation, particularly since the level of both Tigris and Euphrates was falling just at the time when the crops most required to be irrigated; but excessive irrigation led to salinity of the soil, a long-term factor in the eventual decline of Mesopotamia. The temples were able to enforce the corvée for maintaining canals and digging new ones. It is clear, however, that this power and wealth led to abuses, for Urukagina, last ruler of the dynasty of Lagash, instituted the first recorded programme of social reforms designed to correct them.

Umma was the last Sumerian city to hold political hegemony before Sargon of Agade established Semitic ascendancy. The ruler was Lugal-Zaggisi, who avenged Eannatum's sack of Umma by looting the temple of Lagash. He then introduced a major innovation by establishing his capital not in his native Umma but in the larger city of Warka, and by attempting to impose political unity on Sumer. An expedition as far as the Upper Sea, the Mediterranean, suggests the growing interest of the secular rulers in economic expansion and control of such resources as the cedar-wood from the Amanus range of north-west Syria. Lugal-Zaggisi's reign of twenty-five years ended with the seizure of power by Sargon of Agade. The Sumerian world was never to be quite the same again.

59. The Stele of Vultures, though far from complete, shows that two kinds of infantry were used by Eannatum, king of Lagash: light-armed spearmen and heavy infantry in a close-knit phalanx with shield-bearers. In a lower register Eannatum rides in his war chariot. The other side of the stele shows the god Ningirsu ensnaring the men of Umma in a net surmounted by his symbols, the lion-headed eagle above two lions. Thus was expressed the belief that the god of a city would fight for its ruler and citizens. This was monumental art, in that it was intended to convey a public message, to act as propaganda.

New Rulers and Peoples in Mesopotamia: Agade, Ur, Babylon, Assyria

The advent of Sargon of Agade marked the end of an era in Mesopotamia, with the establishment for the first time of a political power overriding the individual cities and even seeking to expand beyond the limits of the Mesopotamian plain. This monarchy proved, however, unstable, with revolts at the accession of each king. Finally an invasion of highlanders from the east brought this Akkadian dynasty to an end. After an interval the Sumerian city of Ur seized power, restoring much of the old Sumerian religion and language, under the rule of the Third Dynasty of Ur. This in turn succumbed to external pressures, from Amorites and Elamites, and was succeeded by more localized dynasties in the cities of Isin and Larsa, with Mari achieving its greatest prosperity under its final ruler, Zimri-Lim. Then it fell, to rise no more, to Hammurabi, the king of Babylon, best known for his codification of Mesopotamian laws: his achievement was, however, short-lived, with the First Dynasty of Babylon soon falling into decline, the far south being lost to the rulers of the Sea Lands, and external trade restricted. After a Hittite raid on Babylon (1595 BC), a partially Indo-European people, the Kassites, gained political control of Babylonia for four centuries, though never adding much to its civilization. Meanwhile Assyria had enjoyed a period of prosperity under Shamshi-Adad I, partly contemporary with Hammurabi: after a period of decline, it rose again to prominence in the power struggles centring in Syria, swallowing up the inherently vulnerable kingdom of Mitanni, erstwhile ally of Egypt and buffer between the Hittite and Assyrian kingdoms. One outcome of the rise of major warlike states was the emergence of international diplomacy, illuminated especially by tablets from two periods, that of Hammurabi and that of the Amarna heresy in Egypt, in the late Eighteenth Dynasty.

THE AKKADIAN DYNASTY
Far-reaching changes in the balance of power between different states are not always reflected in the archaeological record; and the same can be said of internal political changes. Such was the seizure of power by Sargon, whose very name ('true king') reflected his humble origins, one tradition having him start life as a gardener. In truth this unification of Sumer and Akkad marked the culmination of a long process of encroachment by Semites on the northern Sumerian lands. These newcomers, probably already present some centuries earlier, were the Akkadians, whose language is philologically classed as East Semitic, and who were the first Semitic people to master the complexities of the cuneiform script. Akkadian was destined to supplant Sumerian after the older language had been revived under the Third Dynasty of Ur. Language, law and strong government were the chief contributions of the new rulers of Meso-

potamia, who were content in large measure to perpetuate Sumerian cultural traditions [62].

Now for the first time, apart from a brief attempt by Lugal-Zaggisi at the end of the Early Dynastic III period to make Warka the capital of a united Sumer, there was political unity throughout the land. This unity, however, was perhaps less in the hearts of men than at the behest of the Akkadian conquerors, for each new reign was marked by rebellion. The kingship was therefore deliberately exalted to make the ruler a god on earth, a status never claimed, for example, in later centuries by the Assyrian kings. Sargon styled himself 'King of all the Lands of the Earth' and 'King of Kish' to emphasize the legitimacy of his rule. His grandson, Naramsin, called himself 'The god' and 'King of the

Pl 9. Shell inlay at Ur is probably seen at its best on a flat surface, such as the gaming-boards with differently designed squares, for a game whose moves are unknown. Here the technique was deep engraving with a sharp chisel, the lines being filled in with black and red paste: animals are usually outlined in black, conventional trees and landscape in red.

60. The stele of Naramsin, carved in sandstone, shows him standing on the battlefield, trampling on his enemies, with his troops marching up the side of the tall sugarloaf mountain, on which is incised an inscription. He is armed with a battle-axe and a bow, perhaps of the composite type. Two sun-discs, emblems of the god Shamash, are shown above the mountain; and the king is wearing a horned helmet, indicating his divinity.

Four Regions' (Sumer, Akkad, Subartu and Amurru, the last two being the north and west respectively). This title was to live on. The old independence of the Sumerian cities had utterly vanished.

The monumental art achieved by the sculptors of the Stele of the Vultures was further developed, though the surviving fragments must represent only a meagre record of the military reliefs of the Akkadian period. Far more sophisticated than the fragments of stelae of Sargon is the famous Stele of Victory of Naramsin, found not in the Akkadian homeland but at Susa. It shows how sculpture had been brought more clearly than ever before into the service of the state. Another outstanding masterpiece is a cast bronze head, found at Nineveh [60, 61].

The best variety of Akkadian metal tools and weapons comes from the excavations at Tell Brak, on the river Khabur in north Syria, many continuing Early Dynastic forms such as the poker-butted spearhead. Contacts with metal-workers on the Iranian plateau are suggested by a seal from Tell Asmar showing a distinctive type of axe, with three spikes on the butt, a form familiar from the cemeteries of Luristan and now known to occur there as early as this period. There was some reversion from casting to the older technique of hammering, a technique more suitable for copper and suggesting a temporary cessation of the supply of tin. Lapis lazuli is also less in evidence in the Akkadian period than before, and, since its only source was in Afghanistan, with a poorer grade from Siberia, there could be implications for the sources of tin imported into Mesopotamia: most significantly, synthetic lapis lazuli was now first used. But this suggestion is undermined by the absence of evidence from Akkadian royal tombs to provide a range of jewellery comparable with that from Early Dynastic cemeteries. Nor does the available evidence sustain any claim of priority of settlements in Iran in developing metallurgical techniques. The expansionist policy of the Akkadian dynasty hardly suggests a shrinkage of commercial contacts between Mesopotamia and surrounding lands; but a threat from Elam to foreign trade would have been a strong incentive for military ventures.

Tell Brak has also yielded jewellery, including silver disc-beads, gold coil-pendants and earrings and bangles of gold, silver and electrum. A very small silver bead in the form of four contiguous spirals or scrolls is paralleled in Anatolia by examples from Schliemann's 'Treasure of Priam' in Troy IIc (see p. 125) and from the royal tombs of Alaca Hüyük, thus giving a useful cross-dating. Characteristically Akkadian are earrings with a lunate end.

The effects of the conquests of Sargon and his successors are perhaps discernible in the greater variety of materials used for beads. Carnelian, lapis lazuli, silver and gold continued to be the most popular; but agate became common, sard quite frequent. Steatite, haematite, marble, onyx, rock-crystal and glazed frit also occur.

The political order of the Akkadian state is most clearly demonstrated by palaces excavated at Tell Asmar and Tell Brak. The smaller palace, at Tell Asmar, covered an area of about 70 × 25 m., and was probably the residence of a provincial or city governor: as such he would have styled himself 'slave of the king'. This was a functional building, approached only along a narrow alley between the houses closely surrounding it. The private quarters of the governor comprised only a few small rooms; to the south an open court gave access to more living-rooms and to a south wing, perhaps the harem. The sanitary arrangements were unique in Mesopotamia, with lavatories of occidental type provided with seats and with bathrooms. All have drains, most of which were

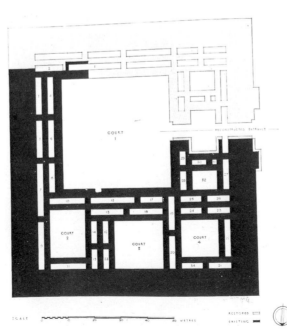

linked to a large main sewer, with a vault of burnt bricks one metre high. Naramsin's palace at Tell Brak was much larger, extending more than 10,000 sq. m., in size and plan closely comparable with the earliest palace at Ashur, perhaps built in the same reign. It was not so much a royal residence as a depot for goods brought as tribute or as loot from campaigns to the north-west, in Syria and possibly also in Anatolia: hence its dissimilarity to the later Mesopotamian residential palaces [63].

62. Cylinder-seals of the Akkadian period display a greater variety of subject matter and material than at any other time, with mere pattern subordinate to narrative. Events in the world of gods or of men are depicted; inscriptions are quite common. The sun god Shamash often appears in a boat propelled by a human prow or ascending a mountain: among his symbols are a plough and a pot. A winged gate, a victorious fight with a bird-man, a god in his shrine and Ea, the water god, are among other themes. The hardest stones might be used, such as jasper and rock crystal; but soft shell–core, so popular for E.D.III seals, had disappeared before the end of the period.

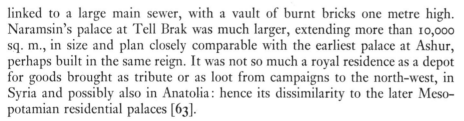

61. Opposite: the style of the hair on this head from Nineveh resembles that of Eannatum on his stele and of Meskalamdug on his helmet. The heavy beard shows a return to the fashion of E.D.I and E.D.II times: in the E.D.III period men were usually clean-shaven.

63. There are four courtyards in the Akkadian depot at Tell Brak, with altogether forty magazines arranged round them. Given 5 m. as the maximum depth of the foundations, slightly later building inscriptions from Lagash would suggest 15 m. as the height of the walls above ground. The external walls were no less than 10 m. thick. The mud-bricks are of flat rectangular form; and many are stamped with the name of Naramsin.

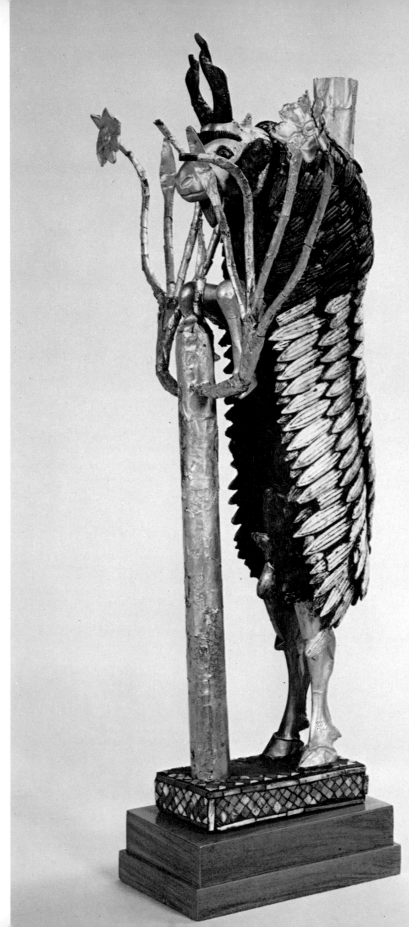

Pl 10. Gold was alluvial and more common than silver, and is easy to beat into thin sheets and to shape over a core, as for example with this well-known goat statuette from the Great Death Pit. A wooden core, carved to the shape required, was also used for the gold head of a bull, with a beard of lapis lazuli, attached to the sound-box of one of the lyres. Bitumen was similarly used for the core of various objects.

84

Little of importance from the Akkadian period has been excavated in Sumer, and even the new capital city, Agade, has yet to be located, though it must have been not far from Kish. From the results of surveys it seems that the distribution of sites still visible indicates a smaller population than in the south for the region around Agade. The density and size of towns and villages were less than in Sumer.

Sargon in his inscriptions was far more communicative about his achievements than his predecessors. Episodes concerning Sargon and Naramsin are preserved in later Omen Texts. The main direction of Sargon's campaigns was

Pl 11. The helmet of Meskalamdug, which was beaten up from a single sheet of gold, and shows the use of the technique of hammering out from within, known as repoussé work, not very common in this period. The fine lines of the hair were rendered by chasing, not engraving as stated in the report: in chasing the metal is in effect stamped or impressed, a chasing tool or die being used.

64. Self-satisfaction is conveyed by all Gudea's statues; he is shown standing or seated, with hands folded in the attitude of prayer and either bare-headed or wearing the woollen cap which was to remain fashionable through the Old Babylonian period. The prayers inscribed on these statues, carved in traditional Sumerian style, show that they had a function as incarnate intermediaries between Gudea and his god Ningirsu.

to the north-west: he himself said that his purpose was to procure timber and metal. Thus the long-lasting commercial links between north Syria and the cities of Sumer and Akkad were reinforced by military measures, and the trade later so amply recorded in the archives of the palace of Mari was made more secure. The traditions of Anatolian campaigns must contain a kernel of fact, and may have created the conditions later enabling Assyrian merchants to found a network of trading posts, centred on Kültepe (ancient Kanesh). Naramasin was engaged in the north-west and also in Elam, which acknowledged his overlordship. He appointed a governor at Susa, erected buildings and had records written in Akkadian, not in the native Elamite language. Thus began seventeen centuries of intermittent hostility and alliances between the rulers of Mesopotamia and Elam, in which economic factors undoubtedly played a larger part than surviving records reveal.

An invasion of highlanders, the Guti, from the Zagros ranges of western Iran brought the Akkadian dynasty to a violent end. Much as the Sumerians resented the domination of the Semitic line, they disliked even more the irruption of the Guti, whom they regarded with good reason as uncivilized. Consequently it is hardly remarkable that, with the possible exception of some grey pottery with incised decoration, nothing in the archaeological record has been attributed to those newcomers.

One city, Lagash, never important enough to hold the kingship in Sumer but briefly prominent at the end of the E.D.III period, was once again to achieve fame through the activities of its governor (*patesi*), named Gudea. His polished black basalt statues are now among the most prized possessions of the Louvre. Gudea never claimed the authority of the Akkadian kings. He was the 'faithful shepherd' appointed by the city's god, Ningirsu, to carry out his commands, particularly the rebuilding of his temple, *Eninnu* [64].

The inscriptions reveal details of the trade which must have played an essential role in the economy of Lagash, as of the other cities of Mesopotamia. Imports included building materials, cedar from the Amanus range, marble from Amurru (Syria) and bitumen from Kirkuk, as well as gravel, in exchange for goods produced in or in transit through Lagash. This is but one illustration of the sophisticated economy supporting the Sumero-Akkadian cities. By ships from the 'lower sea' (Persian Gulf) came timber, porphyry, lapis lazuli and gold dust, this last also obtained from Cilicia. Gudea made much of the fact that he used diorite for his statues: on one he wrote that 'the statue is neither of silver nor of lapis lazuli, bronze, lead or copper did a skilled craftsman fashion it; it is of diorite. . .'.

The long tradition of concern for the offerings due to the god on the building of a temple is demonstrated by the custom, characteristic of this period at Lagash, of depositing figurines, usually bronze or copper, in the foundations. These take the form of a god kneeling, a servant carrying a basket on his head or a sitting bull.

THE THIRD DYNASTY OF UR

The Gutian yoke was thrown off by the Sumerian cities under the leadership of Ur. The Third Dynasty of Ur (2130/12–2021/4 BC) (Ur III) comprised five kings, and never had to face the recurrent internal revolts of the Akkadian period. Pious works only were recorded by these kings, so that Ur III texts lack the interest of those of Sargon and Naramsin. Ur inherited the memory of Akkadian power, and deliberately restored it. Ur-Nammu, the first king, was

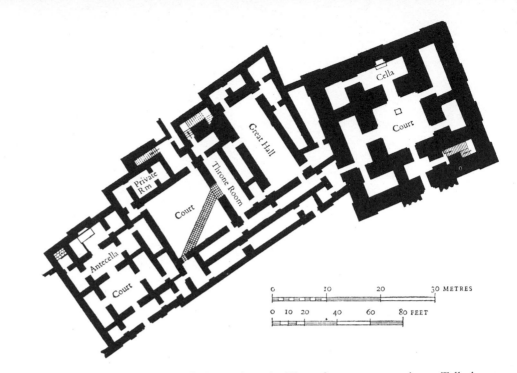

Cella

Court

Great Hall

Throne Room

Private Rm

Court

Antecella

Court

Court

| 0 | 10 | 20 | 30 METRES |

| 0 | 10 | 20 | 40 | 60 | 80 FEET |

active as far north as the Khabur valley, where the great storehouse of Naramsin at Tell Brak was rebuilt; but the main interests of his dynasty seem to have lain in the east, where trade routes had to be protected. His successor had close relations with Susa, appointing one of his officials as governor. The downfall of Ur III came very rapidly, as a result of a combined threat from the Amorites in the north-west and Elam in the east. It was the Amorites who were to make themselves the political masters of Mesopotamia.

The genius of the Sumerians may have been more fully expressed in literature than in the visual arts under Ur III. Scribal activity greatly expanded, administrative and economic texts on clay tablets abounding. Sumerian religious and epic traditions were re-copied or written down for the first time. Sumerian became again the official language, but Akkadian was not suppressed; and Akkadian royal titles and the cult of the deified king were revived [65].

Cylinder-seals were less varied than in the Akkadian period. Haematite was now far the commonest material, remaining so till the end of the Old Babylonian period (see p. 90), and ritual scenes greatly preponderate. The commonest scene shows a minor goddess leading a worshipper by the hand towards an enthroned deity, more often female than male: the throne usually resembles a shrine, the worshippers being bald-headed and clean-shaven. Kings are distinguished from gods by their dress: they wear a fringed cloak and round cap like that of Gudea, rather than a horned crown. Writing appears on most seals.

The achievements of the Ur III kings are most clearly discernible in the city of Ur itself, about 1 × 1.5 km. in area, protected by Ur-Nammu with a great mud-brick rampart, 25 m. thick at its base and surmounted by a wall of burnt brick, a material much more extensively used than before. There were two gates, one on the west on to the Euphrates and the other on the north side. Canals ran along the north and east sides of the city perimeter, and several temples stood just inside the wall. The whole history of the ziggurat and temples of Ur, as well as its walls, is one of repeated rebuilding, sometimes after destruction, culminat-

65. Plan of a square temple at Tell Asmar dedicated to the worship of Gimil-Sin (Shu-Sin), fourth of the Ur III kings; in the adjoining palace of the city governor stood a private temple of the same plan, with the addition of an ante-cella and one room on either side of it.

Pl 12. The war panel on the 'Standard' from Ur, which may depict a typical battle formation of the E.D.III period, with spearmen wearing cloaks and leather helmets, and heavy wagons with four solid wooden wheels, not unlike the cumbersome carts still to be heard creaking and groaning along roads on the Anatolian plateau today. At Ur these were drawn by onagers, depicted on the reverse panel of the Standard as booty, a valuable asset to any Sumerian city-state.

ing in the antiquarian zeal of Nabonidus. To some degree Ur-Nammu and his successors of Ur III were inspired by similar motives, though they sought to rebuild on a grander scale than their predecessors.

The efforts of Ur-Nammu were concentrated on the sacred precinct, the *temenos*, in the north-west part of the city. He made it into a high platform with a great wall, with the ziggurat itself on an upper terrace in its west corner, over the remains of the Early Dynastic terrace. A pylon gateway of burnt brick gave access to this upper terrace, with a buttressed, sharply battered face. The ascent of the ziggurat was by three staircases on the north-east side, one at right angles to the façade and two running up it. A gate-tower stood on a small recessed platform where these three staircases met, at a level necessarily higher than the pavement of the first stages; and the central flight of stairs continued upward to reach the second stage. Numerous small copper crescent moons, about 2 cm. wide, were found on the bitumen floor of a sanctuary on the south-east side of the first stage, suggesting the cult of the moon god Sin, patron of Ur and its kings. No trace remains of the shrine on the top of the ziggurat, the most imposing of its time in all Mesopotamia and functioning as a high place or sacred mountain, built to exalt the shrine of the Sumerian god Nanna (Akkadian, Sin) and to be a landmark from afar. The core of the ziggurat was of mud-bricks laid in the characteristic Early Dynastic herringbone style, with mud as mortar but without the reinforcement of matting, as used elsewhere. The casing, not bonded into the core, was of burnt bricks with bitumen mortar, many of the bricks stamped with the name of Ur-Nammu, always on the underside. Bitumen was also used for surfacing floors, and for an elaborate system of drains to carry off rain water beyond the upper terrace. Weeper-holes running through the casing to the mud-brick core were for drying the interior, which would, even in that climate, have taken many years. Woolley's theory that they were intended to carry off water used for trees planted on the stages of the ziggurat as the sacred mountain is by no means impossible [*Pl 13*].

Within the precinct were three great square temples, below the upper terrace and connected with it by the Court of Nanna [**67**]. Just outside the precinct were the tombs of the Ur III kings, in design comparable with contemporary private houses. They are within a mausoleum of rectangular plan with rounded corners, containing twelve rooms with two annexes. The entire mausoleum had been looted, almost certainly by the Elamites, all eight altars serving the funerary cult having been dug into from the back by the robbers. Hints of the plunder which they removed from this shrine, which tablets of Ibi-Sin prove to have been in use to the very end of Ur III, are discernible in traces of gold leaf which must have adorned the wooden doors of the rooms opening off the central court. In one room were found small gold nails, gold and lapiz lazuli sun's rays incrusted in wood and minute gold stars [**66**].

The power of Ur III may have evaporated as quickly as it came into being. But the monuments of this vigorous yet culturally introverted dynasty, the great ziggurat and the mausoleum, are the most impressive awaiting the visitor to Ur today.

Pl 13. The ziggurat at Ur which, unlike later ones, was not square but rectangular, 62.5 × 43 m. in area and originally rising about 19.6 m. above the upper terrace. Two corners are orientated to the north and south. The sides of the ziggurat were relieved by shallow buttresses, very wide at the corners, a subtle effect of massive solidity being achieved by the very slightly convex facades.

66. In the royal mausoleum at Ur considerable ingenuity had been shown in concealing the entrance from one room of the superstructure, the cult room, to a shaft down to a small platform in the bottom of a great pit, roofed at either end with a corbel vault but open in the middle. Two flights of steps descended from this platform, each leading to a burial chamber with its door bricked in. Holes in the corbel vaults showed where the wooden centring had been inserted during their construction.

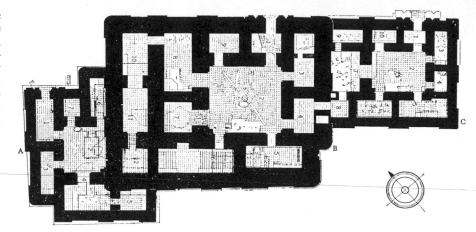

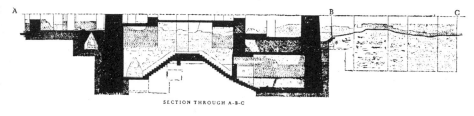

SECTION THROUGH A-B-C

67. Within the precinct of Ur were three great square temples, below the upper terrace and connected with it by the Court of Nanna, surrounded by a casemate wall with intramural rooms, some for storage, and entered by a triple gate crowned by a high tower. Directly to the south-east stood *E-Nun-Mah*, a temple of unusual plan, in that it comprised a small shrine of five rooms on its own, surrounded by long narrow store-rooms. Another temple, *Gig-par-ku*, belonged to the goddess Ningal: more than 75 m. square, it had two entrances and was divided within by a narrow corridor into two sections. The third temple, *E-hursag* ('house of the Mountain'), stood in a projecting portion of the Ur III precinct, at its south-east corner.

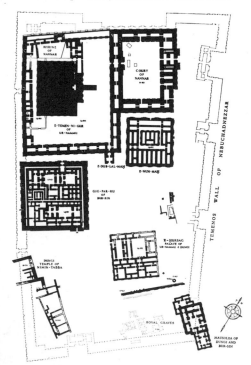

THE OLD BABYLONIAN PERIOD

The fall of Ur III marks the beginning of a new age in Mesopotamia, in which the Amorite incomers from the north-west came to control cities as far apart as Mari, Babylon, Larsa and Ur. The First Dynasty of Babylon became dominant only under Hammurabi (1792–1750 BC on the 'middle' chronology), the dates of whose reign are a matter of continuing controversy. The whole time-span of four centuries is commonly called the Old Babylonian period, during the earlier years of which the cities of Isin and Larsa took the lead, whence the term 'Isin-Larsa period'. This whole period is characterized by the lack of any lasting unity, Hammurabi's conquests being short-lived, and by the growing secularization of the economy and probably of society in general, a process beginning in the Akkadian period. Foreign trade, amply attested by tablets from Mari, Tell Asmar, Sippar, Larsa and Ur, as well as from 'Kanesh–Kültepe in Anatolia, had in some areas shrunk compared with the limits of direct trade under Ur III and earlier, perhaps owing to resistance by Elam and other neighbours to commercial exploitation; but control of this trade had passed from the temples to individual merchants, whose dynastic power was often considerable.

The decline in piety, reversed by the kings of Ur III, is perhaps discernible in the paucity of new religious architecture of the Old Babylonian period, with the notable exception of the temple at Ischali, within the kingdom of Tell Asmar and dedicated to Ishtar-Kititum, a form of the mother goddess [68].

At Tell Harmal (Shadupum), just outside Baghdad, two of the entrances of the temple were guarded by lions, modelled in clay and fired, arranged in pairs. This is an early example of a tradition destined to spread widely through the Near East and to survive many centuries.

Among the major restorations of the Old Babylonian period was that of the temple of Ningal in the precinct of Ur. Nearest its gateway was one complete temple, with two courts, separated by two long rooms, one serving as a lustral chamber. Beyond the second court were the sanctuary and living quarters for the priests, whose tombs, all robbed, were beneath the floors. There was also a sanctuary dedicated to Bur-Sin (Amar-Suen) of Ur III and restored, like the rest of the temple, by Enannatum, daughter of Ishme-Dagan, king of Isin. The second half of the building comprised a temple of different plan, with a sanctuary reached from the large court through three arched doors and with a statue

68. The Ischali Temple included a very large forecourt, which was approached by steps from the east leading up to the level of the platform on which stood the temple proper, surrounded by subsidiary rooms. A second court was reached by another flight of steps: on the north side was the sanctuary, of the broad shallow type, accessible through an ante-cella.

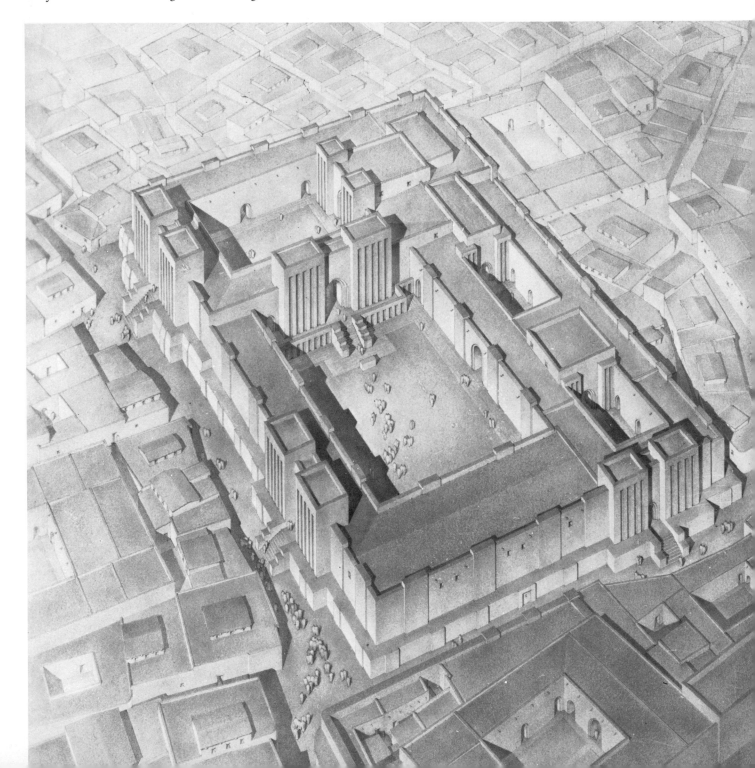

Pl 14. The upper scene of the central panel of the 'Investiture of the King of Mari', which shows the king, no doubt Zimri-Lim, touching the emblems presented to him by Ishtar, goddess both of love and of war, in a ceremony attended by several other deities. Elsewhere are depicted date-pickers climbing a palm-tree with a splendid blue bird in its branches.

of the goddess Ningal on a high brick base facing the court. Fragments of a stone victory stele set up by Hammurabi were found in the court: it had been smashed, probably when the building was sacked about twelve years after the death of Hammurabi, in a revolt against Babylon by the southern cities.

The most remarkable surviving evidence of secular power in this period comes not from Babylon, where the remains of Hammurabi's city lie buried beneath those of the Neo-Babylonian period, but from Mari. The great palace, eventually comprising over 250 rooms and extending more than 34 hectares, was repeatedly enlarged during a lifetime of four centuries, until its destruction by Hammurabi (1757 BC). The ruler of Ugarit asked Hammurabi to present his son to Zimri-Lim, last of the kings of Mari, to enable him to widen his education by a visit to one of the recognized wonders of the world [69].

Any attempt to describe the layout of the palace of Mari, for most of its duration occupied by Amorite rulers but briefly incorporated in Assyria, must begin by stressing its combination of several functions. It was the private residence of the king, the centre of his civil service, the place of reception of foreign visitors and embassies and the depot for taxes and tribute received in the form of food and other commodities requiring extensive storage space. It also included private chapels, school rooms and quarters for the palace guard. Interpretation of the functions of the different parts of the palace is not solely dependent on the archaeological evidence, for some 25,000 tablets have been recovered by the French expedition under André Parrot, providing the fullest data for trade and diplomacy in this period.

Most of the palace was of only one storey, though the rooms were very high, with some doorways over five metres high, to admit enough light. The doors probably did not reach to the top, the doorways being largely covered with matting. Many groups of rooms shared one doorway into a court or corridor, so that some must have been very gloomy; but there were probably clerestory windows wherever practicable. Most rooms had hinged doors, with a wooden door-post turning on a pivot-stone fixed in a socket of burnt brick, where animal sacrifices were often found. Pipes of terracotta or of stone were used for the drains, emptying at a depth of eight to twelve metres. Holes in the walls at close intervals show where roof-beams were laid, supporting a ceiling of burnt bricks. Where there was an upper storey, the roof, though in the normal Near Eastern style with rush matting or hurdles laid on the beams, was covered not merely with mud but with mud-bricks overlaid with plaster. The spring rains were carried off by gutters of terracotta. Firewood must have been plentiful, for burnt brick was extensively used for paving floors and for drains, and as an alternative to stone for foundations. Bitumen coating was used for a dado round many of the walls. The basic building material, however, was mud-brick, the typical brick being large, thin and square (42 × 42 × 10 cm.).

The main entrance was a massive double gateway, with a sentry-box in the

Pl 15. The enclosure and ziggurat of Dur Kurigalzu, the Kassite capital.

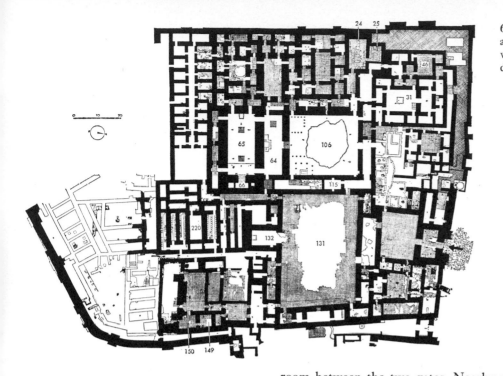

69. The palace of Mari, which was the largest and latest in a succession of palaces, three of which have been discovered underlying it, dating back at least to the E.D.II period.

room between the two gates. Nearby was a group of rooms perhaps used by visitors but, from their position near the gate, more probably for the praetorian guard. As all such buildings in the Near East, the palace comprised units of rooms ranged round an open court. This arrangement allowed for air, light and communication, with security and privacy as prime considerations. This is apparent in the way in which the two doors giving admittance from the small forecourt inside the gateway through a corridor to the largest of the central courtyards are not in line: thus any direct view into the great court was barred. Nor could anyone fire an arrow within. The visitor, having entered the great fortress-palace from the north and reached the vast public court, would have been faced by a room approached by semi-circular steps with a dais at its south end, clearly for a throne, this being the first audience-hall. To reach the king's apartments or the administrative offices one would have to leave the great court by a door close to its north-west corner, whence eventual access to a second large court was possible. Directly west of this lay the administrative quarters or secretariat, a group of rooms centred round a small rectangular court, one room, clearly an archive, containing 1,600 tablets. Nearby the quarter-master's clerk may have checked the inventory of incoming goods, on a low plinth close to a row of huge storage jars. The civil servants had three bath-rooms, one with a lavatory. Immediately to the north, between the secretariat and the royal apartments, were two rooms containing mud-brick benches and a scatter of tablets, suggesting exercises: this was the school; presumably for training youngsters in the difficult and laboriously acquired mastery of the signs of the Akkadian syllabary, of which the Assyrian king Assurbanipal was to write in the seventh century BC as part of the education of a prince. Thus was literary and bureaucratic continuity assured. To the south of the secretariat were the servants' quarters, including some of the kitchens and store-rooms, these occupying over one third of the total area of the palace, its southern portion.

North of the secretariat were the royal apartments, shut off from the public sector by long passages, the rooms grouped round a central, almost square courtyard, and including two bathrooms with terracotta baths. In this part of the palace the chief interest lies in the mural painting: the court was embellished with a frieze painted in cobalt blue, composed of two rope bands of reversed 'S' spirals, each being between two bands of white and separated from each other by a sunken moulding. Two rooms had a triple band in black, red ochre and black. Decorative elements, perhaps rosettes, seem to have been affixed to the walls but subsequently stripped off, leaving holes at regular intervals: this is one of the features of Mari suggesting its role as an influence on the early development of Assyrian art. The paintings of the royal apartments were strictly geometric, but those of the inner great court were representational. On the south side of this court was a group of three rooms originally described as a chapel or shrine with a throne-room beyond; but they appear to be a prototype of the 'standard reception suite', destined to become a typical element in the plan of the Late Assyrian palaces. In line with the doorway into the court was the podium, or throne-base, with holes for two posts to support a canopy over it. Nearby was found the famous statue of a goddess with liquid flowing from a vase in her hands. The throne-base, if such it was, had eight panels on top painted to imitate marble, surrounded by a long multiple-spiral band. Off the east end of the inner room opened a small chamber described as the king's private chapel. The great court was adorned with a painting named by the excavators 'The Investiture of the King of Mari' [*Pl 14*].

To what extent Sumerian and Semitic elements can be differentiated is debatable: more certain is the affinity between the spiraliform motifs of Mari and the art of the Proto-Palatial (Middle Minoan) period of Crete. Trade between Crete and Ugarit on the Syrian coast is archaeologically attested; and Ugarit was on the trade route from the west to Mari and beyond. The belief, however, that the artistic influence originated in Crete rather than in Syria is not beyond argument.

Much light on society and law in the quasi-feudal order of the times is shed by the famous Code of Hammurabi. The provisions of the law code comprise the record of established precedents, in effect case law. Failure to perform the duties required of a feudatory in return for the grant of a fief by the king was punishable by death, and severe penalties fell on those helping runaway slaves. Much indirect evidence is given by the code for the social structure of Mesopotamia in the time of Hammurabi. Rent was paid either at a fixed rate per unit of land or at a fixed volume for the entire holding, a less equitable but simpler and therefore commoner method. Penalties were imposed on farmers failing to grow a crop. Certain groups of men performed specified duties for the king in return for a 'field of maintenance'. The use of the term 'fief' is justifiable, all the more so since these duties often related to war; but analogies with medieval Europe should not be pressed too far. The fame of Hammurabi rests far more firmly on his code than on his military exploits, which culminated in the conquest of Larsa and the south and of Mari [**70**].

Trade, well documented by tablets from several cities, is illustrated indirectly by the houses found in an extensive excavation of the Isin–Larsa town of Ur [**71**]. From tablets it is possible to identify the owners of some houses: one was perhaps a moneylender, another a smith; and one house served as an inn. The houses of the well-to-do, among them the great sea-faring merchants who plied their ships to Dilmun (Bahrein) and beyond in the Persian Gulf as well as up the Euphrates to Babylon and Mari, conformed to a standard design, namely

Pl 16. The most impressive of the fortified enclosures of M.B. date in Syria, through little excavated, is Qatna, near Homs, extending over nearly 101 hectares and enclosing a town which, like Hazor and Ugarit, had greatly expanded.

a two-storeyed house with central court for light and air, where pack-animals and merchandise could be received. Rooms were kept dark and doors shut against the summer heat. On the ground floor were the main reception room, kitchen quarters, lavatory and sometimes also a private chapel. Though a staircase does not prove the existence of an upper storey, this seems probable, and here would have been the private rooms. In the poorer houses burnt brick could be afforded only for the damp course, in the richer for the wall facing, with mud-brick inside. Matting was used to reinforce the joints in the brickwork, which was well laid, with courses of headers and stretchers. Five houses had private chapels, long narrow rooms, brick-floored, with a dais surmounted by an altar in the wall behind which was a square recess with a chimney, perhaps a hearth for burning incense. A squarish base may have supported a statue of the god. By the door of one chapel in Ur a terracotta relief of a human-headed bull performed the same function as in the Late Assyrian palaces, of keeping away the evil spirits.

Intramural burial was usual in the Old Babylonian period, with the dead

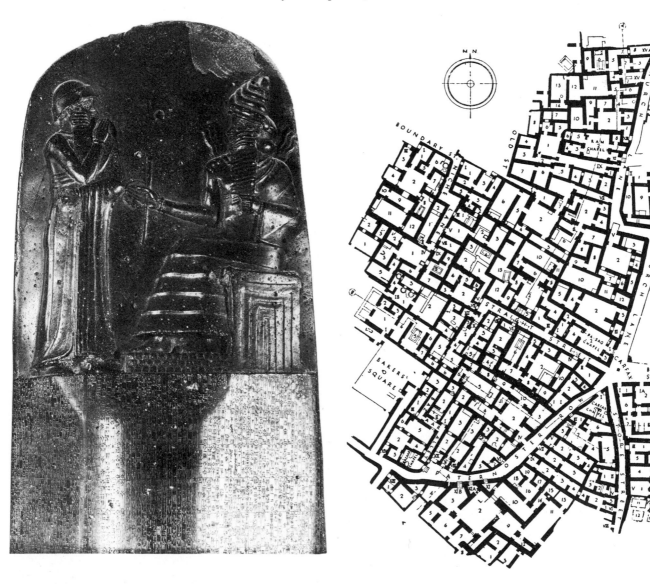

interred beneath the floor of their house, a custom perhaps attributable to the Amorites, since it was so different from that of Early Dynastic times. Many children's graves occur in the residential areas at Ur, one house having thirty-two beneath the floor, many inside jars. Nearly always there was a brick vault underneath the chapel: when not in these vaults the dead were buried under house floors, either in terracotta coffins (*larnaces*) or in small vaults.

It may have been a greater demand for cylinder-seals, as a by-product of the increased commercial activity, which brought about a certain standardization in glyptic art. Two styles are now distinguishable: some seals display degenerate versions of the typical Ur III presentation scene; others represent the Old Babylonian style, which had come into vogue before the reign of Hammurabi, being common at the Assyrian colony of Kanesh–Kültepe. Typical themes are various scenes of worship and standards, such as a crescent staff with streamers.

Tablets from the Mari archives and elsewhere reveal a delicate balance of power in the years before and after the accession of Hammurabi, in the reigns of Shamshi-Adad I of Assyria and his son and of Zimri-Lim of Mari. It was not to outlive Hammurabi's defeats of Larsa and Mari in his thirty-first and thirty-fifth years. Yet for a time there was a developed system of diplomacy, not evident again until the time of Akhenaten and the Amarna tablets in Egypt, four centuries later.

THE KASSITES

The downfall of the First Dynasty of Babylon, long since deprived by the rulers of the Sea Lands of control of the head of the Persian Gulf, was a story of decline in the face of the growing influx of highlanders from the Zagros to the east, the Kassites, a people at least partly Indo-European and expert horsemen. A Hittite raid administered the *coup de grâce* (*c.* 1595 BC). The Kassites inherited political power, and held it through a long period of cultural stagnation but considerable economic activity (till *c.* 1170 BC).

The most distinctive feature of Kassite rule in Mesopotamia was the innovation of the boundary stone (*kudurru*), commonly occurring and recording a new type of grant of land. Cylinder-seals display a greater use of inscriptions. Architecture was principally a matter of refurbishing older structures, although a new capital was founded, Dur-Kurigalzu [*Pl 15*]. At Ur, after the sack of the city by Samsi-iluna (*c.* 1737 BC), houses were of the traditional plan, though of only one storey: beneath the houses were tombs with undistinguished grave goods, including plain pottery; and the Sumerian language, used for letters, contracts and accounts till this destruction, was replaced by Akkadian.

It was not till the reign of Kurigalzu II (1345–1324 BC) that any Kassite king was actively interested in building. Ur benefited along with other southern cities. Burnt brick was commonly used in the buildings erected at this time, but mud mortar had to take the place of bitumen. Old bricks were often reused for the wall faces, which alone were of properly laid brickwork, the core being of mud and brick rubble. Kurigalzu II's work on the ziggurat did not survive the Neo-Babylonian additions. He was primarily a restorer, among his achievements being the refacing of the Isin-Larsa revetment of the precinct terrace. Moulded bricks reproduced the façade of the gateway tower, with its half-columns and niches. The small temple of the goddess Ningal, south-east of the ziggurat, was the one entirely new structure built at Ur in the Kassite period, again by Kurigalzu II, with its sanctuary set at right angles to the main axis of the building, and probably roofed with a dome and barrel vaulting, already seen much earlier in Assyria, at Tell al Rimah.

Dur Kurigalzu, the Kassite royal city probably founded by Kurigalzu II, is marked by the ruins of Aqarquf, west of Baghdad, including a ziggurat. The Kassites left remarkably little mark on Mesopotamian civilization, perhaps because they grasped the cause of its preservation with the zeal of converts. Even their language survives in little else besides personal names and the names of some of their gods. Babylonia fell into an obscurity which, in archaeological terms, was to be little dispelled before the Neo-Babylonian period.

ASSYRIA: THE EARLY PERIODS

The origins of the kingdom of Assyria, whose first rulers dwelt in tents, are far from clear. Certainly the Assyrian people were from the first not entirely Semitic; and during the second millennium BC a new ethnic element, the Hurrians, already detected in the Khabur valley in the Akkadian period, and most clearly manifest in the tablets from Nuzi, near Arrapḫa (modern Kirkuk), played a shadowy but decisive role in the formative phases of Assyria. The institution of the eponym (*limmu*), already evident in the colony at Kanesh in Anatolia, is but one demonstration of the strong thread of continuity from the Old Assyrian period onwards. A sense of its long past history was to give an edge to Assyrian nationalism.

Tell al Rimah, ancient Karana, situated in the steppe forty miles west of Nineveh, has given us for the first time a record of the architectural achievements of the Old Assyrian period. This was a walled town with a high central mound and diameter of about 600 m. Its short-lived palace, containing two archives, was built under Shamshi-Adad I and destroyed in the time of Zimri-Lim. On top of an earlier settlement mound were built a temple and ziggurat, their earliest and most grandiose phase (III) probably dating to the late nineteenth century BC, the time of Shamshi-Adad I of Assyria. The dating of the subsequent phases is not too sure: Phase II was destroyed perhaps *c.* 1475 BC, at the same time as the town of Nuzi near Arrapḫa. More certain is the dating of the final abandonment of the temple to the late thirteenth century BC, from the occurrence of many tablets of Shalmaneser I and Tukulti-Ninurta I of Assyria. Tell al Rimah thus reveals much of the Old and Middle Assyrian periods alike. By Late Assyrian times it had declined to the status of a large village.

The architectural skills demonstrated by the remains of this temple and ziggurat have led the excavator of Tell al Rimah to suggest the employment of southern architects and craftsmen. The use of radial brick vaulting is here plainly the work of builders with a long tradition behind them, whose record is unfortunately missing in the southern cities, but which had already appeared in northern Mesopotamia, at Tepe Gawra, in the late Uruk period. A similar antiquity may be sought for the amazingly elaborate and finely executed façades, with more than 270 engaged columns, fifty of which are of spiral form or of one of two types of palm trunk. The former are without parallel, the latter comparable only with the façade of the bastion of Warad-Sin at Ur, most probably contemporary. The temple of Tell al Rimah, possibly dedicated to Ishtar and associated with the fertility cult, was entered by the east side through a massive gate, flanked by two columns, each comprising two spiral and two palm-trunk shafts. Across a central courtyard, in the middle of the west side, stood the door of the antechamber leading to the much smaller sanctuary, against the foot of the ziggurat, a typically Assyrian juxtaposition for centuries to come. A staircase

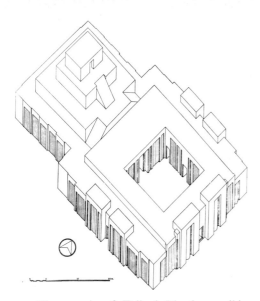

72. The temple of Tell al Rimah, possibly dedicated to Ishtar and associated with the fertility cult, was entered by the east side through a massive gate, flanked by two columns, each comprising two spiral and two palm-trunk shafts. Across a central courtyard, in the middle of the west side, stood the door of the antechamber leading to the much smaller sanctuary, against the foot of the ziggurat, a typically Assyrian juxtaposition for centuries to come. A staircase with two flights indicates the original height of the temple as at least eleven metres above floor level.

73. Though badly preserved, the remains of the northern part of Ashur are very impressive, including the Great Ziggurat (on right), with its temple standing separately on one side and the palace on the other. Here, unlike in the Late Assyrian palaces, the ziggurat dominated the Old Palace (seen immediately in front of it) built round a central court. Beyond this was the Square of the Foreign Peoples, flanked by the double temples of Anu and Adad and of Sin and Shamash, gods of sky and storm, moon and sun respectively. Two ziggurats were associated with the Anu-Adad temple (to left of the Old Palace) and were doubtless reached from the roof. Beyond stood the very large New Palace and next to that the temple of Nabu, the Babylonian god of writing.

with two flights indicates the original height of the temple as at least eleven metres above floor level. In the courtyard was found a gypsum block, set in a recess, with a standing figure in high relief between two palm trees, having a very badly weathered inscription across her skirt. This is almost certainly the goddess Lama, related to the *lamassu*, the protectors of the Late Assyrian palaces: she acted as an intermediary between suppliants and the chief deity [72].

Assyria, after a long interval of weakness, revived in the fourteenth century BC under Assur-uballit I and his successors. The neighbouring kingdom of Mitanni was reduced and in due course eliminated, bringing the Assyrian frontier in the west to the middle Euphrates, and leading, under Tukulti-Ninurta I, to direct conflict with the Hittites. The same king also conquered Babylon and 'took the hands of Bel', otherwise Marduk, in the Babylonian coronation ceremony, a feat not repeated till the time of Tiglath-Pileser III (729–8 BC). Thus the Middle Assyrian period, as it is commonly called, was one of considerable importance in terms of Assyrian power. The archaeological record, however, does not yet reflect this at all adequately. Much of the evidence dates to the reign of Tukulti-Ninurta I (1244–1208 BC), to whom are attributable some of the buildings of the ancient city of Ashur, including the Ashur temple and ziggurat, whose general layout is comparable with the earlier temple at Tell al Rimah [73]. Two altars of Tukulti-Ninurta I at Ashur suggest something of the remoteness of the gods of Assyria even from her kings. The same ruler built himself a residential palace (Kar-Tukulti-Ninurta) two miles upstream from Ashur. Its greatest interest lies in the mural paintings, surely suggesting an ultimate influence from Mari, and demonstrating two motifs, the sacred tree and the crested griffin, which were to become traditional elements in Assyrian art. Continuity in the mainstream of Mesopotamian tradition was modified by a distinctive Assyrian contribution.

The kingdom of Mitanni, at its greatest in the sixteenth and fifteenth centuries BC, exerted a profounder cultural influence on the powers which were to devour it, Assyria and the Hittites, than its rather shadowy remains might suggest. Until full-scale excavations are carried out at the site of its capital, Washshukanni, plausibly identified with Tell Fakhariyah near the upper reaches of the Khabur, there is little to be said of its central homeland. More evidence is, however, available from Tell Atchana (Alalakh), discussed in the next chapter. The Mitannian style of glyptic art influenced that of the Middle Assyrian cylinder-seals. Mitannian influence lingered on in the early first millennium BC, especially at Tell Halaf (Guzana), just south-west of Tell Fakhariyah. The material civilization of Mitanni, with its largely Hurrian population, its mounted warriors (*maryannu*) and its Indo-Aryan ruling class, demands much further investigation.

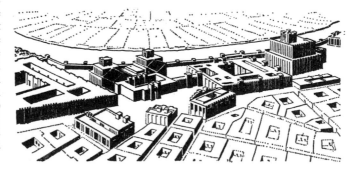

4

The Levant from c. 5000 BC until the end of the Bronze Age

The long 'dark age' in Palestine, following the end of the Pre-Pottery Neolithic B culture, is now seen to have been briefer and less backward than recently supposed. Teleilat el-Ghassul may well have dated back to *c.* 5000 BC, on radiocarbon dating, suggesting that the Ghassulian culture flourished from the early fifth millennium BC. Society may have been tribal, but technology was not neglected, as apparent from metalsmiths' hoards.

Urban life appeared in Palestine from the opening of the Early Bronze Age, now to be dated not later than *c.* 3500 BC, slightly preceding the unification of Egypt. In the Early Bronze (E.B.) III period an intrusive movement brought in northerners, almost certainly Hurrians from eastern Anatolia via north Syria, their traces being evident especially in Amuq H phase in the plain of Antioch. Byblos VI, contemporary with the Old Kingdom in Egypt, marked the height of prosperity in an ancient city flourishing on the cedar trade across the Mediterranean to the Nile.

Before this, in Amuq F phase, the merchants of the late Uruk period in Mesopotamia had been extending their trade up the Euphrates into Syria, where the economic initiative soon passed to the local population, Syria becoming a centre in its own right of urban life and long-distance trade. This is being revealed most dramatically by the tablets from Ebla (Tell Mardikh), a city perhaps overshadowing Mari in the time of Sargon of Agade and destroyed probably by Naramsin.

More familiar is the evidence of Amorite migrations, introducing the Early Bronze-Middle Bronze culture and the abandonment of urban life. This revived on a scale never previously attained in the Middle Bronze Age, after the arrival of the Canaanites. Throughout the Levant such cities as Kadesh, Hazor and Jericho were massively fortified. Here was the homeland of the Hyksos resistance to the expansion of Egypt in the early Eighteenth Dynasty.

The story thereafter is one of economic decline under Egyptian rule in Palestine. Under Hittite suzerainty Ugarit was to grow in prosperity as an international trading city, cut off in its prime by the catastrophic invasion of the Sea Peoples in the early twelfth century BC.

SYRIA AND PALESTINE TILL THE PROTO-URBAN PERIOD

After the end of the PPNB culture Palestine, including Jericho, sank into a long obscurity from which it was to emerge only after a lapse of two thousand years. Tribal divisions are reflected in an archaeological diversity between sites not far removed from one another. This was not understood by earlier archaeologists, who made the mistake of arranging these cultures entirely in series rather than largely in parallel. The minutiae of the prehistory of the Levant, especially Palestine, should not be emphasized without reference to their wider context.

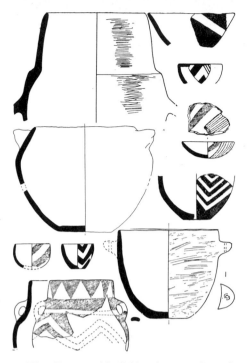

74. The Pottery Neolithic A ware is soft, poorly fired and friable; and there is some ware decorated in burnished red paint. The patterns include chevrons. Similar pottery is found at Tell Ghrubba, also in the lower Jordan valley.

75. Opposite: Chalcolithic underground dwellings near Beersheba.

In terms of relative chronology the Levant must be reckoned backward until the late fourth millennium BC, the Proto-Urban period.

Byblos, on the coast of the Lebanon, continued to flourish as a village community through three phases (Early, Middle and Late Neolithic) throughout the fifth millennium BC and well into the fourth. Here the Amuq A tradition of dark-faced burnished ware continued, with shell-impressed decoration. The Middle Neolithic of Byblos is characterized by coarse incised decoration and the Late Neolithic by coarse red ware. It is in the Byblos coastal region that the origins of the cultural influences on Palestine from the early fifth to the mid-fourth millennium BC must be sought.

First is the Yarmukian culture, whose principal site is Sha'ar Ha-Golan on the Yarmuk river, a north-eastern tributary of the Jordan. The Yarmukian economy seems to have been agricultural and more or less self-sufficient, without evidence of external trade. Representations of the female figure, the human face and a phallus suggest a fertility cult. Yarmukian pottery has incised decoration with herring-bone patterns, reflecting the influence of the Byblos littoral.

A cultural change occurred in Palestine, with the appearance of the 'Pottery Neolithic A' occupation of Jericho IX, marked by primitive pit dwellings later filled with rubble. Clearly these people had only the most rudimentary material culture and were but semi-sedentary. Any sub-division of this pottery into grit- and straw-tempered wares overlooks the variation of supply of straw according to season [74].

The next phase is the 'Pottery Neolithic B' of Jericho VIII, with houses suggesting a more settled population and with pottery distinguished by herring-bone incision and a convex jar neck profile termed the bow rim.

From about the mid-fourth millennium BC came a fairly rapid advance in the level of material culture both along the coast and inland. Although chronological proof is lacking, it is to be surmised that the coast, at least around Byblos, was still ahead of the interior. Nevertheless there now began in Palestine the period aptly termed Proto-Urban, in which the settled population grew immensely. Whether this was the result of increase or merely of concentration is as uncertain as elsewhere in the ancient Near East. Egyptian influence cannot be reckoned as relevant, since the Unification of the Two Lands did not come about before *c*. 3300 BC, nor are direct connections apparent outside Byblos and the copper mines of Sinai. The first phase in Palestine in this Proto-Urban period (formerly termed Middle Chalcolithic) includes a group of settlements round Beersheba, in the northern Negev, of which the most interesting are Tell Abu Matar, where copper was worked, and Bir-as Safadi, where ivory and soft stone were carved. The first three levels (I–III) of Teleilat el-Ghassul, on the north-east side of the Dead Sea, belong to this formative phase, followed by the classic Ghassulian culture of Ghassul IV (formerly Late Chalcolithic) [75].

There are signs of the firm establishment of settled life in different parts of the Levant. Byblos, after a long abandonment, was reoccupied, with the appearance of a new culture termed Byblos B. Paved alleys ran between the houses of the town, now covering the whole citadel mound. Houses followed an unexpected development, from rectangular to round to apsidal plan. Metalworking flourished, not only copper but also gold and silver, the last almost certainly imported from Anatolia. Ceramic parallels provide additional evidence of Anatolian trade. An extramural cemetery containing over 1,800 burials in large ribbed jars was the source of most of the metalwork. Wheel-made pottery appears towards the end of this period. Stamp-seal impressions on some vessels

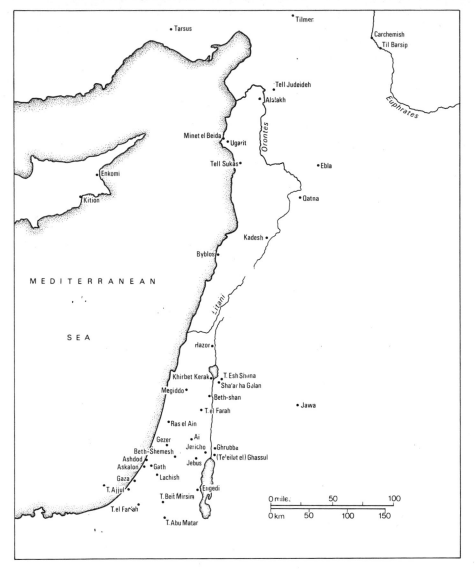

76. Map of the Levant in the Chalcolithic and Bronze Ages.

are of Eanna V (Warka) type, showing links with the Sumerian cities.

The people of Ghassul IV lived in well-built houses of mud-brick, some with foundations of undressed stones; the bricks were shaped by hand, not in a mould. Mural painting was the outstanding artistic achievement of the Ghassul community [77]. The burial customs may suggest continuity in the population of the Jordan valley, for the dead were buried in cist-graves, lined and roofed with slabs and covered with a circular stone cairn. These could be a survival of earlier megalithic dolmens in the Jordan valley; they have also been associated with a nomadic element in the population. Ghassulian pottery is usually hand-made, though the slow wheel may also have been used; painted decoration is rare. Forms include vases in the shape of a bird, 'cornets' and lugged bowls on high pedestals. Querns, pounders and stone vessels were made; but flint arrow-heads were lacking, so that the sling was probably used, as at contemporary sites in Syria and Cilicia. Parallels with Egypt are indicated by disc-shaped and pyriform maceheads and flint 'fan-scrapers', a distinctive type found also in Byblos

77. The most striking example of mural painting at Ghassul includes an elaborate eight-pointed star; among many elements originally surrounding it are a sailing-boat with oars and stylized dragons. Human figures and birds appear in other wall-paintings.

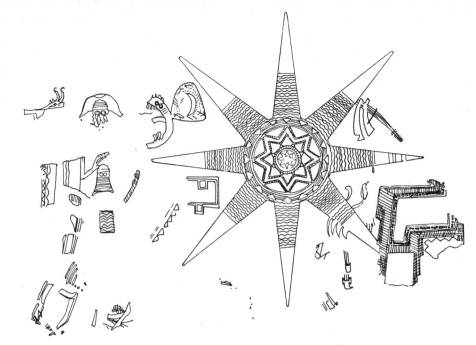

II. The extensive, rather straggling settlement of Ghassul was abandoned before the Early Bronze Age, probably because of the drying up of the streams from the highlands of Trans-Jordan, through climatic deterioration or the drawing off of the water by settlers upstream. Whatever the reason for the desertion of Ghassul, later settlements tended to be at the foot of the hills east of the Jordan instead of out in the plain, towards the deep, winding ravine cut by the river.

Architecture on a larger scale occurs in the form of a hall with columned porch in the surface level at Safadi, near Beersheba, and a temple complex at Engedi above the Dead Sea. This temple has a shrine 20 m. long, with entry in the middle of one long side. A strong hint of the source of wealth for such ambitious structures, with their implication of a degree of communal organization not attested since the Pre-Pottery Neolithic B period, is provided by the famous hoard found wrapped in a mat in a cave in the Mishmar valley, near Engedi, comprising 630 copper objects. This hoard shows that by this time, not later than the Jemdet Nasr period in Mesopotamia, coppersmiths second to none were plying their trade in the Levant. This tradition was later to find its strongest manifestations not in Palestine but at Byblos and Ras Shamra (Ugarit). The Mishmar hoard, however, must warn archaeologists of the much greater role of metalworking in early periods than the chances of discovery and survival have hitherto revealed.

Among indications of newcomers arriving in Palestine are the appearances of a burnished grey pottery, from its distribution named Esdraelon ware, and of collective burial, shared by different groups, in contrast with earlier funerary customs. Esdraelon pottery appears over the whole of the north of Palestine and most of the Jordan valley as far as Jericho. Elsewhere the old Ghassulian culture continued.

The inhabitants of Syria and Cilicia, their culture known from the excavations at Ras Shamra, in the Amuq Plain, at Mersin and elsewhere, were subject

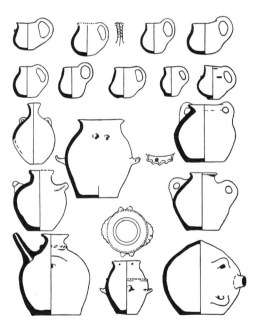

78. Tomb A94 at Jericho, whence this pottery comes, shows the conjunction of old and new funerary customs: hundreds of pots were provided for the dead, round the sides of the tomb; and in the middle was a large pyre on which the decomposed bodies were burned. The skulls, partly charred, had been removed, 135 of them surrounding the pyre. Thus a Neolithic tradition had survived more than two millennia. Collective burial was, however, to become a long-lasting tradition in the Levant.

to successive waves of newcomers from the east. The Halaf culture reached the Syrian coast at the beginning of Ras Shamra IV; and half the pottery of Amuq C, the third phase in that long cultural sequence, was inspired by Halaf types. Local variants emerged in due course, in Amuq D, Ugarit III and Mersin. Then came violent destructions marking the arrival of newcomers bringing the Ubaid culture from southern Mesopotamia, the hallmark of the Amuq E phase. In the Amuq Plain there emerged an idiosyncratic local pottery, found at Tell esh Sheikh and combining Ubaid with surviving Halaf elements. This was followed in Amuq F by Uruk influence, when the long tradition of successive styles of painted pottery came to an end, displaced by red slipped and burnished pottery and plain buff wares, from Tarsus in the north to Byblos in the south. The implications of these movements into Syria, especially the last, for cultural connections between Mesopotamia and Egypt in the late fourth millennium BC have yet to be adequately investigated. It is not too bold to speak of Sumerian influence in the Levant.

PALESTINE: THE EARLY BRONZE AGE

The Early Bronze (E.B.) Age needs to be studied in the Levant as a whole, and not in Palestine alone, if only because the process of urbanization which distinguishes this era, with its sub-periods, seems to have begun earlier in the north than farther south. Mesopotamian influence surely played a more decisive formative role than Egyptian; and the evidence of Jericho, with its maceheads of Egyptian type, should not be over-emphasized. It is anyhow uncertain in which direction the cultural influence went between southern Palestine and Egypt. In the far north, the Amuq G phase marked a considerable advance, with eight successive levels at Tell Judeideh (20–13) containing houses with rectangular rooms. The pottery of Amuq G has similarities to and differences from that of E.B. I–II of Byblos and Palestine. There are lacunae in knowledge of the intervening regions of Syria.

The successive periods of the Early Bronze Age in Palestine and at Byblos led up to a climax, in terms of the size and prosperity of towns, in E.B. III, an era contemporary with the Old Kingdom (Dynasties IV–VI) in Egypt. Byblos best illustrates this: the town growing, in Byblos IV, round the spring on the acropolis. Houses, first of rubble, were later built of cut stone, with many wooden posts on stone bases along the insides of the walls, using the abundant local timber. In Byblos V, dated by Egyptian stone vessels of Dynasties I–II types, the first houses were designed round courtyards. The city was fortified, and strongly so in Byblos VI, the old temple of the 'Lady of Byblos' being rebuilt and enlarged, with two smaller temples. The water supply was redesigned [79].

Defences became a feature of Early Bronze Age towns throughout Palestine, where urbanization had been in progress for a century before the unification of Egypt. Palestine may aptly be termed a cultural backwater for much of its history, but not in relation to Egypt before the New Kingdom. It is in Syria and Lebanon that any external influences should be sought. No doubt these were times of insecurity, explaining the abandonment of villages and concentration in the newly developing cities. In the E.B. I period there were several walled cities in northern Palestine: Khirbet Kerak (Beth Yerah) with a mud-brick wall eight metres thick, and also Beth Shan XV–XIV and Megiddo XVIII. Farther south Tell al Farah and probably Jericho VII were fortified. Round houses occur at Tell Shuna III and Jericho VII, but are rectangular at Beth-

79. This aerial view shows the extent of the city of Byblos. Most significant in Byblos VI were the houses of the merchants, presumably prospering on the trade with Egypt. These houses had up to eight rooms round a long, narrow courtyard; and one had dimensions of 30 × 28.5 m. and was lit by clerestory lighting, the roof being supported by thirty-five wooden columns. This design is reflected in that of the contemporary temples.

Shan XV. The E.B. II period was marked by reconstructed defences at a number of sites; but there is no evidence of violence. The coastal plain and the Negev remained outside this cultural advance.

The length and continuity of the Early Bronze Age in Palestine, in spite of upheavals from time to time, are exemplified by the seventeen phases of rebuilding and repairs distinguished in the fortifications of Jericho, where mud-bricks and mortar of different coloured clay were used successively. In the E.B. III period the appearance of hammer-dressed masonry in a temple at Ai, whose plan is comparable with that of the earlier shrine at Engedi, and with those at Megiddo and Beth Yerah IV, suggests influence from the region of Byblos, where such masonry was common. Pottery shows marked changes from the Proto-Urban period: the wheel had come into use, and red-slipped and burnished ware became typical [80].

The appearance in E.B. III Palestine of a wholly alien pottery with highly burnished yellow, red, brown or black surface and hand-made, provides clear-cut evidence of newcomers. Their pottery is named Khirbet Kerak ware, after the site otherwise known as Beth Yerah, where a massive rectangular structure seems to have been a temple: it incorporates nine circular chambers, probably domed, with basalt masonry preserved two metres high. It would, however, have been appropriate to name this pottery after a site farther north, for it undoubtedly was brought into Palestine by northerners, probably the Hurrians, the Horites of the Old Testament, and is rare in southern Palestine, though found in tombs at Jericho [81].

THE AMORITE PERIOD

The city life of Palestine, at its greatest prosperity in the E.B. III period, came to an abrupt end, marked by destruction debris. At Jericho and elsewhere there was only gradual and partial reoccupation. Pottery and burial customs and the scant architecture all indicate newcomers. Megiddo, Jericho, Lachish and Tell Ajjul have each produced evidence of the cultural period now commonly termed Early Bronze–Middle Bronze (E.B.–M.B.) in their extramural cemeteries. Historical references from Egyptian and Mesopotamian sources and indirectly from the Old Testament make it clear that this can be called the Amorite period. The Amorites were semi-nomadic pastoralists, scorning town life, though later they were to invade the Euphrates valley and to gain power in most of the Sumero-Akkadian cities.

Variations of contents and plan have led to the classification of the E.B.–M.B. tombs of Jericho into five types ('dagger', 'pottery', 'bead', 'square shaft' and 'outsize'). These differences have plausibly been attributed to the practices of individual tribes or clans; and the occurrence of disarticulated burials to the long-lasting practice of carrying the corpses to an ancestral burial ground. The large number of E.B.–M.B. graves is the result of the abandonment of collective burial in favour of single burials, or at most of two persons in one tomb.

The pottery of E.B.–M.B. Palestine has distinctive, if aesthetically unpleasing, forms [82].

It would be mistaken to dismiss the Amorites as entirely backward, however, since metalwork was highly developed and showed a close connection with Syria. Bronze toggle-pins with a swollen or club head, probably used for fastening garments such as cloaks, occur in E.B.–M.B. tombs at Megiddo and in graves at Ras Shamra (Middle Ugarit 1), where they are accompanied by fenestrated axeheads, socketed spearheads, triangular dagger-blades, torcs and heavy brace-

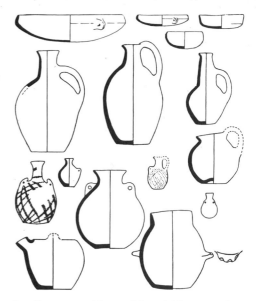

80. Pattern-combing and burnishing came into fashion for Early Bronze pottery in Palestine. Juglets with criss-cross painted decoration in red are common. Hole-mouth jars often had ledge-handles, very long in use in Palestine but more briefly in Egypt, where, however, the stump-based Syrian jugs occur.

81. Khirbet Kerak ware (of which examples from Beth Shan are shown) is the most abundant in the Antioch Plain, in Amuq phases H and I. Similarities in its grooved decoration to that of some contemporary pottery from central Anatolia is explicable by common origins.

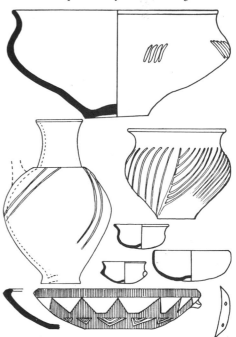

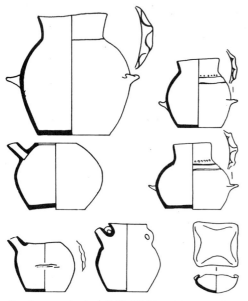

82. Among typical E.B.–M.B. pottery are jars with very wide flat base and prominent ledge-handles of 'envelope' type, with the clay turned over like a flap. The ware is plain, usually a drab buff. Though hand-made, the rims are turned on a slow wheel. A quatrefoil form of pottery lamp is unique to this period.

83. One of the votive deposits which were found at Byblos, associated with the three great temples rebuilt after the destruction of Byblos VI.

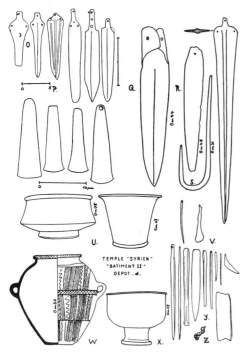

TEMPLE "SYRIEN"
"BATIMENT II"
DEPOT . d.

lets, with cups of the class called caliciform. Palestine, Lebanon and Syria can be discussed as sharing to a large extent a common cultural tradition disseminated from north to south, even though many of the Amorites arrived from the east across the Jordan.

New settlers, after the burning of Byblos VI, built long, narrow houses, up to 15 × 4 m., very different from those of Byblos VI. With them they brought a variety of the caliciform pottery, a wheel-made plain ware so named from the predominance of chalices, goblets and drinking cups; jugs and spouted jars and other forms also occur in the homeland of caliciform pottery, the region from the lower Orontes valley eastwards to the Euphrates [84].

Caliciform pottery is the hallmark of Amuq J, first occurring late in Amuq I. At Ugarit, as elsewhere, its appearance marks the arrival of newcomers, here named by the excavator *Porteurs des torques*, after the bronze arm-rings with curled ends, found earlier at Byblos and thus perhaps originating in that centre of metalworking. They appear also worn by figurines. The term 'E.B.–M.B.' can now indeed be applied to inland Syria as well as the coast, for pottery of characteristic forms has been excavated, at Qatna and elsewhere.

The richest finds of this period have been made at Byblos, where, remarkably, urban life, with the one violent destruction of Byblos VI ascribed to the Amorites, lasted for three thousand years. This demonstrates the commercial role and the long cultural traditions of the Lebanon, inherited by the Canaanites and passed on to their Phoenician descendants. Byblos took second place to Ugarit and later to Sidon and Tyre, from about the fifteenth century BC onwards. Its royal tombs provide a link between the E.B.–M.B. and M.B. I periods, and have yielded jars, bowls and juglets very similar to M.B. I pottery in Palestine and dated by inscriptions of rulers of Byblos to the reigns of Amenemhet III (1842–1797 BC) and Amenemhet IV (1798–1790 BC) of Egypt. There was a flourishing bronze industry, most distinctive in its torcs, at Byblos itself, along the Syrian coast and in the Orontes valley [83].

Who were the makers and disseminators of the caliciform pottery so widespread in Syria? It contrasts sharply with the crude E.B.–M.B. pottery found in most of Palestine. If these two classes of pottery are attributed to Canaanites and Amorites respectively, it means that the Canaanites had occupied most of the territory which they were to make their homeland by *c.* 2300 BC, with Palestine kept in a state of backwardness as the result of the Amorite influx. The civilization of the towns and villages of Syria must, however, have owed much to the mingling of these two distinct yet related ethnic groups.

THE MIDDLE BRONZE AGE

For the next period in the Levant, the Middle Bronze Age, Palestine may be considered first, not so much for its intrinsic significance as for the clarity of the available archaeological evidence. The first phase, M.B. I, was relatively brief, and is represented at rather few sites, suggesting only a gradual penetration. The pottery, however, shows a complete break with the E.B.–M.B. types. It is a wheel-made, red burnished ware, including vertically burnished juglets, carinated bowls and hemispherical bowls with flat base. The most important sites for M.B. I pottery are Tell Beit Mirsim C–F, Tell Ajjul (Courtyard Cemetery) and Ras al 'Ain, as well as Megiddo and one tomb on the *tell* at Jericho. This phase, however, marks the beginning of a continuity which persisted, side by side with imported elements of briefer duration, in the pottery of Palestine until the Roman period.

Ceramic forms in M.B. I Palestine have close parallels at Byblos and Ugarit, and thus with the whole Levantine coast; but inland Syria formed a second cultural province. This divergence seems to have continued in the following M.B. II period, and has led to the suggestion that inland Syria, at least from Homs northward, lay beyond the limits of Canaanite civilization. On the coast, Ras Shamra (Middle Ugarit 2) shows close parallels in its pottery with M.B. II Palestine, and shared with its towns a marked expansion. It was now that the area of Ugarit extended beyond the limits of the older *tell*, with houses and streets carefully laid out, their subterranean tomb-chambers being precursors of the larger examples of the Late Bronze Age. Ugarit now covered nearly 20 hectares, a modest area compared with the 74 hectares of Hazor. At Jericho the length of this period is emphasized by the three successive phases of the town's defences, each with plastered glacis, the latest having a massive stone revetment at its base, founded on the bedrock.

This was the time of the greatest prosperity of the Canaanite world, when communities such as Hazor, Jericho, Tell el Far'ah (near Nablus) and, in the south, Tell ed-Duweir, Tell Beit Mirsim, Tell Fara and Tell Ajjul were flourishing as developed towns. Double or triple gateways, each gate flanked by a pair

84. Caliciform ware occurs throughout north Syria, from the hypogeum of Til Barsib, here illustrated, downstream from Carchemish, to Ras Shamra (Middle Ugarit 1), providing a higher chronological limit for that period than was once suspected, and fitting with the dating evidence, including Khirbet Kerak ware, for Early Ugarit 3.

85. The Middle Bronze Age was the period when the Jebusites fortified their hill city of Jebus (Jerusalem), whose defences were to remain substantially unaltered until the late eighth century BC.

86. Many examples of woodwork shown in this reconstruction of a family room were preserved in the rock-cut M.B. tombs of Jericho just outside the city mound, by the presence of carbon dioxide. A wooden table, of a single plank with three short legs, was a normal item in the equipment of these tombs: other wooden items include beds, boxes, bowls, platters and combs.

of massive piers, were typical of M.B. II fortifications and at least wide enough for one chariot. The former L-shaped gateway was abandoned, as unsuitable for vehicular traffic [85].

The tombs of Jericho have provided a full picture of M.B. II burial customs, marked here and elsewhere in Palestine by a return to collective burial. Often E.B.–M.B. tombs were reused. As each generation passed, the earlier burials were rather unceremoniously pushed to one side to make room for the next generation. War or plague seems the likeliest explanation of a tomb containing a number of intact burials made simultaneously.

Woodwork was an advanced craft in the M.B. II period. Bone inlay was fashionable for the decoration of boxes: the vigorous running fawns on an inlay from Tell Beit Mirsim show that this type of decoration was not confined to Jericho. These contrast with the crude incised carvings scratched on one tomb of E.B.–M.B. date. The change from barbarism to sophistication was swift and undeniable [86].

Fortified enclosures, no doubt military camps, were defended by massive ramparts and are found at sites widely distributed through Syria, Palestine and beyond. The wide distribution of these fortified sites, beyond the boundaries of Canaan, has led to their association with the Hyksos, since they seem to represent the strongholds of a ruling military class. Possibly the inner town of Carchemish, with an earth rampart of this type, dates to this period, though on historical grounds it has more plausibly been attributed to the time of the Hittite conquest of north Syria in the early fourteenth century BC. The Hyksos were a capable group, responsible for introducing the horse and chariot into Egypt: yet the sloping ramparts of their fortresses were designed less against the attacks of chariotry than against mining. The old theory that these were 'shepherd kings' of purely Semitic stock has long been abandoned, and the Hurrian element has been given due prominence [Pl 16].

A very different architectural tradition is represented in the Amuq Plain by the modest palace of the local ruler, Yarim-Lim II of the kingdom of Yamkhad (Aleppo), a contemporary of Hammurabi. This building, excavated in Alalakh (Atchana) VII, demonstrates an early manifestation of north Syrian design destined to become a hallmark of that region in the early first millennium BC. Here stone, timber and mud-brick were combined in a manner more typical of Anatolia than of the Levant or Mesopotamia. Basalt was used for orthostats as a dado for the rooms and courtyard of the principal of the three sections of the palace, and also for column-bases and door-sills; it was to be the favourite material for the mason and sculptor in north Syria for a thousand years to come. This appearance of orthostats suggests a possible origin for the Anatolian reliefs of the Late Bronze Age. Wood was used as reinforcement for the walls and for columns. In a store-room were found five ivory tusks, a hint of the tradition of ivory-carving of later generations. Cement flooring suggests an advanced standard of comfort. Wall-paintings echo the contemporary art of Mari, and occur also in Alalakh IV, in a house contemporary with the palace of Niqmepa. As in Yarim-Lim's palace, the living-rooms of the later building were on the upper floor [87].

THE LATE BRONZE AGE IN PALESTINE
The end of the Middle Bronze Age in Palestine is firmly associated with the expulsion of the Hyksos invaders from Egypt and their retreat into Asia. It is therefore hardly remarkable that this political upheaval, with the establishment

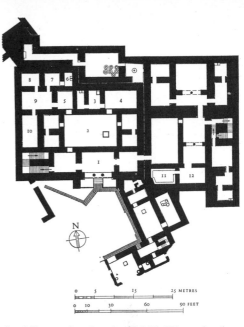

87. Niqmepa's palace in Alalakh IV was in plan a large private house comprising a number of rooms grouped round a central court, the public wing, with official quarters and audience rooms, being added later. Hundreds of tablets were found. This was a period of renewed prosperity for Alalakh, in the late fifteenth and early fourteenth centuries BC, with an elaboration of the architecture of Yarim-Lim's time.

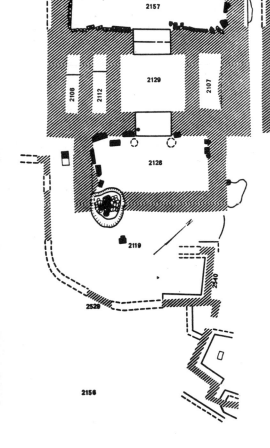

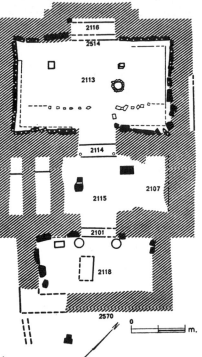

88. The Orthostats Temple of L.B. II–III at Hazor has a plan foreshadowing that of Solomon's temple at Jerusalem. It may have been dedicated to Baal, the Canaanite storm god, whose Aramaean counterpart was Hadad. A statue of a god with an inverted crescent pendant on his breast and a stele with hands upraised to a crescent moon strongly suggest the cult of the moon god Sin, the stele possibly indicating its combination with a goddess.

89. There was much of this cult furniture, carved in basalt, in the final phase of the Stelae Temple of Hazor, though only one of the stelae was carved in relief: these were reused from an earlier phase. Bronze cymbals give another hint of the temple ritual. It is possible that the stelae were memorials to the dead (Hebrew, *masseboth*).

of Egyptian rule on a firmer basis than ever before, is marked in the archaeological record by destruction levels in most of the towns and by a gap in the continuity of occupation, apparent at Jericho on the mound and in the tombs alike. Egyptian influence in the subsequent Late Bronze Age is, however, curiously difficult to discern. It was not till the reign of Thotmes III that Egyptian governors and vassal rulers were appointed in the chief cities (c. 1479 BC). By then the transitional M.B.–L.B. period had merged into L.B. I, without any cultural discontinuity, as the excavations at Megiddo have revealed. Megiddo IX (M.B.–L.B.) probably ended with the sack of the town by Thotmes III; Megiddo VIII marks the L.B. I period. The main period, L.B. II, began in the early fourteenth century BC, continuing till c. 1200 BC or slightly later, and is marked by a deterioration of the material culture. This can perhaps be associated with the gradual infiltration of bands of nomads, many of them called Habiru, who occupied an ever greater proportion of the country, leaving the Canaanite dynasts hopelessly isolated. Their fate is known from vivid passages in the Amarna letters, tablets in Akkadian cuneiform unearthed by villagers at the site of the royal city of Akhenaten: local rulers complain of lack of help from their Egyptian suzerain. Among these rulers was the Hurrian name of Arad-Hepa of Jebus, later Jerusalem. This is a plausible reconstruction of the earlier Israelite occupation of southern Canaan, agreeing with the archaeological evidence.

Some religious continuity from the M.B. II period is suggested by a temple at Megiddo overlying one of the E.B.–M.B. period. The Late Bronze temple has a main hall with shallow niche in the rear wall and two small rooms flanking the entrance; between these rooms may have stood a columned porch. There are three phases (Megiddo VIII–VIIA). Temples have also been found at Beth Shan IX and VII. In the silted-up defensive ditch of Lachish (Tell ed-Duweir) were built three successive phases of the Fosse Temple, of modest size with a rectangular sanctuary and two attached rooms, but with no inner room or Holy of Holies. The latter was essential for the religion of Yahveh and appears in the series of temples at Hazor, beginning in M.B. II and continuing to the end of the Late Bronze Age. Hazor has indeed provided the clearest archaeological evidence in Palestine of the Canaanite background to Hebrew religion, second in importance only to the literary sources recovered at Ugarit. The excavator's chronology divides the Late Bronze Age into three phases, assigning Hazor XV, XIV and XIII to the fifteenth, fourteenth and thirteenth centuries BC respectively (L.B. I–III). In two areas of the lower town were excavated successive phases of two religious buildings, the Orthostats Temple and the Stelae Temple. The plan of these buildings includes an inner sanctuary and outer room with court, foreshadowing Solomon's temple in Jerusalem [88, 89].

The M.B.–L.B. period is distinguished especially by the use of a bichrome painted ware, probably native to Palestine, although found as far north as Ugarit (Late Ugarit 1). Cypriot juglets of White-Painted and wheel-made Black-Polished wares occur in Megiddo IX, to which the tombs attributed by the excavators to the preceding level belong; but they are not found at sites less accessible from the coast, such as Jericho or Tell Beit Mirsim. Imported pottery, mostly from Cyprus, increased in the next period (L.B. I), when narrow-necked Base-Ring ware jugs first appear in Palestine. Yet Middle Bronze forms still persisted; and a degenerate style of pottery with linear and geometric decoration in dull red matt paint appeared and continued in the L.B. II period [90].

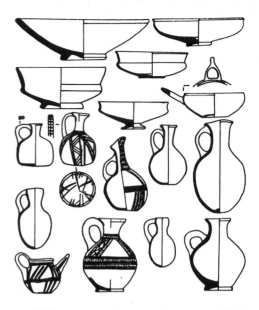

90. Bichrome ware is most abundant at Tell-Ajjul and occurs all along the coast. This pottery is in dull red and black or grey paint, with patterns including fish and birds enclosed in metopes; the so-called 'Union Jack' motif is also characteristic.

The apogee of Mycenaean influence in Palestine, brought about by the fall of Minoan power and probably also by the favourable attitude of the Egyptian suzerain, was early in the fourteenth century BC. Very little Mycenaean pottery occurs in Palestine before *c.* 1400 BC; and by the thirteenth century BC most of the pottery of Mycenaean type found in the east Mediterranean from Egypt to Syria seems to have been made in Cyprus. Among the Cypriot forms was the ubiquitous 'milk bowl', with dark brown-on-white decoration and 'wish-bone' handle.

The chronology of the Late Bronze Age in Palestine is based on a combination of the pottery, especially the Mycenaean imports, with such stratigraphic evidence as the sequence of three phases of the Fosse Temple at Lachish, attributed to a time-span from *c.* 1475 BC to the death of Rameses II (1223/1237 BC). The authors of the report are rightly cautious about the use of scarabs as dating evidence: all that they prove is that, from the occurrence of scarabs bearing the name of Rameses II, the temple cannot have come to an end before his accession (1290/1304 BC).

UGARIT

The fortunes of the great powers in the ancient Near East are nowhere more clearly demonstrated than in Syria, where the heir to the Amorite principalities of the Middle Bronze Age was the kingdom of Mitanni, at its zenith in the sixteenth century BC. At first the adversary of Egyptian expansion, it later became allied through marriages between the two dynasties. This alliance was shattered by the southward thrust of the Hittites under Suppiluliumas in the early fourteenth century BC, assisted by Egyptian preoccupation with internal affairs, and by the expansion of Assyria. In the fifth year of Rameses II occurred the famous encounter between the Egyptian and Hittite armies at Kadesh on the Orontes, a draw in favour of the Hittites, Egyptian pretensions to restoration of the Eighteenth Dynasty's suzerainty over all Syria being permanently abandoned; but the record is that left by Rameses II in the reliefs and inscriptions of Karnak. Sixteen years later a treaty was made between him and Hattusilis III, which resulted in an enduring peace until the fall of Hatti.

The richest city of all Syria was Ugarit, on the Mediterranean coast seven miles north of Latakia. Its material remains illustrate the delicate position of a city whose prosperity depended on trade, carried out largely by foreigners, and which adopted as far as practicable a neutral attitude to the rivalries of the great powers. After the relatively obscure Late Ugarit 1 period came Late Ugarit 2 (*c.* 1450–1365 BC), when the Egyptian hegemony in Syria created ideal conditions for commercial expansion. The earlier seasons of excavations at Ugarit yielded tablets mostly of the fourteenth century BC, and created the belief that Late Ugarit 2 was the period of the city's greatest wealth. More recent discoveries have corrected this by showing that in the thirteenth century BC (Late Ugarit 3) the city attained even greater prosperity, under the aegis of the suzerain power of Hatti. The supposed hostility of the Hittites to Mycenaean trade is not confirmed by the growing presence of Mycenaean merchants in the Late Ugarit 3 period, after first appearing in Late Ugarit 2. Trading links with Cyprus are amply attested by pottery.

Fourteen stone-vaulted chamber-tombs in the city of Ugarit and its nearest port, Minet-el-Beida, are the clearest archaeological indication of the presence of Aegean colonists and merchants. The excavator attributes the design of the chamber-tombs to Minoan rather than Mycenaean influence: they do not

resemble known Mycenaean tombs, but there is a parallel at Isopata in Crete. These tombs, very well built of finely dressed masonry with the floor often paved with slabs, were corbelled, the roof varying from tall and pointed to low and rounded. They are sophisticated examples of a rather primitive structural technique. The owners of these tombs, the richest families of Ugarit, were buried beneath their houses. Less well built but otherwise largely similar tombs were made for the less well-to-do under a courtyard or one of the rooms of the house. Collective burial was customary, continuing the tradition of earlier periods, with successive deposits of funerary goods [91].

The presence of Minoan and, later on, Mycenaean merchants settled at Ugarit provides a partial explanation of the appearance in Egyptian tomb paintings of the *Keftiu* side by side with the *Retenu*, ethnic terms to be translated as 'Aegean' and 'Asiatic'. Ivory-carving and goldsmith's work demonstrate Aegean influence in the Late Ugarit 2–3 periods, discernible in an ivory cosmetic box lid showing a very Aegean mother-goddess in flounced skirt holding up food for animals beside her in very oriental pose. Byblos and Megiddo have also provided examples of fine ivory-carving of the Late Bronze Age.

Ugarit has a good claim to be rated as the most remarkable excavated city of the whole Near East in the fourteenth and thirteenth centuries BC. For indications of foreign trade, the influence of a mixed population, local industry, linguistic and literary attainments, the tolerance of different cults and fine architecture to contain its archives Ugarit is unsurpassed. Canaanite, Mesopo-

91. This is one of the chamber-tombs of Ugarit whose contents suggest that they date largely to the fourteenth century BC. They comprise an entrance-passage, or *dromos*, never more than 3 m. long, with steps leading down to the doorway of the rectangular tomb-chamber. Three of these fourteen tombs had an ossuary for the bones of the owner; in others a pit was cut down from the floor of the tomb-chamber; in others the interment must have been simply in one corner of the chamber.

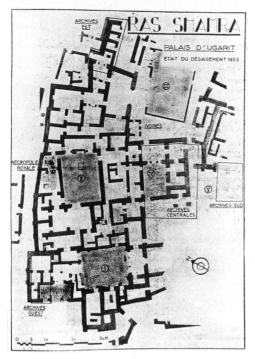

tamian and Hurrian deities occur together in lists of offerings. Literary and lexicographical tablets in Ugaritic, Akkadian and occasionally Hurrian were kept not only in palaces and temples but also in private houses. It is surely from this mingling of languages and literatures that the Ugaritic alphabet developed, the earliest significant alphabetic script, written in cuneiform. Its twenty-seven consonants and three vowels are set out on one tablet. Many religious and mythological texts, mostly of the late thirteenth century BC, were written in the Ugaritic alphabet. West Semitic texts are largely of the Amarna period, when Egyptian influence was still dominant.

The palace of Ugarit, famous in its time and reputedly rivalled only by that of Tyre, was frequently extended and rebuilt; and the standard of life demanded by the rulers of Ugarit is demonstrated by the piped water supply in one court-yard, by cedar and other wooden panelling and by a large walled garden with a pavilion and flower beds. Hurrian tablets give a hint of the musical attainments of Ugarit, at least among the large Hurrian minority. The masonry was fine ashlar, the prototype of Phoenician architecture [93].

The richest houses were ranged in large *insulae* east and south of the palace. One house had thirty-five rooms on the ground floor. Drainage, bathrooms and lavatories were usually included. Store-rooms and offices occupied the ground floor and the main living quarters the upper storey, with an internal court for light and air, having a staircase in one corner. Beneath each house was the family vault, as also in the contemporary town of Enkomi, then a thriving port on the east coast of Cyprus. Smaller houses were crowded along narrow streets in the north-east and north-west sectors of Ugarit. The goldsmiths, silversmiths, bronzesmiths, seal-cutters and sculptors lived round a square in a bazaar quarter to the south. Heaps of crushed murex shells were also found here, evidence of the dyeing of linen and wool, the famous 'Tyrian purple', varying

93. The original palace of Ugarit comprised one entrance hall with staircase to a large court surrounded by rooms, with the royal tombs with three corbelled vaults beneath one room. By the Late Ugarit 3 period, the palace had an area of about 1 hectare, with 8 entrance staircases each with columned portico and with 9 interior courts.

92. Metalworking exemplifies the craftsman-ship of Ugarit, not least a hoard of bronze tools and weapons, including swords, of the fourteenth century BC, and two gold bowls, both of Late Ugarit 2 date, one here illustrated with an elaborate and crowded design resembling certain ivory-work and the other showing a chase, with the hunter in a chariot.

from violet to purple-red. Grain, olive oil, wine, salt and wood (box, juniper and pine) were valuable exports, as were scented oils. Even the poorer citizens lived in more sophisticated, if not necessarily more desirable, houses than the beehive huts of some villages, attested by pottery models and resembling those of villages around Aleppo and eastward today.

The palace of Ugarit was strongly fortified by ramparts in some degree comparable with those of the southern, outer town of Hattusha (Boğazköy) in Anatolia. The superiority of the masonry of the postern-tunnel at Ugarit is one of the indications that Suppiluliumas (see p. 114) was probably influenced by north Syrian military architecture, not vice versa, though it may well have been he who built the rampart of the inner town of Carchemish, established as the Hittite viceregal centre. Dowels, of wood or metal, were used to bind together some of the large blocks of the fortifications of Ugarit.

The power and increasing prosperity of Ugarit rested on economic foundations. Utilitarian metalwork continued to be a significant export from Ugarit, exemplified by a sword bearing the cartouche of Merneptah (*c.* 1220 BC), which never reached the Egyptian customer. Trade was as much the focus of life in Ugarit as it was in the Phoenician cities of Tyre and Sidon [92].

THE SEA PEOPLES

Whatever the historical truth contained in the Old Testament account of the conquest of Canaan by the Israelites under Joshua, much had happened long before. An event with more catastrophic consequences was the arrival of the Sea Peoples, a heterogeneous coalition long known in contemporary sources only from the colourful inscriptions and reliefs of Rameses III on the walls of his mortuary temple at Medinet Habu in Thebes. More recently tablets from Ugarit, from an oven where they were left at the moment of the sack of the city, have shed new light on the events leading to the end of Ugarit. It is apparent that the city had powerful forces, including 1,000 chariots and at least 150 ships: these can be compared with an average of 30 to 50 chariots for each small city-state of Syria and Palestine in the Amarna period and the largest naval contingent mentioned in the Iliad, one hundred ships from Mycenae. Seven enemy ships caused havoc, in the absence of the navy of Ugarit in the waters off the Lycian coast, and of its army in the land of the Hittites.

Widespread destruction is the most obvious archaeological mark of the Sea Peoples. Many sites were reoccupied; others, such as Ugarit and Alalakh, were not. Cremation became more commonly practised, with cemeteries wholly of cremation burials first appearing, as at Hamath and Carchemish. Iron also came into use, particularly through the Philistines and the Sherden (Shardana). The long swords and plumed headdress of the Philistines are prominent on the Medinet Habu reliefs; their skill in ironworking is recorded in the Old Testament, and their abiding influence finds an echo in the very name of Palestine. They were a people at least strongly under Aegean cultural influence: this is reflected in their painted pottery with birds in metopes, or panels, and in the pentapolis of Gaza, Gath, Ekron, Ashdod and Askalon, their chief towns. Pottery coffins with anthropoid lids and tombs with a *dromos* leading down to a trapezoidal chamber with very straight sides were characteristically Philistine, the latter being best exemplified at Tell Fara. Askalon has revealed a major burnt layer sealing the final Late Bronze Age level and overlain by occupation with Philistine pottery. Much of the Levant was never to be the same again after the passing of the Sea Peoples and the abiding settlement of the Philistines.

Anatolia until the End of the Bronze Age (c. 1200 BC) and Contemporary Cultures in Iran and Trans-Caucasia

The Anatolian plateau emerged from the obscurity of the Late Chalcolithic period with the beginning of Early Bronze I, now dated (by calibrated radiocarbon) as early as *c.* 3600 BC. This implies some reduction in the time-span of the Late Chalcolithic phases and a considerable lengthening of the Early Bronze Age compared with previously accepted chronologies. Anatolia was probably divided between numerous small principalities, of which archaeology gives a hint in the wealth accumulated in Troy II, Alaca Hüyük and elsewhere. Mesopotamian traditions of Anatolian campaigns are in no way incompatible with the early development of trade between Anatolian cities, into whose orbit the Assyrian merchants of Kanesh were latecomers. The well-known Cappadocian trade may have been centred at Kanesh more than at Assur, with the Assyrians proving useful instruments of Kaneshite commercial ambition.

The arrival in growing numbers of Hittite invaders from the east brought disorder to central Anatolia, followed by the obscure centuries of the so-called Hittite Old Kingdom. Arzawa had a long history as a major power in the west. Only with Suppiluliumas, in the early fourteenth century BC, did the Hittite state enter a clearer historical stage, with the annexation of territories in north Syria, Carchemish becoming the viceregal centre. This emergence into the wider Near Eastern world contributed to the gradual abandonment of some of the distinctive Indo-European traditions, including the power of the assembly (*pankush*), in favour of a royal despotism under the control of the Sun, as the Hittite kings came to style themselves. Hittite relations with the west are still a controversial subject, with the probability against identification of Ahhiyawa with the Mycenaean power. In Syria the battle of Kadesh was followed by a treaty between Egypt and Hatti, bringing a century of peace through recognized frontiers.

In southern Iran the power of Elam was enduring, and extended farther north and east than formerly suspected, with Anshan (Tell Maliyun) as a major eastern centre. The wide distribution of Proto-Elamite tablets indicates the early ramifications of trade, especially with sources of lapis lazuli, chlorite and metals. Tepe Hissar and other sites in the north-east lay within the homeland of Indo-Europeans from the late third millennium BC; but it was not till one thousand years later that the Iranian tribes overran the plateau.

THE CHALCOLITHIC PERIOD

After the precocious art and technology of Çatal Hüyük and Hacilar, as in the Levant after the eclipse of the PPNB culture, a long dark age ensued on the Anatolian plateau. This lasted until the mid-fourth millennium BC. Even in the better known phases of the Bronze Age the archaeological evidence from Anatolia is at present predominantly that of pottery. Written sources are intermit-

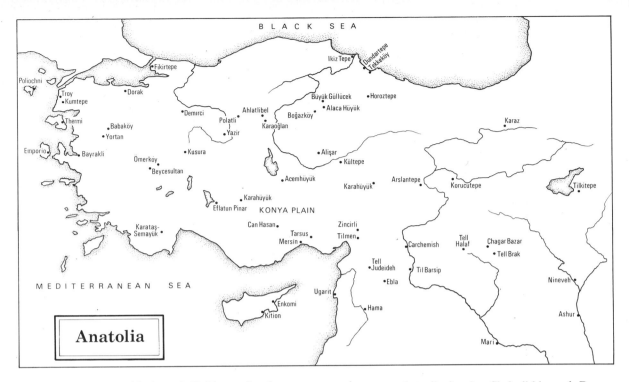

94. Anatolia in the Chalcolithic and Bronze Ages.

tent, art and architecture often unsophisticated. Evidence for the reconstruction of historical geography is scant before the Hittite New Kingdom (fourteenth and thirteenth centuries BC). Perhaps more than anywhere else in the Near East, the major factor determining the limits of cultural provinces was physical geography.

For the obscure fifth and fourth millennia BC two sites, Mersin in the Cilician Plain and Beycesultan in the upper Menderes (Maeander) valley of south-western Anatolia, are of outstanding importance not so much for the intrinsic significance of the remains excavated as for the long continuity of their occupation. Their value for comparative chronology is immense. The sequence at Mersin had already begun in the Neolithic period and is paralleled at neighbouring Tarsus. That at Beycesultan extended through twenty-one Late Chalcolithic levels, the earliest (XL) yielding some white-painted pottery and probably not long post-dating the final desertion of Hacilar, the latest (XX) being immediately followed by the Early Bronze I period (XIX–XVII). Suggestions that this whole sequence should be fitted in to the third millennium BC do not square with the evidence, quite apart from the number of levels and the ten metres' depth of deposit.

The south-west Anatolian cultural province in the fifth and fourth millennia BC seems to have been very conservative. After a hiatus some Early Chalcolithic sites near Hacilar itself were reoccupied by Late Chalcolithic settlers. At Beycesultan the excavators have distinguished four phases spanning the period c. 4900–3500 BC (Late Chalcolithic 1–4). Pottery and architecture alike display strong continuity throughout the twenty-one levels. There can be no doubt of the northern origin of the population bringing pottery into south-western Anatolia and the corresponding wares into the Konya Plain. In both regions new settlements were established, often occupied only during this period. The Late Chalcolithic 4 phase in the south-west is well represented by the large, unexcavated mound of Ömerköy, close to Beycesultan, at a time when the transition to E.B. I pottery was beginning [95].

Can Hasan, near Karaman, may be reckoned the type site for the cultural province centred in the Konya Plain. The Early Chalcolithic of Can Hasan 2B was followed by the Middle Chalcolithic of Can Hasan 2A, with five levels and continuing till *c.* 4500 BC or slightly later. The site was then deserted, the next occupation being of the Late Chalcolithic period, in the earlier half of the fourth millennium BC, this being Can Hasan 1, with six distinct building levels. The greatest concentration of settlements of this Late Chalcolithic culture was in the Çumra district, around the ruins of Çatal Hüyük. The most northerly extension of the influence of this culture is known at the excavated site of Yazir, near Sivrihisar, in the bend of the upper Sangarius (Sakarya) river. The humble village houses of Can Hasan 1, built of small mud-bricks without timber reinforcement or stone foundations, were grouped round courtyards containing ovens and bins, and were frequently modified.

Another cultural province was centred in the Cilician Plain, where Mersin first provided the key to the whole Chalcolithic sequence. Its importance has been diminished by the discovery, since 1951, of Early and Late Chalcolithic cultures on the plateau, so that it has long since ceased to be reasonable to apply the Cilician cultural sequence to the whole plateau. Mersin remains, however, an invaluable barometer of the mingling and confrontation of elements from north Syria and Mesopotamia with others from the Konya plain and remoter parts of Anatolia. The so-called 'Middle Chalcolithic' culture of Mersin XIX–XVII, exhibiting strong Halaf influence from the east, was succeeded by the more indigenous culture of Mersin XVI. Now the settlement was fortified, and seems to have endured throughout the later fifth millennium BC. One piece of evidence for its long duration was the considerable wear on the paving stones of a road up through a gate from the river [96].

Metalworking seems to have advanced, exemplified by copper axes and chisels, demonstrating the possible priority of Anatolia in this branch of technology. A metal hoard from Beycesultan XXXIV and a copper shaft-hole axe from Can Hasan add to this evidence. The long dark age of Anatolia was not entirely backward: changes were quiet and slow but enduring.

After the violent destruction of Mersin XVI (*c.* 4000 BC) the fortifications were twice rebuilt and destroyed in XV–XIII, when eastern influences of ultimately Ubaid origin became ever stronger, transmitted through the culture of the Amuq Plain (Amuq E), best known from Tell esh Sheikh. In the final phase of the Late Chalcolithic period in Cilicia there was once more a cultural diversification, apparent in pottery of widely differing types and origins: the eastern part of the Cilician Plain, exemplified by Tarsus, remained largely under eastern influences, however decadent, whereas Mersin, as before, was more open to elements from the Anatolian plateau. At Tarsus a local painted pottery was inspired by lingering Halaf traditions; there were also 'wheel-finished plain slipped bowls', with a very wide distribution, from Cilicia through Amuq F to Tepe Gawra in northern Mesopotamia, providing the sole link in Cilicia with the Uruk culture. Clearly not too much significance should be attached to every survival, development and change in the output of one class of craftsmen, the potters.

In eastern Anatolia the cultural succession is very patchily documented for the whole pre-Bronze Age sequence, although evidence from the Keban Dam excavations near Elazığ has greatly clarified the prehistory of that fertile plain

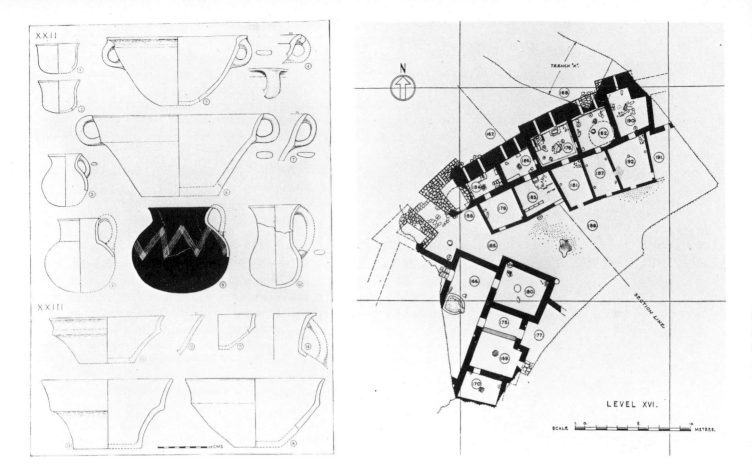

from the aceramic Neolithic phase onwards. At Korucutepe a great burning marks the end of the Chalcolithic period, with one radio-carbon determination suggesting *c.* 3000 BC as the date for the arrival of the subsequent Early Trans-Caucasian I culture. Close to Lake Van the very small mound of Tilkitepe (Shamiramalti) had three main levels, the earliest (III) yielding burnished Halaf pottery of the finest quality. Very large obsidian cores were abundant. At Karaz, near Erzurum, one of the first sites to draw archaeological attention to the Early Trans-Caucasian culture, there was an earlier phase dating back into the fourth millennium BC.

In the Urmia basin of north-western Iran the beginnings of village life in the sixth millennium BC, represented by Hajji Firuz close to Hasanlu and by the smaller site of Yanik Tepe near Tabriz, were followed by the Dalma culture, named after another small site very close to Hasanlu, in the Solduz Plain immediately south of the lake. Radio-carbon determinations suggest that Dalma Tepe flourished in the later fifth millennium BC. No comparison with Halaf pottery bears scrutiny. This was a local culture, yet more widespread than first suspected, for it is manifest at Seh Gabi, a site near Godin Tepe, in the Kangavar district, thus extending over the northern Zagros highlands. At Yanik Tepe the typical pottery was red-slipped and burnished, with only a small percentage of black-on-red painted ware. This was indeed the characteristic pottery of the eastern half of the Urmia basin. On the west side of Lake Urmia it occurs in the earliest phase (N) at Geoy Tepe, just south of Reza'iyeh. But it was

95. Above left: At Beycesultan, white-painted decoration occurs from the first (Level XL); and heavy bowls with increasingly exaggerated carination were typical of Late Chalcolithic 3-4.

96. The fortifications of Mersin XVI were of mud-brick on stone foundations reinforced by a glacis. The sling had supplanted the bow as the main weapon, with sling-stones heaped beside embrasures in the 'barrack rooms' ranged along the inside of the perimeter wall. The bow and the sling were not mutually exclusive throughout the Near East, though at Mersin they may have been so.

97. Dalma pottery is distinguished by a range of limited forms, such as hole-mouth bowls, with dark purplish-black painted decoration of lozenges, triangles, sweeping bands and chevrons, the paint covering much of the surface and the ware being extraordinarily friable. Finger-impressed decoration is another surface treatment, as well as comb-impressed.

superseded by black to brown-on-cream to buff painted pottery in Geoy Tepe M, in a broad Ubaid tradition. Presumably this reflected, if indirectly, the economic expansion of this period from the Sumerian world into western Iran. The major excavated site is Pisdeli Tepe, in the Solduz Plain. An indigenous origin for the black-on-red ware in the Urmia basin may be indicated by the nine Chalcolithic levels of Yanik Tepe, some with sub-phases, with their strong ceramic continuity. More sophisticated forms, such as stem goblets, had come into fashion towards the end of the period, contemporary with Pisdeli [97].

In Trans-Caucasia, in the middle Kura valley, were the settlements of Ṣomutepe, with its coarse pottery, obsidian from the Sevan region, mats and textiles, and Shulaveri, slightly later in date. In its earlier period (I), this site was distinguished by small, closely crowded round houses and by rather crude pottery, decoration taking the form of incision, with knobs, pellets or notches along the rim. The chipped-stone industry in obsidian and the ground-stone industry in basalt and serpentine, partly used for celts, were developed and prolific. Antler sleeves probably served as digging implements. Shulaveri II had oval instead of round houses. Local peculiarities in pottery occur at each site of this culture, such as Aruchlo and Sadachlo. In the Araxes valley, Kültepe (Nakhichevan) IA yielded copper artefacts and demonstrates a long occupation, with over eight metres' depth of deposit. Several sites, especially Shengavit I, just outside Erevan, represent a phase in the prehistory of the Armenian S.S.R. immediately before the appearance of the Early Trans-Caucasian I culture, with an improved ground-stone industry and a developing agriculture, which had originated in the fifth millennium BC.

ANATOLIA IN THE EARLY BRONZE AGE
The cultures of the third millennium BC in western, southern and central Anatolia lack any unity, in contrast with the vast Early Trans-Caucasian cultural zone to the east. They appear, at least to the newcomer to Anatolian archaeology, to form a bewildering patchwork, each piece centred round one or more sites, often imperfectly excavated, sometimes known only from surveys. Geography played perhaps a greater role than at any other time in determining the boundaries of cultural provinces. Small principalities flourished enough to give rise to notable concentrations of wealth, eventually creating the conditions which gave rise to the growth of cities in the Early Bronze III period, especially in the Konya Plain and in the Cappadocian region. But this was a slow process. Some regions, such as Cilicia and north-west Anatolia, moved ahead of parts more isolated, such as central Anatolia within the bend of the river Halys (Kizil Irmak). One or two sites have attained a prominence quite undeserved, such as Troy, which in the time of Schliemann's First Settlement was a modest citadel barely 100 m. in diameter. Not till it was looked at in its true context, as an Anatolian site relevant to the study of the north-west Anatolian cultural province, could Troy be put in proportion to its contemporaries, among them the much larger Beycesultan, in the south-west Anatolian cultural province. Only a few sites can be dealt with even briefly here; but any approach centred round a small number of distantly separated settlements without due regard to the intervening territory is sure to be distorted.

From the number of excavated sites within its area, the E.B. I culture named after Troy I deserves first mention. Soundings have been made at Bayrakli (Old Smyrna), Kumtepe IC in the Troad and elsewhere; but the major excavations have been at Troy itself and at three island sites, Poliochni in Lemnos, Thermi in Lesbos and Emporio in Chios, from north to south. The long time-span of the Troy I culture is indicated by the number of building levels: there are ten at Troy I, comprising three major phases; six at Thermi, with three phases; and three at Poliochni (II–IV), the earliest (II) being of long duration. Partly because of the long duration of the following Troy II culture, now recognized, an approximate dating of *c.* 3600–3100 BC may well be reasonable for the Troy I culture. This was well established, with a distribution showing its largely maritime character, and with Poliochni as the most impressive site, Troy I itself being still largely concealed by the later levels. Stone was much used in building, for wall footings, built-in cupboards, benches and sleeping platforms. Troy I, Poliochni II–IV and Thermi V were all fortified, with towered gateways, approach ramps and bastions. A building inside the gate of Poliochni has benches ranged along the whole of one long side, suggesting an assembly hall. Archers manned the defences when required, as shown by slit windows at Poliochni, where the town walls still stand five metres high. Contact with distant regions, if not necessarily as far away as Bohemia, is proved by the one technical advance beyond the Late Chalcolithic period, the occurrence of tin-bronze at Thermi and Troy I.

The most widespread material is the pottery, hand-made and with burnished slip, the colour often being an olive-green shade in the earlier phases but later mostly black. The earliest common form is a rather heavy bowl with a much thickened rim and a carination just beneath it. Other typical forms are bowls with sharply everted rim, some on a hollow pedestal base with 'windows' in it, and jugs with three knob feet and with a cut-away or plain rising 'beak' spout. The latter is characteristic of the Early Bronze Age of western Anatolia as a whole, especially in the cemeteries of the inland Yortan area. These have proved a rich source of illicitly dug material, the jugs and other pottery commonly being decorated in white paint. The Yortan culture survived as a conservative element through the time of Troy II [98].

The Troy I culture seems to have been the achievement of a people depending primarily on a self-sufficient economy of mixed farming but with trading connections far beyond their own province. Anatolian connections are the strongest: with a source near Kütahya, even the obsidian need not have come entirely from Melos. The Troy I culture was Anatolian, extending into Thrace, not Aegean. Perhaps this is most clearly demonstrated by the grouping of the houses round a main hall of the *megaron* plan, with a central hearth and door at one end entered through a large porch formed simply by prolonging the line of the walls. The Anatolian derivation of the *megaron*, which remained fashionable into the Iron Age, is now beyond doubt.

During the time of the Troy I culture the indigenous development of south-western Anatolia is discernible in the distinctive pottery of the E.B. I period at Beycesultan (XIX–XVII), a thin, highly fired and burnished ware, with horizontal and vertical fluting on jars and jugs, altogether metallic in appearance. A single shrine foreshadowed the double shrines of the following period, and yielded miniature copper tools and fiddle-shaped marble figurines of Aegean type. The defensive wall of Beycesultan XIX was very modest compared with the walls of the Troy I settlements.

Archaeology and philology have been combined to support an ingenious reconstruction, as yet not disproved, of the sequence of events in western Anatolia, beginning with the violent destruction of nearly all the coastal Troy I

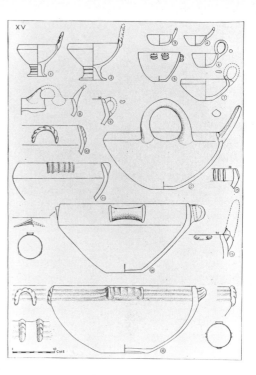

98. Incised decoration, white-filled, is the commonest style of ornamentation for Troy I pottery, but grooving and white paint occur also. A variety of lugs is typical of the Troy I culture, though at Troy their development was not the same as at Thermi, where horned lugs appeared first (Period A: Levels I–III), followed by trumpet lugs (Period B: Levels III–IVA), then by ribbed trumpet lugs (Period C: Levels IVB–V), then by solid lugs and those set below the rim. At Troy a long straight lug came first; later the ends were enlarged and finally exaggerated. Some bowls have a partly pinched out rim, with a crude incised representation of a human face. With a stone stele of the middle phase of Troy I they seem to foreshadow the well known 'face-urns' of Troy IIg–V.

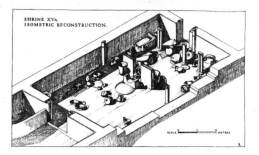

SHRINE XVA.
ISOMETRIC RECONSTRUCTION.

99. The shrines of Beycesultan, perhaps dedicated to a chthonic cult, contained a number of vessels as offerings, with stelae of clay and a local grey-blue clay as mural decoration, as used to this day in the district.

100. At Troy the *depas amphikypellon* was a characteristic pottery vessel. At Polatli thirty-one levels, grouped into four periods, yielded evidence of connections especially with Troy and south-western Anatolia rather than with the central region. *Depata* appeared at the end of Period I; and 'red-cross' bowls are the clearest dating evidence for Period II, linking it with Troy V (*c.* 2100–1900 BC).

sites. Although Troy itself was immediately rebuilt, elsewhere the cultural break was complete. In the south-west Anatolian province, however, the E.B. II of Beycesultan XVI–XIII was in effect the Troy I culture removed from its original homeland, the pottery being very similar, though the double shrines of Beycesultan are a local feature [99].

The arrival of the north-west Anatolian E.B. I (Troy I) culture in the south-west can be explained as a refugee movement in the face of attack by newcomers from the Balkans, a movement resulting in the displacement of some of the E.B. I population and their migration westwards across the Aegean, bringing the Early Helladic I culture into Greece. Most of the sites of the Troy I culture were deserted. Troy II itself was one of the few settlements of the Troy II culture, whose distinctive pottery has made its diffusion in the following E.B. III period throughout the greater part of southern and western Anatolia, as far as the Cilician Plain, easily discernible. This took place as the result of a second, more far-reaching invasion, and may plausibly be associated with a people known from the Hittite Old Kingdom onwards and even from a hieroglyphic seal from Beycesultan VI: these were the Luvians, mentioned also in the Kül-tepe–Kanesh tablets. They were Indo-Europeans, who must have arrived from an earlier homeland in the Pontic steppes of south Russia, and who absorbed Anatolian traditions during the long duration of Troy II, before their expulsion by the second invasion. Such a reconstruction of events, in the absence of written records, has the merit of taking into account all the available archaeological evidence, from surveys as well as excavations. It is contrary to the traditional outlook of those scholars whose training and interests are centred round the Aegean. But no later period for the arrival of the Luvians, thus preceding the Hittites by several centuries, makes archaeological sense. The general cultural continuity from the opening of the E.B. III period to the end of the Late Bronze Age is an unanswerable objection to a later date for the Luvian invasions, which were destined to leave a permanent impress on the population of western and southern Anatolia.

Although the first wave of newcomers into north-western Anatolia may have brought with them an economy only partially sedentary, thus accounting for the desertion of many settlements, the inhabitants of Troy II were far from uncivilized. In Troy IIb new elements first appear, with the technical advance of the use of the potter's wheel. In this Troy II was virtually alone in Anatolia in the E.B. II period: this phenomenon—manifest especially in a form of shallow bowl of plain ware, continuing till Troy V, mass-produced and sometimes coated with a red wash—seems to have resulted from maritime trade with Cilicia, always important as a means of cultural contact between Syria and different parts of Anatolia. The other Troy II pottery can be classed as in the local tradition. A very easily recognizable form of two-handled goblet, Schliemann's *depas amphikypellon*, appeared in Troy IIc and lasted as late as Troy V. The citadel of Troy IIa–c, the main phases, was still of modest area, little over 100 m. in diameter, with a building complex best described as a manor house set in a courtyard reached by a propylon just inside the fortified gateway. The perimeter, polygonal in its circuit, had stone footings surmounted by mud-brick with massive beams laid horizontally every three courses (with occasional cross beams also) and every four courses in the walls of the two *megara*.

The wealth of western and central Anatolia in the E.B. II period is best illustrated by the metalwork, jewellery, gold, silver and bronze found at several widely separated sites. From west to east the most important finds have been those of Troy IIg, Dorak south of the Sea of Marmara, Alaca Hüyük and Horoztepe. All appear to fall within the period *c*. 2900–2600 BC. The famous treasures found by Schliemann had been buried in the final phase (IIg) before the destruction of Troy II: they comprised nine hoards of caches, certainly manufactured no later than Troy IIc, since the subsequent phases marked a time of impoverishment [101].

In technical skill the Trojan jewellers cannot be compared with those of Ur. A silver spearhead with rounded shoulders, bent tang and two slots in the blade, paralleled at Alaca Hüyük and at Gerede in northern Anatolia, is from Treasure A. Another hoard, Treasure L, included highly polished dark green stone shaft-hole axes, one of lapis lazuli, bone tubes of Cycladic origin and amber from the Baltic or the Ukraine.

Some six cultural provinces have been distinguished in western Anatolia in the E.B. II period (Troy II, Yortan, Akhisar-Manisa, Caria, Marmora and Demirci Hüyük), the last being in the Eskişehir plain and forming a link with central Anatolia through the Ankara cultural province, best known from excavations at Karaoğlan and Ahlatlibel. The sequence at Polatli, on the west side of the same province, has provided invaluable evidence for the third millennium BC and later, showing the cultural conservatism of an Anatolian village.

The central Anatolian and Pontic cultural provinces, closely associated with each other, had emerged from the obscurity of the Late Chalcolithic period, continuing through the centuries elsewhere termed E.B. I. This rather confusing terminology has one merit, its emphasis on the undeniable backwardness of central Anatolia, perhaps partly the result of its remoteness from trade with the Mediterranean and the Levant. Later written sources suggest a Hattian, non-Indo-European population. In Alişar 'O' and Ia there were eight Chalcolithic levels, a sequence nevertheless beginning only in the late fourth millennium BC, and divided into Early (Levels 19–15) and Late Chalcolithic (14–12). Fruitstands, thick and bulbous at first but in later levels becoming tall and slender, are typical of Alişar and Alaca Hüyük too. Less sophisticated pottery, with a variety of incised decoration, occurs at Büyük Güllücek, near Alaca Hüyük. Jars and two-handled bowls were among other forms at Alişar. As with all the central Anatolian Chalcolithic sites, black to blackish-brown is the dominant surface colour of the pottery, the ware being black and soft-baked.

Perhaps the most obvious change in the central Anatolian E.B. II culture, termed the Copper Age in earlier publications, is in the surface colour of the pottery. Far and wide through western and central Anatolia red burnished wares became typical, though the old taste for black pottery did not vanish. The total impression is one of a substantially common culture over much of the Anatolian plateau in the early third millennium BC, the E.B. II period. To some extent, therefore, the differences between cultural provinces are less significant than their common factors. Central and western Anatolia, however, did develop as two rather different zones.

The excavated sites within the bend of the River Halys would be more valuable if they had been more consistently dug and published. The stratigraphy of Alişar Hüyük was unnecessarily confused by the American excavators, who finally classified the numerous building levels into several main periods (O, Ia, Ib, III, II, IV and V, in that order, with a hiatus between II and IV). Alişar Ib is the E.B. II period, with five levels (11M–7M) equivalent to the four levels (8–5) of Alaca III. Thus a duration of five centuries (*c*. 3100–2600 BC) for the

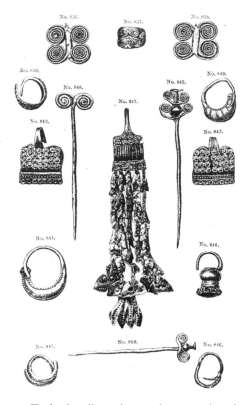

101. Trojan jewellery: the most important hoard is Treasure A (Schliemann's 'Treasure of Priam'), originally buried in a wooden chest; here were two elaborate gold diadems, with a fringe of chains ending in a leaf- or flower-shaped pendant and with long tassels at either side; and here too were fine earrings, bracelets, a gold 'sauce-boat', hairpins with rosettes and spirals, double-spiral and other pins. Gold was beaten into sheets and cut out to make these personal ornaments; wire coils were also used.

E.B. II period could be rated as excessive. The E.B. II pottery, important if only for its ubiquity, has a limited variety of forms, without the taste for lugs and fluting found in western Anatolia and as far east as Polatli. Simple bowls are the most common; a shallow bowl with sharp carination just below the rim is typical of Alaca Hüyük and other sites; two-handled cups in the latest E.B. II levels are related to those at Tarsus rather than to the *depata* of Troy and Polatli in the west. A Cilician prototype seems likely for both forms. Painting is rare on E.B. II pottery, but the red cross pattern appears on some of these cups. A painted ware found at Maltepe, close to Sivas, is confined to that district.

The royal cemetery at Alaca Hüyük, whose rich contents form one of the major attractions for the visitor to the Ankara Museum today, comprised thirteen tombs, sited on the edge of the town. They were almost certainly provided with markers, since no tomb impinges on any other. This cemetery thus conformed neither to the burial custom of extramural cemeteries normal throughout western Anatolia—those of Troy and Beycesultan, for example, remaining undiscovered—nor to that more traditional in central Anatolia, of intramural burial. The extramural cemetery at Tekkeköy, one of the Late Chalcolithic-E.B. II sites on the Black Sea coast near Samsun, has been quoted as evidence of influence from western Anatolia by maritime connections. The tombs of Alaca Hüyük seem to represent a funerary custom originating from the steppes north of the Caucasus, though their contents are of Anatolian workmanship. The same can perhaps be said, to some extent, of the great Maikop barrow in the Kuban valley, north-west of the Caucasus range. It is therefore not impossible that a small group of Indo-Europeans penetrated the Halys region as early as the E.B. II period, at least seven centuries before the first documented presence of Hittites in the time of Kültepe II (*c.* 2000–1900 BC). If so, they could have been instrumental in bringing Anatolian metalwork to their original homeland. Certainly they brought nothing beyond the design of their burials into the Near East. The graves were pits roofed over with beams and covered with earth. Animal bones on top suggest a funeral feast after each burial.

A chronological sequence spanning the period *c.* 2800–2600 BC is evident from the metalwork, with one E.B. II level preceding the cemetery and with the partially contemporary burials at Horoztepe continuing slightly later. There are several parallels between the Alaca tombs and the treasures of Troy II. A variety of metallurgical techniques is apparent in the Alaca tombs, including hammering and casting in open and closed moulds and by the *cire perdue* method, the latter used for the difficult casting of a copper stag and standard combined. Chasing, but not engraving, was also practised, together with soldering, sweating, inlay and repoussé work. Granulation, filigree and cloisonné in granulation, though not found at Alaca, occur in the north-west, at Troy and Dorak. There the variety of materials used, other than metals, was greater than at Alaca Hüyük, and included ivory, amber, lapis lazuli and turquoise. Thus the trading connections of north-western Anatolia seem to have been wider than those of central Anatolia, a fact strongly suggesting a major role for maritime trade and routes to Mesopotamia at this time by-passing central Anatolia. The metalwork of Alaca Hüyük, however, shows skills not far removed from those of Ur [*Pls 17, 18*].

Diadems of sheet gold with openwork decoration, 8-shaped brooches and bracelets, pins and beads of many types demonstrate the versatility of the goldsmiths of Alaca Hüyük, also displayed in jugs and goblets of gold, silver, electrum, copper and bronze. Thus the influence of metal vessels on pottery is amply documented, even if fluting is commoner on western than on central Anatolian pottery, the only serious question-mark over the local workmanship of these vessels. Swords, daggers, maceheads, spears and battle-axes provide a formidable armoury, though arrows are lacking. Two daggers of terrestrial iron with gold-plated handles, one being crescentic and paralleled at Ur, are among the earliest dated examples of the use of this metal.

The E.B. II town of Alaca was destroyed by incomers, who seem not to have settled in the area, for the site was only spasmodically occupied in the period *c.* 2600–1850 BC. The easily recognizable criterion of the E.B. III period in central Anatolia (*c.* 2600–2000 BC) is the Alişar III (or Cappadocian) painted pottery, even if it does not signal the emergence of an entire new culture. This pottery is hand-made, with a buff or light red burnished or wet-smoothed surface and geometric patterns in dark brown or black paint, sometimes combined with red and a cream or buff panel as background in the trichrome decoration. Bowls have a narrow band of painted decoration just below the rim; other typical forms are small cups and large jars and jugs, with most of their outside surface painted. Alişar III itself comprises two levels, with three at Kültepe. This pottery occurs chiefly in the south and south-west parts of the Halys basin.

In north-west Anatolia, Troy II was violently destroyed, and followed by relatively impoverished periods (Troy III–V, *c.* 2600–1900 BC), comprising respectively three, five and four levels. This, the main Luvian invasion, swept south and east through south-west Anatolia and as far as the Cilician Plain. The very marked decline in the number of settlements of this period compared with those of the E.B. II period underlines the catastrophic nature of this invasion. Whole areas, including much of the Konya Plain, were abandoned. At Beycesultan the pottery most clearly demonstrates this abrupt change, from the E.B. II levels (XVI–XIII) to the E.B. III levels (XII–VI). The Indo-European newcomers had occupied the upper Maeander valley: more isolated areas, such as that of the Yortan culture and Kusura B, near Afyon Karahisar, preserved essentially E.B. I traditions for another three centuries, till *c.* 2300 BC, when Kusura was burnt.

The E.B. III levels at Beycesultan have been divided into three phases: the earliest (XII–XI) had little architecture in the area excavated; the next (X–VIII) had a group of houses on the *megaron* plan, here a standard design for urban houses; the final phase (VII–VIB–A) is most noteworthy for its pottery. These three phases correspond to Troy III, IV and V respectively, the last correlation being clinched by the occurrence of 'red-cross' bowls in Beycesultan VII–VIA. Most of the pottery is hand-made, reddish in colour and with a tendency to reflect metal prototypes. Tall beak-spouted jugs, bowls and two-handled cups are most characteristic, with new types, such as jars with volute feet, appearing in Beycesultan VIA, when handles and rivets imitated on bowls add to the evidence of the influence of metal vessels which have not themselves survived. Anatolian pottery frequently reveals much of metal prototypes, whose significance would otherwise be grossly underrated [102].

The most distant impact of the Luvian invasion was in the arrival of the E.B. III culture in the Cilician Plain, best represented at Tarsus, where Anatolian influences had predominated since the start of the E.B. I period in the late fourth millennium BC. Cilician E.B. I pottery includes 'red gritty' ware, derived from a finer variety found in the eastern half of the Konya Plain and extending into north Syria. Among Cilician E.B. II pottery is this same ware, often coated with purplish paint, as well as wheel-made plain wares and deep bowls of black

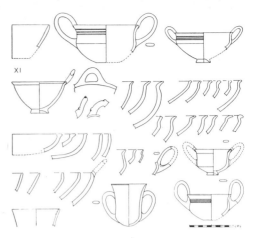

102. 'Proto-Minyan' two-handled cups occur from Beycesultan XII onwards, being dull red to reddish-brown and either hand- or wheel-made. Grey Minyan ware, very rare at Beycesultan, seems from surface finds to be commoner in the Tavşanli-Kütahya region, one hundred miles to the north. Thus a west Anatolian origin for the well-known Minyan ware of Middle Helladic Greece seems perfectly acceptable, indeed probable, on the archaeological evidence. Here in the south-west, as elsewhere in Anatolia, there was no real cultural discontinuity between the E.B. III period and the Middle Bronze Age.

burnished ware profusely decorated with white-filled 'cross-stitch' incision, found also across the Amanus range at Zincirli and as imports in Amuq I, contemporary with Khirbet Kerak ware. Probably allied to the 'red gritty' ware of the Cilician Plain was the reddish-orange brittle ware found throughout the Early Bronze Age at the sites of Gedikli (Karahüyük) and Tilmen Hüyük in the Islahiye district of Gaziantep province. Gedikli is interesting for its cremation cemetery, in use for a long period, at least *c*. 2400–1900 BC, with quasi-spherical pottery urns, the earliest evidence of this burial custom in Syria and Anatolia. The E.B. I and E.B. II levels at Tarsus have a similar depth of deposit, eight metres, the E.B. II period comprising ten building phases. The more modest depth of deposit of 2.5 m. for the E.B. III period at Tarsus, divided into three phases (E.B. IIIa–c) by the excavators, appears to comprise no less than seven phases, the last five being grouped together as one (E.B. IIIc).

The appearance of the 'red-cross' bowl in the first, transitional Middle Bronze Age level at Tarsus is a clear parallel with Troy V (*c*. 2100–1900 BC); and Late Cappadocian one-handled bowls, with a cross painted on the inside or outside or both, provide comparable cross-dating with central Anatolia. Small bottles of plain ware, of Syrian origin, illustrate trading connections through Cilicia to central Anatolia, since they occur in the E.B. IIIc phase at Tarsus and likewise in the Early and perhaps also the Middle Cappadocian levels on the city mound of Kültepe–Kanesh. These ceramic parallels prove that the Cilician E.B. III period ended by *c*. 2100 BC, and suggest an early version of the trade network established between the cities of Ashur and Kanesh. The E.B. III period was as different in its architecture as in its pottery from the E.B. I–II periods, when houses at Tarsus were built with two rooms, a large front room with a square hearth and a small room at the back; the E.B. III houses were of the *megaron* plan, with hall and porch. This combination of architectural with ceramic change underlines the cultural transformation from the Cilician E.B. II to E.B. III periods. What more likely time for the arrival of the Luvians from the north-west? Their importance in Kizzuwatna, as the Cilician Plain was known to the Hittites, is obvious from the archives of the Hittite capital.

THE EARLY TRANS-CAUCASIAN CULTURE

Scattered excavations and wide-ranging archaeological reconnaissances have revealed a remarkably far-flung material culture in the highlands of eastern Anatolia, in Trans-Caucasia and in north-western Iran, crossing modern frontiers and enduring over most of this territory for a thousand years or even longer. This cultural province, far larger than any other in the Near East in the third millennium BC, exhibits a predictable progression, from uniformity in its first phase through growing diversity to fragmentation into smaller cultural sub-provinces in its third and final phase. Elsewhere the writer has proposed the terms Early Trans-Caucasian I–III for these phases, partly for brevity but also because the most probable centre for the origin of this culture lay in the fertile Araxes valley around Erevan, where Shengavit II–IV constitutes a type site. Admittedly the evidence, predominantly ceramic, is not nearly as abundant or varied as could be wished; and new discoveries will no doubt overturn cherished theories. One difficulty is the absence of sites with a complete, unbroken stratified sequence extending throughout the duration of the Early Trans-Caucasian culture. Recent discoveries in the Elaziğ region partially remedy this deficiency. Transhumance played a major role, accounting in part for the meagre stratigraphic evidence.

Pl 17. The religious objects from the Alaca tombs will always generate discussion: copper figures of animals, a bull or a stag, were inlaid, sometimes partly sheathed, in electrum. Concentric circles may have had some esoteric significance. The massive dowels at the base of these figures may indicate attachment not to poles, as standards carried in procession, but to wagons; but an equally probable explanation is that they surmounted the wooden framework for a canopy over each tomb.

The first period, Early Trans-Caucasian I, witnessed a rapid expansion from the original centre into Georgia in the north-east and to the Erzurum Plain to the west, with the fertile Altinova (nowadays the province of Elaziğ and the focus of the recent Keban Dam rescue excavations) also being occupied. Kültepe (Nakhichevan) II has fourteen levels of this period. Dark ware, hand-made, with relief and grooved decoration is the most typical. Architecture is the other hallmark of this culture, with rectangular houses in the west and round houses in the east, from the Georgian S.S.R. through the Armenian S.S.R. into the Urmia basin. There, however, this type of house does not appear before the Early Trans-Caucasian II period, when there are nine principal building levels at Yanik Tepe, in the plain between Tabriz and Lake Urmia. Clearly these newcomers had arrived on the east side of the lake from the north; and they were to press on as far south as the Kermanshah–Hamadan region, where their typical pottery and plastered hearths appear in Godin IV, if only rather briefly. This was one of two major thrusts from the earlier homeland of this culture, coinciding approximately with the transition from Early Trans-Caucasian I to II: the other thrust was the movement into the Levant of the people who introduced the Khirbet Kerak pottery characteristic of Amuq H.

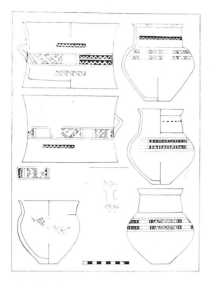

103. At Yanik Tepe the kitchen fittings were standard in design and arrangement, and the whole appearance of the round houses suggests that their prototype was in the nature of the Turkoman *yurt*. With the evidence for skill in woodcarving, this points to nomadic origins for the Early Trans-Caucasian II settlers in Yanik Tepe. The confined space within the round houses, only some of which were large enough to require a central post, may have dictated strict allocation of certain areas to specific members of the household, as occurs today in Mongolia.

A considerable time-span for the Early Trans-Caucasian II period is indicated by Yanik Tepe XXIV–XIV, comprising three phases. The round houses increase in diameter and density through these phases, though the distinctive incised pottery ceases at the end of the second. The decorative repertoire invites comparison with that from Jerahovid and elsewhere in the Araxes Plain of the Armenian S.S.R., where boldly swirling designs make the work of the Yanik Tepe potters appear for the most part crabbed and confined to the limitations imposed by earlier traditions of woodcarving, including bands of excised ornament round the shoulders of small jars, the most typical form [103, *Pl 19*].

In the terminology used by Soviet archaeologists the Early Trans-Caucasian I and II periods are classified as 'Aeneolithic', while the following period is the Early Bronze Age. This term is justifiable by the marked increase in metallurgy and the introduction of bronze; but the pottery shows a general cultural continuity from the preceding periods, precluding any major change in population. There are now, however, distinct cultural provinces within the vast Early Trans-Caucasian zone. In the Urmia basin the earlier forms continued, but without decoration apart from finger-depressions; the massive Nakhichevan lugs are less prominent; and a graphite burnish gives a silvery sheen to some pottery, a deliberate imitation of metal prototypes, paralleled in the contemporary cemeteries of Tetri-Tsqaro and Amiranis-Gora in Georgia. More significant than ceramic changes was the apparent stability of this period in north-western Iran, with the change from round houses to far more solidly constructed rectangular buildings, with successive alterations but without the destruction levels of the preceding period, at Yanik Tepe and Haftavan VII alike. Urban life seems to have taken root in this part of the Early Trans-Caucasian zone, although most of eastern Anatolia probably remained sparsely settled. An exception was the south-western region, where, around Elaziğ and Malatya and straddling the upper Euphrates, a local style of painted pottery evolved, hand-made and highly fired, quite different from the pottery of the rest of the zone but contemporary with various styles of painted pottery on the Anatolian plateau. In Altinova, where the excavations at Korucutepe and other sites in advance of the inundation of the plain by the Keban dam have proved very informative, urban life seems to have developed, and population reached a density long unsurpassed. Already in the Early Trans-Caucasian II period small bowls of distinctive profile had been produced in this area, which seems early to have evolved somewhat along its own lines.

Phosphorus brickettes, from the bones of animals ground and mixed with clay, were used at Metsamor in the smelting of cassiterite: recent experiments have proved that this method leads to a significant reduction in the temperature required for smelting. The source of tin is not yet known: the amber trade is not enough evidence to make it likely that tin was brought from as far away as Bohemia. Some nearer source was certainly available, perhaps including alluvial deposits from north-eastern Anatolia; and there were innumerable sources of copper in the Caucasus, from the Black Sea eastwards.

The metallurgy of the Early Trans-Caucasian I and II periods was one of simple copperworking, exemplified by artefacts from burials at Kvatskhelebi in eastern Georgia: from a grave contemporary with the earliest level (C 3) and thus dating to *c.* 3000 BC came a copper double spiral pin, of a type common in western Georgia and very widely distributed in the late third millennium BC. This seems to be the earliest example. A copper diadem from Kvatskhelebi has a horned animal and bird, rendered by punching dots, and comparable with

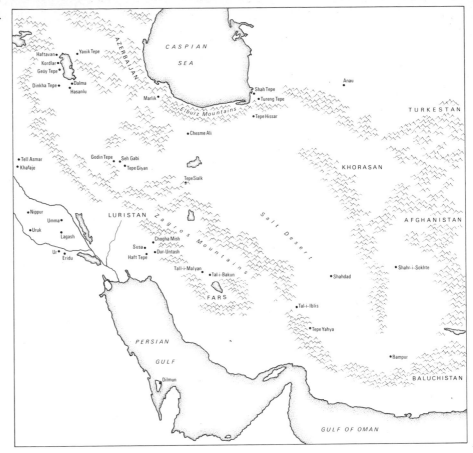

104. Iran in the Chalcolithic and Bronze Ages.

some in the incised ceramic decoration at Yanik Tepe. In the Early Trans-Caucasian III period metalwork became more advanced and abundant, Sachkere in eastern Georgia being the richest source, and with finds from Tetri-Tsqaro foreshadowing the wealth of Trialeti: socketed axes could indicate ultimately Mesopotamian influence, though it is highly unrealistic to imagine Sumerian smiths at work for long in Trans-Caucasia, if at all. Hammer-headed bronze pins represent a type probably originating in the western Caucasus and imported thence into Anatolia, at Alaca Hüyük, and into Europe as far as the north German plain. Double-spiral pins, in contrast, were common in the lower Danube valley, as well as in Anatolia, and could indicate an eastward export from the early metalworking centres in Europe. The Caucasus region as a whole was not the universal ancestor of metallurgy it was once supposed to be; but its importance was far-reaching, and the foundations of technical skills were laid in the Early Trans-Caucasian III period.

Evidence from animal bones recovered from excavations suggests a trend away from arable farming to stock-breeding during the third millennium BC and thereafter, with a decline of self-sufficient village communities in a context of expanding trade and widening cultural contacts. The Kurgan (barrow) culture of the steppes north of the Caucasus, in its later phases influencing Trans-Caucasia, was based more exclusively on stock-breeding, allowing mobility. Economic factors were probably more important agents of change in Trans-Caucasia than migration or conquest.

The religion of the Early Trans-Caucasian people is most vividly attested by

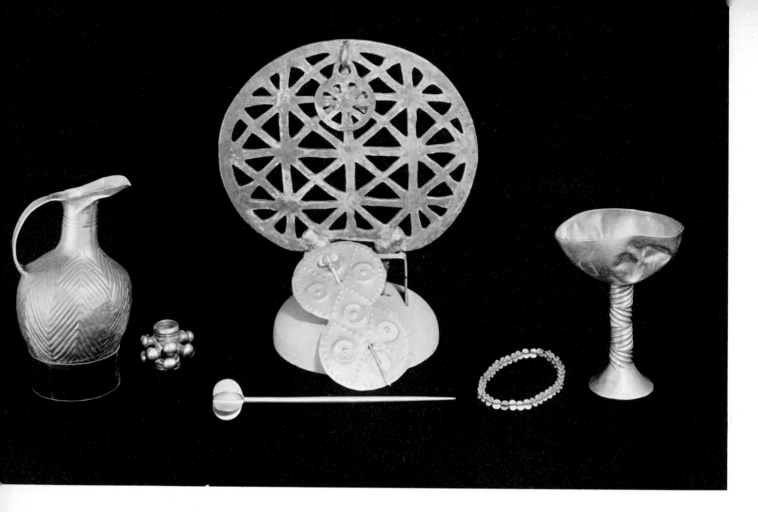

Pl 18. The trellised discs from Alaca Hüyük may possibly indicate a solar cult. These gold vessels and jewellery demonstrate the skill of the goldsmiths of Alaca Hüyük.

a shrine at Arslantepe (Malatya), with painted and relief decorations on its walls. More widespread, however, is the evidence of a domestic cult focused on hearth and home and adapted to the extremes of the climate, especially the bitter winters [105], with a series of shrines at Pulur (Elaziğ).

There are no inscriptions to prove the identity of the Early Trans-Caucasian population, during the first beginnings and rapid expansion of the cultural zone from about 3400 BC until the disintegration from *c.* 2000 BC onwards. Parts of eastern Anatolia, such as the Van region, perhaps continued their cultural tradition for several more centuries. Written records of different periods from surrounding regions indicate the presence of the non-Semitic and non-Indo-European race, the Hurrians, in the Khabur valley as early as the Akkadian period; in upper Mesopotamia in increasing numbers during the second millennium BC; on the Anatolian plateau and in Kizzuwatna (Cilicia) as an influence on the Hittites; and, much later, as the population of Urartu. The identification of the Early Trans-Caucasian people as Hurrians has at least the merit of avoiding inconsistency with the available evidence, though leading to some inescapable consequences. Among these is the dating of the first movement of Hurrians, the Horites of the Old Testament, into the Levant to the E.B. III period of Palestine, when the Khirbet Kerak pottery appeared. From their wide highland homeland this people was to have a profound, if inadequately understood, influence on their neighbours, in the arts of peace and in religion perhaps more than in politics and warfare.

KÜLTEPE–KANESH

Written traditions concerning the penetration of Anatolia by Sargon and Naram-sin have been mentioned in a previous chapter. Their accuracy is open to some doubt; but they probably contain a kernel of historical fact, which would be unsuspected but for the discoveries resulting from excavations at Kültepe, ancient Kanesh, twelve miles north-east of Kayseri, in the Cappadocian region of classical times. Other sites—Boğazköy (Hattusha), Alişar II (Kussara?) and Acemhüyük (Purushshanda?)—have also yielded relevant material. Kül-tepe-Kanesh, however, is the most important of these sites, for here was established the first and greatest colony of Assyrian merchants. They lived in an enclave of their own, termed in Akkadian a *karum*, just outside the walls of the native Anatolian city. Their presence is known from some fifteen thousand tablets found in *Karum* II and IB: the complete dearth of tablets in the earlier levels (*Karum* IV–III) is strange, perhaps explicable by the use of tablets of wood. The occupation of these early levels by Anatolian merchants of Luvian birth is a possible theory, if unproven. By the time of the establishment of the Assyrian merchants in Kanesh (*Karum* II, *c.* 2000–1900 BC) they occupied the north and central areas of the *karum*, with native Anatolian traders in houses in the southern quarter. The tablets contain many personal names, revealing onomastic evidence of the intermarriage of Assyrians with Anatolian women of Hattian, Hurrian or Hittite race. Some archives indicate overwhelming Syrian and Assyrian and others Anatolian trading connections.

Pl 19. Birds and horned animals in highly stylized form are frequent on Yanik Tepe pottery, and probably gave the inspiration to later ceramic decoration in paint, on 'Urmia ware' of the early second millennium BC. The yield of pottery within the round houses was abundant, owing to the frequent destructions by fire, often accidental, as the wind caused the fire in the hearth to flare up and set alight the wattle-and-daub superstructure above the mud-brick lower walls.

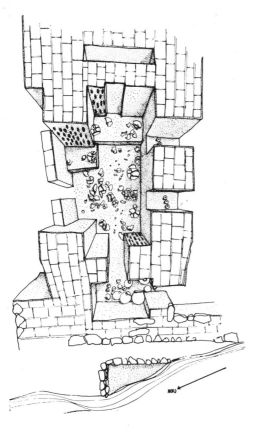

105. The shrine at Arslan Tepe (Malatya). Decorated hearths and pot-stands occur from Trans-Caucasia to the Amuq Plain (Amuq H), where they are in association with Khirbet Kerak ware. Miniature models of the central hearth were found at Kvatskhelebi C1, where, the excavators believe, a fertility ritual was being enacted at the moment that a fire destroyed the village. The anthropomorphic figurines found there are male.

106. Opposite above: Various types of rhyton are found at Kültepe-Kanesh, the painted vessels in the shape of a lion, as here, and deer, usually found with the tablets, being peculiar to *Karum* II. Painted pottery boots, perhaps used as tokens, also occur in the archives.

107. Opposite below: The local Anatolian glyptic style includes a great range of themes, among them the weather god driving a chariot drawn by bulls. War, hunting, ritual and mythology are treated, and there is a taste for arrangement in registers. Most seals are uninscribed.

After earlier, imperfectly conducted excavations, the Turkish expedition began work in 1948 at Kültepe, already identified through tablets dug up by villagers as the city of Kanesh. The volume of material and the literature on this site are already immense; and there has been the predictable proportion of theories from those not directly involved, unsupported by enough first-hand knowledge or common sense. Priority must be given to the interpretation of the discoveries by the excavators themselves; and for valid suggestions on the routes followed by the Assyrian merchants more intensive surveys are still necessary. The likeliest trade route from Assyria would have taken the donkey caravans through the densely populated highland plain of Elbistan. In the Konya Plain, however, the wealth of the Middle Bronze Age culture is exemplified by the excavations of Karahüyük II–I and by at least twenty-five other major sites, and clearly demonstrates contacts with the Cilician Plain via the Calycadnos (Gök Su) valley. Thus a more westerly route for some of the caravans to Kanesh, through the Cilician Gates, cannot be entirely ruled out. The city of Karahüyük, defended by great walls with double gates and bastions at regular intervals, was as extensive as Kültepe-Kanesh.

The impetus behind the Anatolian trading network connected with north Syria and Ashur came initially as much from the growing prosperity of towns in central Anatolia and farther west as from Assyria. Without the existence of a large and profitable market this trade would never have developed: it was channelled rather than created by the mercantile dynasties who established themselves at Kanesh, to the advantage of all concerned. The growth of trade and urban life in Anatolia, as in much of Iran, came in the late third millennium BC, in the E.B. III period, whose beginning (*c.* 2600/2500 BC) indeed marks a cultural watershed in Anatolia not repeated until the advent of the Iron Age in the twelfth century BC. The characteristic Alişar III (or Cappadocian) painted pottery appears at Kültepe in the levels termed Early and Middle Cappadocian, and continues through the Late Cappadocian phase, which includes the first two levels (IV–III) of the *karum* of Kanesh. This Alişar III pottery underwent three phases of development conforming with the sequence of levels at Kültepe-Kanesh. The native city of the Early Cappadocian phase included a public building of *megaron* plan, either a temple or a palace, paralleled in Troy IIg and Poliochni V and suggesting western influence on central Anatolia, perhaps a side-effect of the Luvian invasions.

The appearance in *Karum* IV at Kültepe-Kanesh of a monochrome wheel-made ware, mostly red-slipped and highly burnished, is commonly attributed to contacts with Cilicia and north Syria, though the treatment of the surface continued the tradition of the Anatolian E.B. II hand-made pottery. This wheel-made ware, which became widespread in central Anatolia in the time of *Karum* II, was the forerunner of the fine products of the Middle Bronze Age potters of Kültepe-Kanesh; the influence of metalwork was never far removed. The written sources hardly indicate the arrival of Hittites before *Karum* II, though this depends on negative evidence, the absence of tablets. Therefore the pottery, even of *Karum* II and its successors, must be reckoned as indigenous central Anatolian side by side with imported wares; and it seems safer to avoid the term 'Hittite' in this context. This nowise precludes the strong influence of the civilization of Kültepe-Kanesh on the Hittite state.

The best documented period, archaeologically and in number of tablets, is *Karum* II. From the names of those holding the uniquely Assyrian office of *limmu*, appointed for one year only, it is clear that the minimum duration of this period of the *karum* was eighty years: a century is a reasonable estimate [*Pl 21*].

Metallurgical workshops are found in the *karum*, indicated by crucibles, hearths and moulds, where bronze weapons, vessels and jewellery such as those in the cist-graves of Kanesh were produced. The city was as much a centre of industry as of trade.

The pottery of *Karum* II includes a number of forms derived from earlier types, such as tripod vessels, spouted jugs and fruit-stands, Alişar III painted jars, north Syrian and north Mesopotamian forms, and new forms, such as the distinctive 'teapot'. Jugs with beak spout and carinated body are characteristic [*Pl 22*].

The glyptic art of Kültepe-Kanesh compromises four classes of seal; the Old Assyrian, Old Babylonian, Syro-Anatolian and local Anatolian styles. The seals of Ur III type have added weight to the arguments supporting the 'high' chronology, favoured by most Turkish archaeologists and certainly more acceptable than the other extreme, the 'low' chronology, which necessitates an improbable compression of the generations of the Hittite Old Kingdom, following the end of the *karum* of Kanesh. The Syro-Anatolian style is peculiar to *Karum* II [107].

The city of Kültepe-Kanesh, contemporary with *Karum* II, was protected

Pl 20. A typical village of eastern Anatolia near Malazgirt. Note the large haystacks for winter feed and the stockpiles of dung-cakes for fuel.

by two defensive lines, the inner wall being built on large unhewn stones, reused in the later defences of Kanesh IB. One excavated building seems to be a palace, with residential quarters and a large paved open square. A palace and five temples are mentioned in the tablets. The entire city and the *karum* outside the walls were burnt in a violent destruction, perhaps the result of a Hittite attack, though this cannot be proved.

There is uncertainty concerning the immediate sequel to the destruction of Kültepe-Kanesh II. The evidence from the *karum*, where graves were sunk into the burnt debris of *Karum* II, in their turn overlaid by the houses of *Karum* IB, points to a hiatus of some length, perhaps fifty years. This is supported by the fact that the graves preceding *Karum* IB were not robbed of their contents. Against this, the stratigraphy of the city mound does not indicate a gap in continuity of occupation, or indeed between Levels II and IB. The palace containing tablets of king Warshama of Kanesh most probably, however, belongs to a phase (IC) when the *karum* was deserted, and the merchants had retreated within the walls of the Anatolian city.

The number of tablets from *Karum* IB and the information which they provide on the caravan trade are much less than in *Karum* II. But it would be a mistake to conclude that this trade had shrunk in volume or variety. Two facts suggest the contrary: first, the expansion of the area of the *karum* of Kanesh to

a diameter of over one kilometre, within a wall built on massive andesite blocks, at the same time as the native city grew in size; second, the establishment of other trading posts or colonies, each a *karum*, at Alişar II, Boğazköy (Hattusha) and Acemhüyük, this last near the south end of the Salt Lake. *Limmu*-names make it possible to synchronize Kültepe IB, Alişar II and Tell Chagar Bazar in the Khabur valley with the reign of Shamshi-Adad I of Assyria, partly contemporary with Hammurabi of Babylon. The buildings of *Karum* IB were more crowded than before; and uprights in the walls were no longer of timber but of stone.

Pottery in *Karum* IB, when there was less difference between Kanesh and the surrounding sites than in the preceding period, includes many earlier forms, though the Alişar III painted ware was no longer made. Pottery is generally less highly burnished. The most marked innovation is the rather slap-dash style of painted pottery termed Khabur ware, indigenous to north Syria and north Mesopotamia for the following three centuries. The diminishing security of life in Anatolia may be underlined by the preponderance of weapons among the moulds in the workshops of *Karum* IB. Among new themes on seals is the heraldic rendering of the double-headed eagle. Imported Syrian seals, with the Khabur ware, suggest trade with Mari and other cities (*c.* 1850–1800 BC) more than with Ashur.

Pl 21. In Level II at Kanesh the *karum* was laid out with some streets wide enough for wheeled vehicles, with wheel ruts visible in places, and with narrower streets also. The general layout was crowded, though not without evidence of planning. The houses had from two to six rooms, were rectangular in plan and had their courtyard not in the centre, as in Mesopotamia, but on one side. Timber was much used in the walls, as a frame for the mud-brick superstructure on top of stone footings; and the upper storey was of wooden frame construction. The absence of staircases suggests wooden ladders as the common means of access. The main houses included their own archive, the tablets being stored in large jars or in envelopes, baked like the tablets themselves and often found unopened.

Historical problems are raised by the discovery in a public building of this period (IB) of the city of Kanesh of a bronze spearhead of Anatolian type, with bent tang, inscribed in cuneiform: 'Palace of Anitta the King'. This is usually taken to be the son of Pitkhana, and thus one of the earliest Hittite rulers in Anatolia; and conforming with this interpretation is the identification of the city of Nesha with Kanesh and thus with the name applied by the Hittites to their language, Neshili. The public buildings of Kanesh IB are on the west half of the mound, with private houses to the east.

After another destruction by fire, the final occupation of the *karum* (IA) was relatively brief and impoverished, without any tablets to shed light on the scale and organization of the caravans. The trade—in tin and textiles from Ashur in return for copper and black donkeys—is commonly thought to have been brought to an end as a result of political changes. But economic changes, possibly among them the use of Anatolian sources of alluvial tin in the Pontic mountains, are equally likely to have ended the Assyrian trade, which had earlier shown itself resilient enough to survive two setbacks.

The Middle Bronze Age was likewise a prosperous period in south-western Anatolia, where the palace of Beycesultan V (*c*. 1900–1750 BC) was built on a lavish scale. On the larger west summit stood other public buildings within their own enclosure. There was also a temple. An outer defensive perimeter included a lower terrace near the river. The violent destruction, preceded by abandonment of the town and by very thorough looting, left virtually nothing of value in the ruins. The historical evidence supports, though it cannot prove, the theory that Beycesultan was one of the principal cities of Arzawa, the great kingdom of western Anatolia and rival to the Hittites: if this were so, the sack of the palace may have been the work of Labarnas I, legendary founder of the Hittite Old Kingdom, to whom later written sources credit military successes in the west. The archaeological record at least proves that Beycesultan IV marks a long period of relative poverty, and that even in the best phase of the Late Bronze Age (II) the town was on a humbler scale than in Level V [108].

The Cilician Plain was important as a cultural and economic intermediary between the Anatolian plateau and north Syria, all the more so with the complete cultural break with the E.B. III period, marked by the introduction of a painted pottery of north Syrian derivation. At first this was like the pottery of Alalakh XVI–VIII in the Amuq Plain; but later the standard deteriorated into wheel-made ware, with matt black, brown or red paint, resembling Khabur ware. The destruction of Middle Bronze Tarsus, the main source of evidence for Cilicia throughout the Bronze Age, may have been the result of the southward expansion of the Hittite Old Kingdom.

In north-western Anatolia there was a cultural change between Troy V and VI, though not as complete as sometimes suggested. The most impressive feature of Troy VI, which lasted over six centuries from *c*. 1900 BC, was the fine masonry of its fortifications, a contrast with the stonework at Beycesultan, where stone was mainly used for the footings of mud-brick walls and heavily reinforced with beams—massive timbers not to be found locally today. The grey Minyan pottery, traditionally thought to have been introduced from Middle Helladic Greece, almost certainly originated on the west Anatolian plateau. Its arrival on the Aegean coast is reasonably attributable, with widespread supporting evidence, to the same westward movement which caused the destruction of sites such as Polatli 15, bringing Period II at that small but significant site to an end. It is hard not to associate this movement, however indirectly,

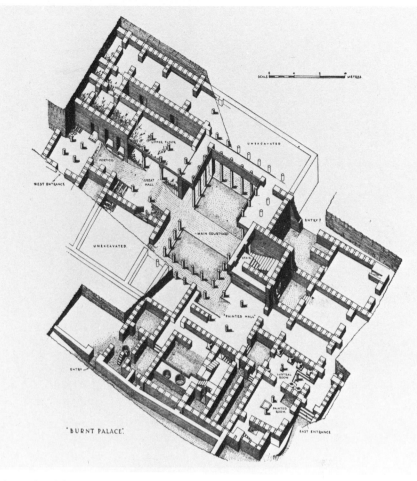

108. The plan of the palace of Beycesultan, in general terms comparable with that of Minoan palaces such as Mallia, just east of Knossos. Fragments of mural painting gave a hint of the decoration of this palace, which occupied the east summit of the site, with a diameter of 75 m.

with the coming of the Hittites into their new homeland in central Anatolia in the twentieth century BC.

At Boğazköy the pre-Hittite levels on the citadel rock of Büyükkale (Vf–Vc) were followed by those contemporary with the *karum* (Vb–IVd). Little has survived of the Hittite Old Kingdom citadel (Büyükkale IVc, with three phases). Written sources mention several temples, as yet not found. In its material civilization the Hittite state looked back to earlier traditions, not forward to the remodelling of the city of Hattusha after *c.* 1400 BC.

THE HITTITES

The civilization of the Hittites in and beyond their central Anatolian homeland within the great bend of the Red River (Kizil Irmak), the classical Halys, is more widely attested for the New Kingdom or Empire, especially from the time of Suppiluliumas (*c.* 1370–1335 BC), than for the obscure generations of the so-called Old Kingdom. Nevertheless much that is loosely termed Hittite cannot be attributed to that people. Even the Hittite royal family seems to have been of Hurrian parentage, all but one of the kings (Urhi-Teshub) taking a Hittite name on his accession. There is reason to suspect that the greatest cultural innovations for which the Hittites can be given credit were in matters of law and government. In the archaeological record, apart from the evidence from the tablets, it is in architecture rather than sculpture or the minor arts that an

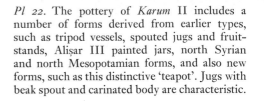

Pl 22. The pottery of *Karum* II includes a number of forms derived from earlier types, such as tripod vessels, spouted jugs and fruit-stands, Alişar III painted jars, north Syrian and north Mesopotamian forms, and also new forms, such as this distinctive 'teapot'. Jugs with beak spout and carinated body are characteristic.

original contribution by the Hittites is discernible. They were, it seems, a humane if not wholly imaginative people, who for a brief while introduced their own Indo-European traditions, before succumbing to the harsher cultural environment of the Near East. This absorption of neighbouring cultural elements is nowhere more clearly visible than in the use of the winged sun-disc as the royal emblem, in the exaltation of the Hittite king with the title of the Sun and in the decline of the role of the *pankush*, the assembly of peers of the realm. The high opinion of their own status held by the Hittite kings is underlined by the rebuke of Hattusilis III to Adad-nirari I of Assyria, when the latter presumed to address him as 'brother'.

The principal source for the archaeology of the Hittite New Kingdom is the capital city of Hattusha (Boğazköy), whose ruins, revealed by successive German excavators working for most of this century, are today one of the major tourist sites of Turkey, easily accessible from Ankara; and only fifteen miles away is Alaca Hüyük. Each building on the citadel, Büyükkale, was an individual unit with connecting short walls or narrow, covered passages: the whole group, however, formed one complex, related to its axis along the line of four courts. This axis began with the fortified gateway into the citadel, with gate chamber between two gates, admitting to a small quadrilateral entrance court, its shape dictated, like much on Büyükkale, by the contours of the rock. Thence, through a hall, a lower court was reached; and at its north-east end a gate building gave access to the middle and upper courts. Red marble flagstones were used

for the road across the entrance court inside the gateway to the gate building, reconstructed on sound evidence as a triple gateway with cubicles for the porters on duty: this divided the public lower part of the citadel from the private royal quarters including the middle and upper courts. One of the more remarkable structures is Building D, facing south-east on to the middle court. Here the parallel walls of the ground-floor magazines were quite massive enough to have supported an upper storey on a grand scale: it has taken the experience and ingenuity of the German excavators to make the most of the surviving remains, in large part no more than the stone foundations, as in many other parts of Hattusha. The area of the upper court, on the summit of Büyükkale, is destroyed down to the bedrock. The upper storey of Building D, opening directly on to the middle court, was most probably a large audience hall, nearly 32 m. square, with five rows of five wooden columns. The king would have come into this hall by the main entrance from the middle court; but those seeking his presence would more probably have used a back entrance reached from the lower court, which had a staircase up to the vestibule, thus avoiding the private precincts. Two of the other buildings (A and E) connected with inner courts housed archives: in A, the tablets were kept in the two central rooms, with two rows of columns; in E, they were kept in the upper storey. Building A adjoined the gate building on the south-east side; Building E stood on its own just north of the audience hall (D). A third, smaller archive was lodged in the central room of Building K, in the perimeter of the citadel and just south-east of A. Here were remarkable indications of the original cataloguing of the cuneiform tablets and their arrangement on wooden shelves: clay labels listing the contents of each shelf were found during the excavation of Building K. Wooden tablets, frequently mentioned in the Hittite sources, have yet to be recovered [**109**].

Pl 23. Rock reliefs occur at widely scattered spots in Anatolia, usually overlooking a river or spring. The most impressive water shrine, here illustrated, is Eflatun Pinar ('Plato's Spring'), near Beyşehir, with its winged sun-disc and fine masonry with drafted edges. Its platform may have been surmounted by two monumental statues, one of which has been found some miles away at Fasillar.

109. Overleaf (top): the fullest stratigraphic sequence at Hattusha has been obtained on the citadel, Büyükkale, where the earlier buildings were succeeded by those of the New Kingdom levels (IVb–IIIa). These buildings were extended by stages until they formed a governmental and residential complex, which in the thirteenth century BC (IIIb–IIIa) occupied the entire citadel rock, and had maximum dimensions of 250 × 150 m.

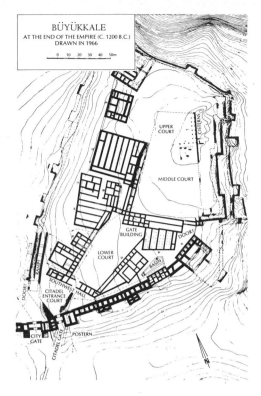

110. Below: Temple I at Hattusha was perhaps dedicated to the weather god (Teshub). Built in the fourteenth century BC, its store-rooms were partly redesigned in the time of Hattusilis III (c. 1275–1250 BC). This was the prototype of the temples in the southern upper city, and stood in the old lower town, overlooked by Büyükkale.

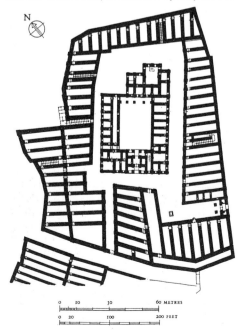

One of the most imposing buildings of Hattusha is Temple I. It was a massive structure extending 64×42 m. and separated by a paved area from a surrounding complex of store-rooms. Near the south corner stood the gate-house, with a square stone basin inside, on the line of entry: water was brought to it from a well by baked clay pipes, and here, on the evidence of a text describing a religious festival, the king must have ritually washed his hands on his arrival. The temple itself comprises a series of rooms round three sides of a rectangular central court with a colonnade of square stone piers on the fourth side. A small separate building in the court is paralleled in the shrine at Yazilikaya. Beyond the colonnade and off the axis of the main part of the temple stood the sanctuary, cut off from the eyes of those gathered in the court by the indirect entry. In this respect Temple I differs from Temple II–V in the upper city, which probably had windows in the interior wall between the statue of the god in his sanctuary and the court. At the end of the main room of the sanctuary of Temple I stood a stone base, presumably for the cult statue. Granite was used for the lower courses of this part of Temple I, limestone for the remainder. Some of the store-rooms contained pithoi, no doubt in part for the liquid tribute allotted to the temple. Two staircases led either to an upper storey or straight on to the roof. The whole complex was bounded by residential quarters with two main phases, both contemporary with Temple I, the later dated by bullae bearing the seal impression of Tudhaliyas IV (c. 1250–1220 BC) [110].

The religion of the Hittite court, under Hurrian inspiration through dynastic alliance with the former protectorate and later province of Kizzuwatna, is best understood by a visit to the rock shrine of Yazilikaya, a mile from the city of Hattusha. These reliefs are by far the most impressive of the many rock carvings distributed from the Ionian hinterland to the upper Euphrates, both in quality and scale. Most of the deities are accompanied by their name, written in hieroglyphs of the Luvian variety, commonly but incorrectly called Hittite. The gods wear the horned headdress of Mesopotamian origin, the chief of the pantheon and leader of the procession of gods being Teshub, storm- and weather-god, standing on two anthropomorphized mountains, followed by his local counterpart of Hattusha. Facing him is the goddess Hebat, standing on a lion: among elements in her procession is a double-headed eagle. The tradition of representing divinities standing on an animal seems to have been of Hurrian origin, explaining its subsequent appearance in Urartu and Assyria [111].

It is hard to be sure how firmly founded is the claim that the Hittites were the originators of relief-carved orthostats and that they bequeathed this tradition, through Carchemish and other Syro-Hittite cities, to the Assyrian empire. But the evidence suggests this was so, and is reinforced by the Late Bronze Age reliefs of Alaca Hüyük [113, Pl 23]. But one argument against the claim for Hittite innovation in monumental sculpture is a reference in a text of Hattusilis III to his importation of Kassite sculptors from Babylonia to adorn the gates of his capital city. It is the defences of the outer town of Hattusha which are most impressive for the visitor: there are five gateways, of the double plan with one gate-chamber and massive polygonal masonry, commonly called 'cyclopean' and carefully fitted together, the gate being set back from the outer face of the wall. A postern tunnel, seventy metres long, with a rough corbelled roof of undressed stones, survives intact and goes out to the fosse running around the southern perimeter. The exact height of the great wall cannot be known; but the parapet along its crest can be tentatively reconstructed from a fragmentary model of a battlemented tower, showing its projecting roof beams [112, Pl 24].

111. The interpretation of Yazilikaya is by no means yet entirely agreed. Texier, the first European to visit the site (1834), believed that here was depicted a meeting of the Amazons and Paphlagonians. The rock faces in the larger chamber of this open-air sanctuary are occupied by reliefs with a unified theme, two processions meeting each other, the gods on the left facing right and the goddesses on the right facing left.

112. The King's Gate at Hattusha has a figure of a helmeted god carrying a battle-axe with spiked butt, in distinctively Hittite ultra-high relief, in effect half a statue in the round.

113. Below right: The Late Bronze Age reliefs of Alaca Hüyük, earlier than Yazilikaya, depict acrobats, including sword-swallowing, a boar hunt and a god with an altar surmounted by a bull, associated with the weather god.

The Hittites were perhaps not a very imaginative people in the visual arts, employing a largely identical iconography both for rock reliefs and for miniature art in the forms of jewellery and seals [114].

The belief that the Hittites possessed a monopoly of ironworking is scarcely credible, though it may contain a kernel of fact. Written references could be taken to suggest the practice of this craft as early as the Middle Bronze Age in central Anatolia. Ironworking almost certainly originated as an accidental by-product of copper-mining, when iron-bearing ores were encountered. These are harder to work than other copper ores, so that here may be a hint of exhaustion of some of the easier sources of copper. It is an attractive suggestion, though quite unproven, that the iron-bladed dagger in the tomb of Tutankhamun was a present from the contemporary Hittite king, Suppiluliumas.

The term 'Hittite' should by no means be used as a synonym for 'Late Bronze Age' on the Anatolian plateau, much of which was seldom, if ever, under Hittite rule. Typical Late Bronze Age pottery occurs, for example, in the Gasga lands, later the heart of Pontus, immediately north and north-east of the central Hittite homeland. To the east, across the Euphrates, the land of Isua is securely identified with the Elaziğ Plain and thus with the area of the Keban dam rescue excavations; it has yielded evidence of a flourishing Middle Bronze Age civilization, especially at Korucutepe, followed by central Anatolian pottery whose introduction can plausibly be attributed to the Hittite conquest by Suppiluliumas. It is seldom that archaeological and historical evidence coincide so neatly.

In the south-west, within the borders of the powerful but tantalizingly obscure kingdom of Arzawa, the settlement of Beycesultan was never again to see the prosperity of the period (V) of its palace. Beycesultan IV was a long stretch of humble village occupation. Then there was a revival, if on a relatively modest scale, with buildings of *megaron* plan as part of a close-knit town in Beycesultan II. Then in Beycesultan I, dating just after the fall of the Hittite state, there is a hint of a refugee movement, like those of earlier times in Anattolia, in the changes in pottery. Beak-spouted and foliate-mouthed jugs of central Anatolian types make their appearance. Thus ended the long history of prehistoric Beycesultan, reoccupied only in the Byzantine period.

IRAN BEFORE THE IRANIAN MIGRATIONS

The vastness of Iran in itself precludes any thorough examination of the cultural sequences of the whole land or even of the western regions alone. Iran is only now beginning to be understood in terms of prehistoric archaeology, with much of the available evidence derived from chance finds or private collections. Precise provenance and circumstances of discovery have often deliberately been kept obscure. Such excavations as have been carried to a conclusion have either been little published or are geographically remote from other excavated sites, with surveys of the intervening territory seldom completed. These deficiencies have already largely been rectified in a few regions, notably Khuzistan, Luristan and the central Zagros highlands; and such regions as the Urmia basin are better known than a few years ago. An intensive survey of much of the Kermanshah Plain may well mark the beginning of similar work over much of Iran, work which will assuredly take years. The northern and eastern regions of Iran, save for a number of very important excavated sites, are still largely unmapped. If length of stratigraphic sequence and thus of time-span of a settlement is a major criterion, it is possible to select a few sites which represent much of Iran.

114. The Hittite kings use stamp-seals with slightly convex face and with hieroglyphs in the centre surrounded by one, two or three lines of cuneiform Hittite, thus providing evidence for the interpretation of the hieroglyphs. Hattusha and Ugarit have yielded such seals.

Pl 24. Opposite: The Lion Gate of Hattusha, with characteristic cyclopean masonry and guardian lions.

145

Among these must be included Susa, Tepe Giyan, Godin Tepe, Hasanlu, Haftavan, Sialk, Tepe Hissar, Tureng Tepe, Shahr-i-Sokhte and Tepe Yahya. Not all these are equally significant; but each provides a yardstick for its cultural province. Other sites will soon have to be added to this list, among them the vast city ruin of Tall-i-Maliyun in the Persepolis Plain.

There is sure to be wide and continuing discussion on major questions of interpretation of archaeological discoveries in Iran. For example, how great a part was played by Sumerian economic expansion in Iran? What role can be attributed to Elam? What was the role of Iran as the go-between in overland trade between the Sumerian cities and those of the Indus valley? How much credit, if any, can be given to early metalworkers in Iran as innovators influencing other regions? Whence came the first Iranian migrations, and how clearly can these be related to ceramic and other data? What roles are attributable to settled urban communities and to nomads before and after the arrival of the Iranian tribes? Such are some of the problems demanding at least a cursory acknowledgement. There can be no space for a level-by-level account of each major site, let alone the many others.

The tradition of painted pottery in local styles was already becoming firmly rooted in the sixth millennium BC, where our previous consideration of the Neolithic cultures of Iran ended (see p. 43). A village economy spread far and wide, into areas without evidence of earlier settlements. In some regions the phase of seasonal habitation sites, with transhumance, was probably very long-lived. Then came the intrusion of alien merchants, presumably seeking raw materials in return for manufactured goods: these may have been in the first instance Sumerians of the Uruk period, whose trading activities were also being extended into the middle Euphrates valley; but they were surely soon succeeded by Susian or, more accurately, Proto-Elamite traders, attested by tablets in the Proto-Elamite characters from Susa Cb, Godin Tepe V, Sialk, Maliyun and, much farther east, from Tepe Yahya IVC and Shahr-i-Sokhte I (Phase 9). The presence of numerous blank tablets at Yahya IVC proves that clerks were at work there, and did not merely import written records from Mesopotamia or western Elam. This was not, however, the earliest phase of trade between the Sumerian cities and their northern neighbours on the one hand, and different parts of the Iranian plateau on the other. Lapis lazuli reached its greatest popularity in the E.D. III period in Mesopotamia, as already noted; but it had been imported from late Ubaid times until late in the Uruk period through Tepe Gawra (XIII–IX), which may even have commanded a monopoly of this trade. The late Uruk–Jemdet Nasr trading post, whether or not it was manned by men of Susa, discovered on the summit of the settlement mound of Godin Tepe V provides a hint that by that time a more southerly route for this trade was coming into use; and links with Iran become less evident at Tepe Gawra. Theories of monopoly in prehistoric periods are perhaps dangerous and very hard to substantiate. But the link with Mesopotamia is confirmed at Godin V and Yahya IVC alike by the familiar bevelled-rim bowls.

The abrupt ending of Sumerian trading posts in western Iran can hardly be proved at present; but the excavations at Tepe Yahya have produced strong evidence in support of the belief that it was the growing political and economic power of the kingdom of Elam which forced the pattern of trade into channels chosen by the highland population of the southern plateau of Iran rather than by the Sumerian cities. Elam had a long history, a king-list from Susa recording kings of Awan and later of Simash, a district of Luristan, from the mid-third millennium BC onwards. The individuality of Elamite civilization is shown by the development from the slightly earlier Uruk IVa pictographic script of the Proto-Elamite script during a phase (Susa Cb) equivalent to the Jemdet Nasr period. Later an Elamite 'linear' script appeared. Although the cultural influence of Mesopotamia on western Elam became overwhelming in the Akkadian period, the identity of Elamite civilization was never entirely obliterated. It emerged as an enduring element in the Near East until the sack of Susa by Assurbanipal (*c.* 640 BC), a kingdom constantly at enmity with the cities and states of Mesopotamia. Yet Elam benefited from mutually advantageous trading relations, to such an extent that Elamite colonies seem to have existed in several cities, especially Tell Asmar (Eshnunna); and place-names ending in -*ak* (e.g. Shuruppak) are said to be of Elamite derivation. Unification of the lowlands of Susiana (Khuzistan) with the highlands to the east (Fars), rich in agricultural produce and in raw materials respectively, came about in the form of a federation cemented by dynastic alliances. Cultural cohesion took time to achieve. Timber and metal ores were always in demand from the eastern highlands, whose people in their turn were attracted by the lure of lowland booty. The Elamites were a people whose origins remain very uncertain: they may have been proto-Lurs; their language, unrelated to known tongues and not yet entirely deciphered, was agglutinative. Their cultural conservatism is revealed in linguistic continuity over two thousand years, demonstrated in the bilingual and trilingual inscriptions of the Achaemenid period; but Elamite literature remains undiscovered.

The expansion of Elamite trade has become very much more apparent as a result of the discoveries at Tepe Yahya, situated 140 miles south of Kerman and only six days' walking distance north of the coast of the Indian Ocean. Steatite (chlorite) in finished form was a major export. These steatite bowls first became known from examples excavated at Tell Asmar, Mari, Kish, Ur and Susa; they

115. This relief of a public building, carved in steatite, was found in Tepe Yahya IVA. There is an opencast steatite mine fifteen miles north of the site. The art of carving steatite, popularly termed soapstone, can be traced there from its early manifestations in Yahya VI in the late fifth millennium BC; and typical round button seals have been found incompletely carved.

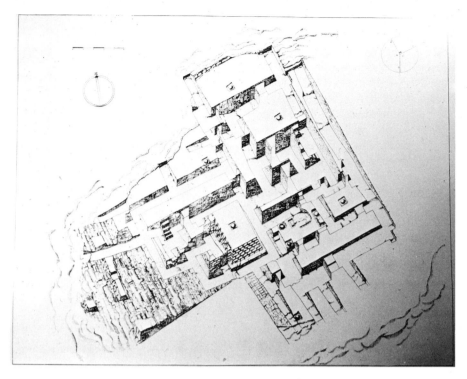

116. This building of Shahr-i-Sokhte IV was excavated at a site which extended at its maximum over two square kilometres of natural hill, largely covered with a thick layer of sherds, and with a cemetery very possibly containing over 200,000 burials, on the evidence of the area excavated. Four periods extended over some fifteen hundred years (c. 3300–1800 BC), subdivided into eleven phases (10–0 in chronological order), with the population reaching its maximum in Phase 3 (Shahr-i-Sokhte III), in an environment more akin to central Asia than to Iran or the Indus valley.

117. Opposite above: in the north-east, Tepe Hissar IC shows the persistence of early traditions, especially in painted pottery, in a period equivalent to late Uruk and Jemdet Nasr, when such pottery had long vanished in western Iran. Chalices are among typical Hissar IC forms; decoration includes horned animals in vigorous style.

occur also as far away as Iranian Baluchistan, at Mohenjo-Daro and at sites along the south-east coast of the Arabian peninsula, yielding exact parallels with Tepe Yahya [115].

Another comparison is provided by a black-on-grey pottery from Yahya IVB, occurring to the east and north-east at Bampur V–VI and Shahr-i-Sokhte respectively, and at Hilli, in Abu Dhabi. There are also parallels with finds from the Barbar Temple on the island of Bahrein, ancient Dilmun. The more archaeological investigations proceed in the Arabian peninsula, the greater will be the proof of a far-flung maritime trade, at its zenith in the Early Dynastic period of Mesopotamia but largely under Elamite control. Whatever the eastern geographical limits of Elam, it is quite clear that the vast zone including Kerman province, Iranian Baluchistan, Sistan and Kandahar must no longer be reckoned as a backward hinterland, remote and significant only for being situated on the land routes between the two civilizations of the Tigris–Euphrates and Indus valleys. Rather were there local nuclei of urban communities, reaching their greatest prosperity at sites such as Tepe Yahya, Tall-i-Iblis, Shahdad, Shahr-i-Sokhte, Mundigak and Bampur. Shahr-i-Sokhte stands out as the most important ·of these sites. From the end of Phase 8 till Phase 5 the wealth of Shahr-i-Sokhte depended partly on the working and export of alabaster and lapis lazuli, whose virtual absence from Tepe Yahya, as steatite from Shahr-i-Sokhte, could suggest antagonism between the two communities or at least commercial rivalry. Decline began in the later third millennium BC (Yahya IVA, Shahr-i-Sokhte IV), probably to be associated with the rise of the Indus valley civilization. In the Sistan Plain the great city declined drastically, though the number of settlements increased. The development of town life may be epitomized in steatite vessels from Tepe Yahya showing a type of building suggesting nomadic antecedents and in a representation of a 'temple-palace complex' façade, attributed to Yahya IVA [115, 116].

Metalworking is best known in Luristan, where a long sequence has been established from the E.D. III period onwards. The debate on the affinities and chronology of the metallurgy of western Iran has been largely resolved. Luristan produced metal artefacts generally comparable with those of Elam, Mesopotamia and north Syria in the centuries c. 2500–1000 BC, its distinction lying simply in the large quantity of copper and bronze tools and weapons preserved in tombs of successive periods. In other words, Luristan and the rest of western Iran shared in the common Near Eastern tradition. For the earlier phases of metalworking in Iran, however, one must look outside Luristan. In the central province of Kashan, at Tepe Sialk, the earlier cultural traditions, such as red ochre burials, ended with III (3). In Sialk III (4–5) innovations include many stamp-seals similar to those from Tepe Giyan and Tepe Gawra, the potter's wheel, found in Susa B and Gawra IX (Uruk period), and the technique of casting copper, known in Susa A, Gawra XII and Tell Arpachiyah. Whether or not these innovations were all of Mesopotamian origin, there is evidence of cultural conservatism in the juxtaposition of Ubaid and Uruk elements in Sialk III (4–5). Shaft-hole hoes found there and in Susa B have been used, rather boldly, as indicating the priority of Iran as the first region where the casting of shaft-hole tools and weapons in bivalve moulds was achieved. Here again Iran is superior to Mesopotamia in specimens preserved; but that does not justify sweeping conclusions. More significant than any other evidence, however, are the traces of a domestic industry at Tall-i-Iblis, fifty miles southwest of Kerman, where hundreds of pieces of crucibles with copper stain were recovered, in a dump with radio-carbon determinations of the late fifth millennium BC, contemporary with the later Ubaid period in Mesopotamia. By the use of copper containing natural impurities, arsenical bronze was produced in Yahya V; but by Yahya IVB tin was being used as an alloy to make bronze. Iran, if behind Sumer in metallurgy, can have been only just so.

A decisive invasion of newcomers from the Turkoman steppe to the north was suggested by the excavators of Tepe Hissar as the most likely explanation of the change from painted pottery (Hissar IC) to plain grey ware (Hissar IIA) in the early third millennium BC. Even then the influence of metal vessels is clear, especially in the goblets. This grey ware continued for a very long time, and was typical of the Gurgan cultural province, being found at the excavated sites of Shah Tepe, Tureng Tepe and Yarim Tepe and also at unexcavated sites in the Gurgan Plain, as well as at Tepe Hissar on the plateau to the south. A first invasion seems to have come from the east, since Hissar IIIB and Yarim Tepe were destroyed, only the former being reoccupied, as Hissar IIIC. Shah Tepe and Tureng Tepe, farther west, continued an unbroken occupation, with Hissar IIIC representing the later phase of the Gurgan culture, attested mainly by hoards and burials [117–119].

Another cultural province on the Iranian plateau was that of Giyan IV–III, centred in Luristan and enduring from the mid-third millennium BC till the Iron Age in much of Luristan. The Giyan II culture may represent an intrusive element, and was certainly geographically more restricted. The Giyan IV class of pottery was derived from the painted ware termed Susa D, associated with Khuzistan in the earlier third millennium BC: the wide distribution of this pottery, from the Hamadan region to Susa, is clear evidence confirming Elamite penetration of the central Zagros zone and making it possible to put the earliest phases of the Luristan cemeteries with their metalwork in their wider context. Giyan III pottery has polychrome decoration, and was widespread in north-

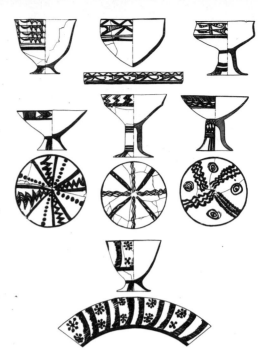

118. Hissar pottery shows developments, with forms such as open-spouted vessels and tall bottles and with fine pattern-burnished decoration: this too points to no great hiatus between the final end of the Gurgan culture and the beginning of the Iron I period, with ceramic prototypes in Hissar IIIC. Chronological problems demand further investigation in the field.

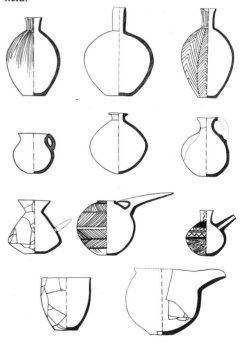

119. Hissar IIIC was a time of prosperity, with metals available in greater quantity, though tin-bronze hardly occurs: copper was used for blades with bent tang, buttons, round stamp-seals, axe-adzes, roll-headed pins and 'wands' with figures cast at the top. Vessels and small objects were also made of gold, silver and lead. Offering-tables, cylindrical and spouted jars, miniature columns and large handled discs were made of alabaster. Carnelian and agate beads and amber occur, the last indicating trade with south Russia and even the Baltic region and suggesting a date for the end of Hissar IIIC after 1500 BC.

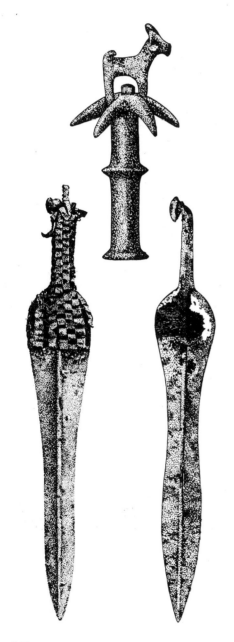

west Iran. During the early second millennium BC there seems to have been a decrease in the number of settlements, not owing to decline in population but to concentration in towns. Nomads must always have played a greater role than the archaeological record is ever likely to indicate, perhaps especially in Iran. In the higher valleys the first cemeteries seem to be unconnected with any permanent settlements. This was to remain an abiding factor down to the rise of the Achaemenid state. In much of Iran there seems to have been a growth of urban communities, with consequent concentration of people formerly inhabiting villages, in the later third and early second millennium BC, a trend which influenced patterns of settlement until the coming of the Iranian tribes and the dawn of the Iron Age, from about the fourteenth century BC onwards.

To the north of the limits of Elamite penetration the merchants of Ashur were seeking tin (*anākum*) for the Anatolian market, as described above, as well as for the cities of Sumer, Akkad and their own homeland, and for Mari and Syria [120]. Indirect trade with the bronze-smiths of Metsamor in Trans-Caucasia (Armenian S.S.R.) is suggested by the ceramic evidence for contact between the Urmia basin of north-west Iran and Trans-Caucasia, with the polychrome painted pottery characteristic of Geoy Tepe D, continuing in C and almost certainly originating around Lake Urmia (Reza'iyeh). Hence the name 'Urmia ware' is appropriate. It is tempting to attribute the destruction levels of this period in north-west Iran to a people known for their horsemanship, the Kassites, en route for the plains of Babylonia, where they settled during the seventeenth century BC before gaining political control.

ELAM
The civilization of Elam reached its apogee in the early thirteenth century BC, when Untash-gal, who extended the limits of the kingdom and invaded Kassite Babylonia, built a new royal and religious city, Dur-Untash (Chogha-Zanbil). This stood twenty-five miles south-east of the ancient city of Susa, which was also architecturally improved. The ziggurat of Susa was of Mesopotamian design, the shrine on its summit (Elamite: *kukunnu*) at first faced in baked bricks, but replaced by Untash-gal with enamelled plaques in metallic colours. Fragments of similarly glazed bricks were found in the debris fallen from the *kukunnu* at Dur-Untash: these must be the bricks of gold and silver mentioned on inscribed bricks from the summit.

Dur-Untash comprised three concentric enclosures, the city between the outermost and the second perimeter wall never being completed. A group of three temples stood on the north-west side of the inner enclosure, where the ziggurat was situated, and a group of four others in the middle enclosure. Like the ziggurat at Susa, that of Dur-Untash was dedicated to the joint worship of the Elamite gods Khumban and In-Shushinak. The original design for the innermost enclosure at Dur-Untash was of a building comprising groups of rooms arranged round a courtyard. In the south part of the south-east side a complex of rooms opening from the court is identifiable from inscribed bricks in the walls as a temple of In-Shushinak; next to it was another temple of this god, entered not from the court but from the pavement surrounding the ziggurat. The other rooms cannot be identified. Then came a dramatic change in the design, with the rooms opening on to the courtyard filled in with mud-bricks and a solid ziggurat above, forming the second, third and fourth storeys, the last completely vanished. The first stage of the ziggurat rose 8 m. above the pavement, the second 11.55 m. and the third and fourth probably the same height.

Thus the total height was about 43 m. Staircases were built within the ziggurat, another feature marking Dur-Untash as departing from the Mesopotamian pattern of ziggurat. Doors were built of arches of irregularly alternating wedge-shaped and complete bricks [121].

Three palaces were found at Dur-Untash, in the outermost enclosure, the two largest in the east corner. The other palace included rooms along the west side of its great courtyard, in which were several carefully concealed stairs leading 6 m. down into subterranean rooms, about 17 m. long and 4 m. wide and high, with a vaulted ceiling and arched door of baked brick plastered over. Heaps of ash and charred bones indicate cremation, but inhumation was the normal custom in Elam. One tomb contained a brick platform or fumerary couch, on which lay a complete skeleton and two burnt bodies. At Haft Tepe, another Elamite site in Khuzistan, twenty-one skeletons were found on a large platform in a vaulted tomb, with traces of red ochre.

Elamite sculpture, bronzeworking and jewellery reached a high standard. A fragmentary stele of Untash-gal has several registers enclosed by two long, winding snakes. In the top register the king stands raising his hands to a seated goddess. In the next register the king is shown with his queen, Napirasu, whose bronze statue, clad in ankle-length skirt and embroidered dress and weighing. not less than 1,750 kilogrammes, demonstrates the Elamite mastery of the technique of casting on a large scale, of necessity using many small crucibles.

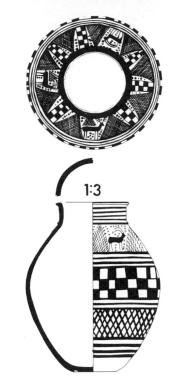

1:3

120. Khabur ware, found in Kültepe-Kanesh IB and throughout north Syria and upper Mesopotamia in the early second millennium BC, occurs in the Dinkha culture at the type site, in the Ushnu valley twenty miles west of Hasanlu, whose distinctive painted pottery is illustrated here. Khabur ware is also paralleled in the Giyan II culture of central western Iran; and it may be significant that the granite highlands north of Hamadan are a possible source of tin deposits, or at least of alluvial tin. Khabur ware seems a fair indicator of cultural contact.

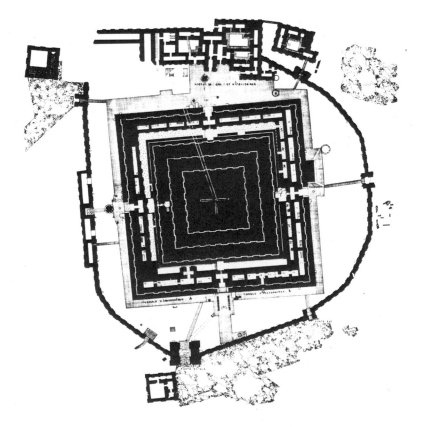

121. The outer wall of Dur-Untash enclosed an elliptical area of about 1200 × 800 m., and probably served to defend the city; within this stood an enclosure 400 m. square; and inside this stood the ziggurat with its surrounding pavement.

On the stele are also semi-divine protective beings, among them a siren or mermaid, with two streams of water flowing from four vases. Many badly damaged statues in the round give a hint of the attainments of the Elamite sculptors, the lower part of one statue of Untash-gal having a bilingual inscription in Akkadian and Elamite.

However damaged by successive Babylonian and Assyrian attacks, the surviving remains of Elamite civilization show beyond doubt that after further excavation Elam will surely come into its rightful place as a major factor in the Near East for many centuries. A kingdom open to Mesopotamian influences, it was based firmly in southern Iran and preserved its own distinctive character and its economic and political role on the Iranian plateau, as much in the plain of Fars and eastward as in the lowlands of Khuzistan.

THE IRON I PERIOD IN IRAN

The evidence for the Iron I period in Iran is very widespread and can be summed up in terms of the distribution of grey ware, a readily recognizable pottery with five type-shapes, including the 'button-base' goblet and the jar with long, unbridged spout. With modifications to radio-carbon determinations the chronological limits of the Iron I period have been raised to *c*. 1350–1100 BC [122].

The distribution of Iron I grey ware over much but not all of western Iran, from the Urmia basin and Marlik in the north to Sialk in the east and Hamadan and the Kangavar valley in the south has been taken as an index of the earliest phase of settlement by Iranian tribes. These probably came in from the northeast, as suggested by the very early tradition of grey ware in the Gurgan culture and especially by that of its late phase. But such a route for this migration would be reinforced by a lowering of the date of the end of Hissar IIIC to *c*. 1500 BC. Another route, additional if not alternative, for the arrival of the Iron I newcomers would have been via the Caucasus, a possibility not diminished by the cultural connections between Marlik and Trans-Caucasia. Their common homeland, probably either east or north of the Caspian Sea, is generally accepted on the evidence of the uniformity of the Iron I culture. Permanent habitations were scarce, with nomadism almost certainly predominant. The absence of fortifications and the extent and character of the building remains confirm the unsettled society of this period. At Haftavan V, for example, only the west side of the mound was occupied; and there was a complete change from the architectural tradition of mud-brick in Haftavan VII–VIA to one of stones set in mud. Large pits and scattered burials are typical of this period at Haftavan V and at Dinkha Tepe. At Hasanlu V a prototype of the columned buildings of the Iron II citadel has been excavated, suggesting that the social structure of the later period, with its local cultural sub-provinces, was already emerging. The evidence from the Urmia basin tends to indicate a relatively short time-span for the Iron I period, which in remoter sites, such as Haftavan V, may not have begun till *c*. 1200 BC. Earlier red wares were never entirely displaced at Haftavan, where the intrusion of Iron I grey ware was a brief episode.

It is tempting to identify the Iron I newcomers with the Medes; and the absence of Iron I pottery from sites west of Kangavar, in the western part of the central Zagros region, is consistent with their very gradual penetration of these highlands. Marlik, with its rich grave goods, may represent the first flowering of Median art, though in the absence of inscriptions this cannot be proved. Middle Assyrian influence on the goldsmiths of Marlik is certainly apparent.

122. Pattern-burnishing is the characteristic decorative technique of Iron I pottery in Iran. Extramural cemeteries are normally of simple inhumations, though at Marlik, near the Caspian Sea, there are stone-lined tombs: such cemeteries occur at Hasanlu V, Giyan I³–I⁴ and Sialk V, the main excavated sites, and also at Khorvin-Chandar near Kazvin and at Yanik Tepe; at Dinkha Tepe, too, were found Iron I burials.

For comparative material one can look to the cemeteries of the Talysh, beside the south-west Caspian shore; but the dating of the finds from that area is not helped by the methods of excavation or by the frequent reuse of tombs in the early first millennium BC. Marlik itself was not a settlement but a natural spur overlooking a fertile valley, where fifty-three tombs were found, usually marked by an irregular group of stones. The corpse was sometimes laid on a slab inside the tomb, which was filled with earth and stones after the funeral, crushing the skeleton. Over the body and all the grave goods was sprinkled brownish earth, 25 cm. thick, brought from elsewhere and representing the tradition of ochre burials imported from the northern steppes.

Theriomorphic pots, such as hump-backed bulls, are associated with Amlash, whence they first reached the antiquities market; are numerous in the cemetery of Kalardasht, south of the Caspian Sea in Mazanderan; and occur also at Marlik. The gold bowl found at Kalardasht, with the lions' heads crudely riveted to the vessel, is provincial work compared with the beaker from Marlik, where three styles of gold vessels have been distinguished. The third is best exemplified by the gold bowl from Hasanlu. Another parallel with Hasanlu is a gold dagger found with the gold bowl at Kalardasht: the distinctive way in which a ring joins pommel and blade occurs likewise on one of a group of three daggers depicted on the Hasanlu bowl. It is on such evidence that the rich finds at Marlik, perhaps accumulated by a ruler from the northern steppes coming into contact with the local variety of Near Eastern civilization, can be put into some sort of relationship to Hasanlu and thus to the Iron II culture of north-west Iran [*Pl 26*].

TRANS-CAUCASIA IN THE SECOND MILLENNIUM BC

The cultural pattern in Trans-Caucasia became more complex during the second millennium BC than in the Early Trans-Caucasian periods; but there are signs of strong continuity, presumably representing the persistence of the older population in the face of newcomers. Cemeteries provide the bulk of the material; but there are enough excavated settlement sites to confirm the general framework of chronology. No single cultural province extended throughout Trans-Caucasia, where there was more diversification than along the north side of the Caucasus range, with its one North Caucasian Bronze Age culture. Even this had three sub-divisions: the north-western (Kuban), the central and the north-eastern (Kayakent-Chorochoi), this last being the most backward.

The Colchidic culture extended over western Georgia and Abkhazia, lasting from approximately the eighteenth until the seventh century BC. One of its major contributions was to be the inspiration of the later metal industries of the Koban region and the Kuban valley and thence of regions as far north as the Ukraine. Pottery and burial customs differed from those of the Koban culture; and Colchidic metalworking was of local origin.

Forty miles south-west of Tiflis, in the Georgian S.S.R., lies the district of Trialeti, where a rescue excavation in 1936–40, supplemented by a later expedition, uncovered nearly fifty barrow (*kurgan*) burials. Three phases have been distinguished, the earliest being attributable to the Early Trans-Caucasian III period, without painted pottery. Most of the barrows fall in the second phase (*c.* 2000–1600 BC), and display ample evidence of wealth [**123**].

Urmia ware is associated especially with the cemetery of Tazekend, north of Erevan. Kizil-Vank, in the Araxes valley, provides parallels through its painted pottery, suggesting the date of the third phase of Trialeti barrows (*c.* 1600–1400

123. Barrow 17 in Trialeti yielded a gold cup set with carnelians and turquoise in filigree, silver pins with heads of gold ornamented with carnelians and granulation and a silver situla with naturalistic scenes in repoussé of animals in woodland and open country. From Barrow 5 came a silver goblet showing a procession of offering-bearers coming before a seated figure, with a row of animals below. There is some similarity between this goblet and the Hasanlu gold bowl. Boldly painted spiraliform decoration on some of the pottery from Barrow 17 has no known parallels in the Near East; but the rest of the painted pottery from the Trialeti tombs belongs to the style probably of north-west Iran, Urmia ware.

BC). Most, though not all, of the Trialeti barrows had a pit cut into the ground for the burial chamber, in a few barrows being lined with stones, undressed but carefully fitted. Wooden wagons drawn by oxen and the very tradition of building barrows indicate origins in the northern steppes, and suggest an intrusive Indo-European ruling class.

Equally impressive are the discoveries in the cemetery of Lchashen, in an area exposed by the lowering of the waters of Lake Sevan, in the bleak highlands north of Erevan. Here a fairly continuous sequence of cultural phases has been differentiated, from the late third millennium BC till *c*. 1200 BC; but, if different types of burial prove in the end to be contemporary rather than in series, the evidence, coming mostly from burials, will have to be re-examined. The majority of the burials are in simple pit-graves, with four phases discernible from the pottery. The second phase (*c*. 1700–1500 BC) is distinguished by black ware with white encrustation round the necks of bowls. The third phase (*c*. 1500–1400 BC) has pottery comparable with that from the last period of Trialeti and from Kirovakan, thus quite widely distributed. Indeed by the fourteenth century BC, the end of the Trans-Caucasian Middle Bronze Age, both painted pottery and metalwork, such as bronze axes, suggest a degree of cultural unity throughout Trans-Caucasia and extending to the Talysh and the Urmia basin. Such unity had probably originated from elements spreading northward from Iran, with painted pottery rarer in Georgia than to the south, in the Armenian S.S.R. Metalwork is less reliable as a criterion of cultural affinities, if only because of the movements of itinerant smiths. Such settlements as Artik, in Armenia, and Ouzerlik Tepe in the Azerbaijan S.S.R. show that any theory of a general abandonment of settled life during the second millennium BC in favour of pastoralism with transhumance can be discounted.

A great increase in bronzeworking and the emergence of two cultures, the Koban-Colchidic in western and the Ganja-Karabagh in much of central and eastern Trans-Caucasia, marked the beginning of the Late Bronze Age (*c*. 1300–900 BC). The burials of the chieftains in the Lchashen cemetery belong to Late Bronze I (*c*. 1300–1150 BC), the final and most brilliant phase in the Sevan sequence. The humbler pit-graves contained vividly decorated pottery, black ware with mauve and white encrustation; and pottery painted with black, red and white panels. The vehicles buried in the richest tombs are themselves eloquent testimony of the woodworking skills of the period [**124**].

Parallels between Lchashen and north Syria (Late Ugarit 3 period) are provided by tridents, which must have served as goads; bidents occur too. Daggers with square shoulder and open-work sheath occur at Lchashen, Artik and Tazekend.

Among other sites of the Trans-Caucasian Late Bronze Age, the cemetery of Samtavro, near the medieval Georgian capital of Mtskheta, lasted through five phases (perhaps *c*. 1300–500 BC). In the Armenian S.S.R., Artik may prove as significant as Lchashen. In the Araxes valley, the Late Bronze II period (*c*. 1150–1000 BC) followed the last phase at Lchashen, and was succeeded by the Late Bronze III period (*c*. 1000–900/850 BC) and then by the Early Iron Age. By then the appearance of iron on a large scale had brought lasting changes to Trans-Caucasia.

124. The earlier two-wheeled A-frame carts of Lchashen were followed by four-wheeled wagons in the richest phase. Wheels were either solid, made of three pieces, or spoked. Oak and elm were used for wheels, axles and draught-poles, and pliable yew for wickerwork sides and arched roofs. From Barrow 11, for example, came a wagon typical in measurements and meticulous craftsmanship, using seventy pieces with twelve mortices. Joints are dowelled or mortice-and-tenon, with pegs and treenails.

6

The Near East in the Period of the Assyrian Empire and its Neighbours

A political vacuum in the Near East from the twelfth till the tenth century BC resulted from the fall of the Hittite empire and the pressure of Aramaean and Chaldaean nomads on Assyria and Babylon. This facilitated the growing prosperity of Carchemish, Sam'al (Zincirli), Hamath, Guzana (Tell Halaf) and other cities within the orbit of Syro-Hittite civilization. It also made possible the brief period of Israelite power under David and Solomon.

From the reign of Adad-Nirari II (911–891 BC) Assyria began to reassert itself, the Aramaeans were steadily pushed back and many were deported. Assurnasirpal II (883–859 BC) rebuilt Nimrud, and did much for the improvement of the Assyrian homeland. His son Shalmaneser III (858–824 BC) continued the policy of expansion into Syria, culminating in the attack on Damascus by Adad-Nirari III (810–783 BC). After a period of weakness in Assyria, the throne was seized and the frontiers restored and extended by an able ruler, Tiglath-Pileser III (744–727 BC). Administrative reforms included direct rule in the provinces through appointed governors, in place of reliance on annual tribute. This policy was continued under Sargon II (721–705 BC): among the victims of this king was the kingdom of Israel, which had endured varying fortunes under the lengthening shadow of Assyria, since the foundation of Samaria by Omri (880 BC).

Round Lake Van arose in the ninth century BC a wholly new power, the kingdom of Urartu, called Van by its own rulers. This reached its widest limits under Sarduri II (c. 765–735 BC), controlling regions from the Zagros in Iran to north Syria. Its language and people were at least related to the Hurrians. It had close cultural connections with north-western Iran, where the Manneans formed the indigenous population, overlaid by incoming Medes and later by nomads from the northern steppes.

The kingdom of Phrygia, with its capital at Gordion on the Sakarya river in west central Anatolia, had a long history. This remains obscure, however, until the late eighth century BC, when the Assyrian records and a few Phrygian inscriptions give hints of a power expanding over much of the Anatolian plateau west of the Euphrates. An attack by Cimmerian nomads from south Russia, first on Gordion (traditionally 685 BC) and later on Sardis (652 BC), brought havoc to Phrygia and Lydia respectively. The former never entirely recovered.

THE SYRO-HITTITE CITIES

The greater number and range of written sources, among which pride of place a must surely go to the Assyrian annals, make it apparent that by the early ninth century BC the Near East had largely, though not entirely, entered the early historic period. The preceding three centuries, following the fall of the Hittite empire, were not as dark as once supposed, except in Anatolia. Continuity can be traced side by side with new developments in technology, especially the spread of ironworking, and in art and architecture. Stylistic analysis has been applied to the wider historical data in attempts to distinguish separate national or ethnic cultural traditions. But such an approach may run directly counter to proven archaeological evidence; and it can underestimate the impact of migrations and, later, of the policy of the Assyrian kings of deporting rebels from tributary states to the Assyrian homeland or to distant frontier districts. Voluntary or forced movement of Phoenician and other craftsmen was another factor in breaking down regional traditions in material civilization. Distinctive traditions persisted, but in increasingly modified, cosmopolitan forms.

The continuity of Assyria remained unbroken, in spite of the upheavals associated with the Sea Peoples in Anatolia and the Levant. They had not over-run the lands east of the Euphrates. Yet a threat to the very survival of the state which had rivalled Egypt and Hatti as a great power in the thirteenth century BC came from the ever-growing influx of a new people, the Aramaeans, from the fringes of the Syrian desert. These were Semites, more important for their language and sheer numbers than for any cultural distinctiveness. They provided the ruling class of many cities in Syria, but became merged in its already heterogeneous civilization. They adopted an alphabetic script akin to Phoenician not later than the ninth century BC, a vehicle for the easy dissemination of their tongue, which eventually, under the Persian empire, replaced Akkadian as the *lingua franca* of government and diplomacy. East of the Euphrates Aramaean pressure on Assyria reached its most severe point in the late tenth century BC, the recovery of Assyrian power beginning with Adad-nirari II (911–890 BC). The emphasis of successive campaigns on subduing Aramaean rulers underlines the gravity of this danger to the Assyrian state.

Carchemish, commanding a major crossing of the Euphrates, was perhaps the richest of the Syro-Hittite cities. It had been the centre of Hittite power in Syria in the Late Bronze Age, much of whose cultural traditions persisted. Its economic importance, with trading connections with Anatolia, is indicated by the large quantities of silver, copper and iron exacted as tribute by Assurnasirpal II from Sangara, king of the land of Hatte.

Several of the kings of Carchemish are known only from inscriptions carved on stone in 'Hittite hieroglyphs,' used also in other Syro-Hittite cities. These had already been largely deciphered before the discovery of the bilingual inscriptions, in Phoenician and hieroglyphs, at the small citadel of Karatepe. This stood in the hills above the east end of the plain of Adana in Cilicia, the land of Que of the Assyrian annals, Kizzuwatna in the Late Bronze Age. Karatepe was built soon after *c.* 750 BC, though earlier and later dates have been suggested, each being related to Assyrian references, from Shalmaneser III to Esarhaddon. Asitawandas, ruler of Karatepe, seems to have been under the overlordship of Awarikus of Adana; he was also open to the influence of Phoenician merchants, if not settlers too. The early occurrences of the hieroglyphs suggest that they were introduced into Syria from Anatolia; and there is reason, from their appearance and from references in Hittite texts, to believe that they may first have been carved on tablets of wood. Philological and archaeological evidence combine to indicate that the hieroglyphs must be associated not with the Hittites, but with another, rather shadowy Indo-European people, the Luvians, already mentioned in western Anatolia in the late third millennium BC. (see p. 127) By the fourteenth century BC Luvian had become the dominant spoken language of the Hittite state. Cilicia played a crucial role in the

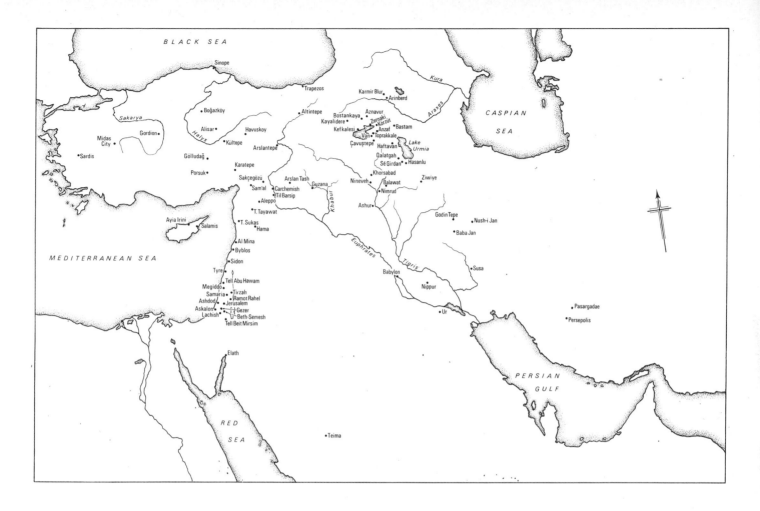

125. The Near East in the Iron Age.

transmission of both Luvian and Hurrian influences on the Hittite capital to the north, and in the Iron Age very possibly a similar one in relation to north Syria.

Thus a hybrid civilization developed in Syria and south-east Anatolia, with Hittite, Hurrian, Luvian and Aramaean elements variously mingled in each region. The scholars of the last century had approached this civilization from the viewpoint of the Old Testament, before the distinction between the Hittites of the second millennium BC and their descendants in Syria in the Iron Age was grasped. As time passed the Aramaeans widened their political power, until suppressed by Assyria in the eighth century BC; but the impact on the arts of the Hittite and Hurrian influences was by far the strongest. Both are reflected in the carved orthostats of Carchemish, the principal discovery of the ill-fated British expedition on which Hogarth, Woolley and T. E. Lawrence served. The survival of themes ultimately derived from Sumerian art has not made analysis and dating easier. Chronologically the famous Long Wall reliefs at Carchemish fall before the reign of Assurnasirpal II (883–859 BC), when the revived military power of Assyria was first felt.

The motive of these Assyrian expeditions was largely economic, to establish control over the trade route west from the Euphrates to the north-east corner of the Mediterranean: their military impact fell mainly on the Aramaean states, especially Bit-Adini, centred on Til Barsip, twenty miles downstream from

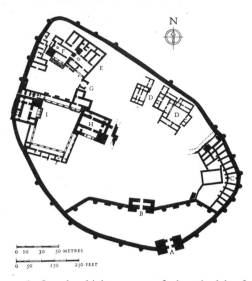

N

0 10 30 50 METRES
0 50 150 250 FEET

126. On the highest part of the citadel of Zincirli a large *bit hilâni* was later replaced by a building constructed by a ruler of Zincirli but later probably used by the Assyrian governor, whose troops were quartered in the adjacent barracks in the upper storey, with their horses below and chariots perhaps just outside. The palace of Kilamu, at the north-west corner of the citadel, was enlarged a century later by Barrakib, to comprise two *bit hilâni* side by side, facing on to a large court entered originally by a portal with guardian lions. A more grandiose access was built to the south by Barrakib, with a vast court enclosed by colonnades and with his principal palace, on the *bit hilâni* plan, at the north-west corner. Inscriptions clarify the dating of these buildings.

127. Assyrian influence is most clearly seen in the winged griffin next to the lion on the right of the portico at Sakçegözü. Next to this is a slab depicting two squat figures, not Assyrian in appearance but standing on either side of a stunted version of the sacred tree, holding tendrils descending from the winged sun-disc. Here the emblem of Assur suggests his original nature as god of fertility, of earth, trees and mountains, rather than as the war god of the Assyrian state.

Carchemish. Syro-Hittite civilization reached its zenith in the early ninth century BC, the strength of these cities being manifested in their stiff and not unsuccessful resistance to Shalmaneser III (859–824 BC), though later Assyrian kings were able gradually to subdue these small states, which were hampered by lack of any lasting unity. The art of Carchemish reflects full Assyrian influence only when this had become a political reality.

Just as the successive phases of a medieval cathedral may represent many centuries of development and stylistic change merged together, so too did the reliefs of Carchemish, the earliest being at the Water Gate. The Herald's Wall, older than the Long Wall, has no unity of theme from one orthostat to the next, a contrasting effect being achieved by juxtaposition of limestone and basalt. These slabs must represent a survival from the period before the remodelling of Carchemish by Suhis II, and include bull-men and other monsters of Sumerian and Hurrian ancestry. The crested helmets of the soldiers on the Long Wall antedate the appearance of similar helmets on the Assyrian reliefs by over 150 years. Even if future excavations at Nineveh and elsewhere should disclose a flourishing Assyrian school of sculpture before the ninth century BC, the tradition of relief-carving in north Syria, if not distinctively Hittite, owed most to Anatolia. Since the time of Yarim-Lim's palace at Alalakh VII the building methods of north Syria had been more Anatolian than Mesopotamian, combining timber, stone and brick. Successive stylistic developments at Carchemish are discernible in the bolder reliefs of Astiruwas (Asadaruwas) on the Great Staircase (c. 820–800 BC), with their taste for covering the whole background with hieroglyphic inscriptions, and in those of Araras (c. 780–760 BC) close to the building described by the excavators on inadequate evidence as the Lower Palace, in a more restrained style marking a return towards that of Katuwas or Suhis II. Nearby stood the temple of the storm god, identified as such by an inscription of Katuwas recording its restoration. Its plan, with the sanctuary approached through an outer and an inner cobbled court, exhibits certain similarities to Solomon's temple at Jerusalem, which is almost contemporary: these cannot have had any direct connection, but a common Canaanite origin. The cult of the Anatolian mother goddess Kubaba is suggested by a fragmentary statue, her shrine perhaps having been on the citadel. Included in the Long Wall is the naked goddess. The Long Wall and Great Staircase formed one complex, the work of one dynasty. The independence of Carchemish ended with an unwise anti-Assyrian coalition, followed by its sack by Sargon II (717 BC). Reoccupation, as at Hamath and other cities thus destroyed, was on a restricted scale. If doubt persists about the survival of the Hittite character of its civilization, the North-West Fort is relevant, containing as it did the 'Gold Tomb', looted after the defeat of the Egyptian army of Necho by the Babylonians under Nabopolassar (604 BC): here was a wealth of tiny gold ornaments, many of designs reproducing those of Yazilikaya, including the king embraced by his protective god.

Zincirli (Sam'al) is the best preserved of all excavated Syro-Hittite cities, its public buildings mostly the work of two of its kings, Kilamu and Barrakib, contemporaries of Shalmaneser III and Tiglath-Pileser III respectively. The citadel was defended by an approximately oval wall with semi-circular towers, with an inner wall along the south sector and two fortified gateways, the outer one decorated with carved stone orthostats. Here, after the greatest days of Zincirli were over, Esarhaddon set up a victory stele to commemorate his conquest of Egypt (670 BC). The characteristic building plan in Syro-Hittite architecture comprised two long rectangular rooms, the front one being a portico, having from one to three columns and often approached by steps. Other, smaller rooms could be added, but this unit could not be adapted as part of a more complex plan, only repeated. This was the *bit hilâni*, reproduced at Nimrud and Khorsabad in late eighth century BC Assyria. Whatever its precise origins, it became as typical of north Syria as the *megaron* was of Anatolia [126].

At Sakçegözü, not far north-east of Zincirli, a modest palace of the *bit hilâni* design stood at the north-west corner of the small citadel, its gateway in the south wall. Here the style and subject matter of the reliefs indicate a date in the late eighth century BC, when Assyrian influence on the arts was in the ascendant [127].

Syro–Hittite civilization extended far on to the Anatolian plateau, including the region covered by the kingdom or federation of Tabal, from the Cilician Gates to the Kayseri region and the Uzun Yayla, the highlands south of Sivas. Its military architecture owed much to Hattusha; its sculpture was derived from north Syria [128].

Tell Halaf, ancient Guzana, on the Khabur river was a city with largely Hurrian population under the Aramaean dynasty of Bahiani, retaining Hittite traditions in its reliefs. The outcome was a rather flamboyant version of Syro-Hittite art at its easternmost centre, with Mesopotamian elements more evident than elsewhere and with greater variety of repertoire. The palace, badly denuded, is the greatest *bit hilâni* so far excavated, approached by the Scorpion Gate and decorated along the façade of the supporting terrace with reliefs in alternating basalt and reddish limestone. A statue-base or altar in front of the

128. In the Taurus mountains, near Bor, the Ivriz rock relief illustrates the juxtaposition of Syro-Hittite and Assyrian styles, represented respectively by the vegetation god Tarhundas, holding a bunch of grapes and ears of corn, and by the smaller figure in attitude of worship, Urpalla king of Tyana.

129. The most striking works of the sculptors of Guzana are the three statues supporting the architrave of the *bit hilâni* palace portico: they lack the usual horned headdress of deities, and may represent members of the Kapara dynasty. Above these figures were conical 'capitals'; the statues themselves were nearly 3 m. high, two standing on a lion and the middle one on a bull, each animal being 1.5 m. high.

palace portico was decorated in green, yellow and white glazed bricks. The description of this building as a palace rather than a temple is supported by its similarity of plan to others elsewhere and by inscriptions [129].

Hamath, on the Orontes, was one of the major cities of Syria, yet displayed a rather different civilization from that of the other Syro–Hittite cities farther north. The Danish excavations revealed a very long succession of cultural periods, from Hama M (Neolithic) to Hama E (*c.* 900–720 BC), the greatest of all the periods [130]. The ground floor of the palace of this period was entirely of store-rooms, the living quarters being in the upper storey, whose splendour is hinted at by red, blue and white painted plaster and gold leaf. A massive pier of brickwork 48 courses high, fallen into one of the rooms below, suggests the great height of the upper rooms. The lower, surviving flight of stairs contributes to the evidence that the whole façade stood almost fifteen metres high. The absence of any columned portico precludes description of this as a *bit hilâni*. Across the central court stood a temple (Building III), with a stele reused as a threshold between its anteroom and court, depicting two figures seated at table beneath the crescent moon, emblem of the god Sin. Aramaean religion, with Hadad (the Phoenician Ba'al and Hurrian Teshub) as chief deity, was an agglomeration of the beliefs of the older populations overrun by the Aramaean tribes.

The citadel of Hamath, with an inner gate (Building IV) to an upper area, was badly destroyed in later times. A second palace (Building V), only partially excavated, resembled Building II. Lions of archaic style were reused on the outside of the gateway (Building I): the others, including the colossal lions in front of the palace, are probably all more or less contemporary. Except the colossi, the heads alone are carefully rendered, the bodies rudimentarily. The colossal lions, carved in the round, suggest the sculptor trying to gain independence of the architect. Outside the citadel were cremation cemeteries, as such comparable with the contemporary Yunus cemetery at Carchemish: at Hamath four phases were distinguished, the first two dating from the coming of the Sea Peoples to the end of Hama F (*c.* 900 BC), the third to the ninth century BC and the fourth to *c.* 800–720 BC. Homeric comparisons are suggested by offerings of

130. Though two gateways (termed Buildings I and IV) on the citadel of Hamath originated in the tenth century BC (Hama F 1), the remains of this Iron Age citadel belong essentially to the ninth century BC, with restorations in the eighth, largely during the reign of Eni-ilu (743–732 BC), shortly before the destruction by Sargon II (720 BC). The most impressive building (II) was a palace, probably the 'king's house' of the Aramaic inscriptions on two red polished bricks. A basalt throne and large window grille, found in fragments in the central court, surely came from this palace.

Pl 25. At Dinkha Tepe and in the contemporary levels of Haftavan VIB, near the north-west corner of the lake, there are signs of a period of prosperity with structures on a large scale destroyed by fire. Haftavan VIB has yielded a variety of painted and burnished pottery, with motifs including birds and a representation of a wheeled vehicle drawn by two horses.

meat put beside the urn containing the ashes of the dead, a practice evident elsewhere and demonstrating belief in an afterlife, apparently not inconsistent with cremation.

The art of ivory carving flourished in Hamath, as evidence from Assyria and from fragments recovered from the smaller palace shows. Volutes, wings, bulls and palmettes were fashionable motifs. There is no need to postulate a Syrian style, distinct from the Phoenician, to admit that Hamath must have been a major centre. Elephants still extant in Syria provided a local supply till the eighth century BC, when they became extinct. This was a craft with origins in the Levant in the second millennium BC, its products ever more widely distributed by the commercial energy of the Phoenician merchants.

PHOENICIA AND PALESTINE UNTIL THE DEATH OF SOLOMON

The Phoenicians, deprived of most of the hinterland held by their Canaanite ancestors, were obliged to depend for survival on manufacture and export of finished products. They were skilled miners, metalworkers, builders and carpenters, as well as experts in construction of cisterns, more effectively waterproofed with slaked lime instead of the gypsum used in the Bronze Age for plaster. These were essential for the intensive cultivation, which they developed to make best use of their limited land.

The archaeological record tells relatively little of the Phoenician homeland, owing to the great overburden of the remains of later periods, from the Ptolemies to the Crusaders. The same is true of the Philistine territory along the costal plain to the south, after their distinctive painted pottery went out of use in the mid-eleventh century BC. But the excavations at Tell Mor, ancient

Ashdod, one of the cities of the Philistine pentapolis, have revealed very strong Canaanite influence, further indicated by the biblical references to the worship of Ishtar and Dagon. The Aegean heritage of the Philistines did not, however, disappear. Tell Mor VI was burnt at about the time of the Israelite invasion; then, after a period of desertion, Tell Mor V–III cover the centuries of Philistine power, till about the time of David; Tell Mor II was destroyed probably during the campaign by Shishak of Egypt, soon after the death of Solomon. Ironworking was a major skill of the Philistines.

The continuity of Phoenician civilization was centred on two cities only, Byblos and Sidon. Tyre may have been refounded by the Sidonians in the early twelfth century BC. The Egyptian tale of the adventures of Wenamun shows that conditions in the east Mediterranean were still unsettled a century later (*c.* 1070 BC). By the time of David and Solomon, Tyre was evidently the leading Phoenician city: Phoenician records depict Hiram I (*c.* 969–936 BC), the ally of Solomon, as a military ruler suppressing colonial revolts and building several temples at Tyre. It is to the recurrent importation of Phoenician craftsmen, first into the united kingdom of Solomon and later into Israel and Judah, that much of the surviving evidence of Phoenician civilization is due.

The archaeology of Palestine in the twelfth and eleventh centuries BC is typically that of a region where law and order and settled life have fallen violently into decline, and with them material civilization. Not till the reign of Solomon (*c.* 960–936 BC) were peace and stability firm enough to allow the restoration of urban life at a few major sites, although on a more modest scale than in the Canaanite heyday of the Middle Bronze Age. David and Solomon were able to take advantage of the political vacuum caused by the simultaneous weakness of Assyria and Egypt. The unhappy history of Jerusalem in later times, destroyed by Babylonians (587 BC) and Romans (AD 70), is enough to explain the absence of any direct archaeological evidence of the capital of Solomon's kingdom, with its famous temple. Here the administration was centred, with a civil service trained in Egypt; and hither came most of the Phoenician craftsmen imported by Solomon. In the provinces, in spite of reorganization, the governmental districts reflected the tribal pattern of the Israelite settlement, perpetuated later in the Assyrian provinces after the fall of the northern kingdom of Israel. The Old Testament (I Kings 9, 15) records Solomon's taxation for his building works at Jerusalem, Hazor, Megiddo and Gezer [131].

The feature linking Megiddo VA–IVB, Hazor X and Gezer is a common design of fortified gateway, with three gates. At Hazor X there were public buildings, following an earlier 'idolatrous' Israelite shrine on the citadel. But not even the whole citadel was reoccupied; and the great lower town was left abandoned for ever. Macalister, the excavator of Gezer in 1902–9, attributed the Solomonic gateway to the Maccabaean period. Even today the complexities of ceramic typology, though largely of the archaeologists' own making, are sometimes hard to reconcile with the historical evidence.

Solomonic buildings have been found also from Ein Gev, on the east side of the Sea of Galilee, to as far south as the head of the Gulf of Aqaba, where a supposed smelter has been excavated in the first of a sequence of phases, Ezion–Geber I. Copper was available from Sinai and from the Wadi Arabah. A farming settlement at Ramat Matred demonstrates resettlement of parts of the Negev, which was abandoned to nomads whenever government was weak. Solomon's control of all the lands east of the Jordan and Dead Sea, from Hauran south to Edom, gave him the grasp of the caravan trade routes from Arabia to Syria, with

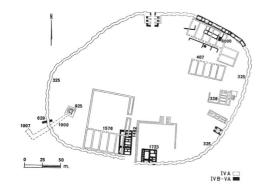

131. Megiddo. Recent excavations have clarified some of the problems left by the reports of the American expedition, and created largely by an incomplete application of the principles of stratigraphy. In the end it seems that Strata VA–IVB at Megiddo constitute the Solomonic period; the remains include a recently uncovered palace and the famous stables, probably correctly described as such, in spite of the absence of any horse trappings.

the Red Sea trade attested at Ezion–Geber by ship's rope and pitch for caulking. Tyrian support was certainly involved in the foundation of this port and the smelter. Important as this maritime trade was, suggestions that it extended to India should be treated with caution. The buildings of Hama F1 may conceivably have owed their construction to Solomon, though it is hard to believe that his hold over Hamath was ever very firm. It may have served as an entrepôt for the trade in horses imported from Que (Cilicia), many then being exchanged at the rate of four to one for Egyptian chariots.

Solomon's kingdom proved unable to survive him, however, and was divided into Israel and Judah, with consequent loss of peripheral territories. In the archaeological record little trace may have survived of the time of the division, save perhaps in fortifications built by Rehoboam in Judah.

ASSYRIA

The citadel of Nimrud included buildings spanning most of the Late Assyrian period, though the most impressive was the North-West Palace, erected by Assurnasirpal II (883–859 BC) as his royal residence, when at the outset of his reign he refounded the city as the capital of his expanding kingdom. He campaigned vigorously, especially against the Aramaean principalities along the Euphrates, and secured access to the Mediterranean; and he deported Aramaeans and other subject peoples to increase the population of the Assyrian homeland. He was the first Assyrian king to leave a pictorial record to supplement the cuneiform inscriptions of his deeds in war and peace.

The citadel was the most prominent part of the town of Kalhu, as Nimrud was known to the Assyrians, and far the most thoroughly investigated in the excavations of Layard in the nineteenth century and of Mallowan and Oates since the Second World War. Only four large buildings have been excavated in the outer town, though these include Fort Shalmaneser, the palace and arsenal constructed by Assurnasirpal's son and successor at the south-east corner of the town. The perimeter wall of Kalhu was no less than 4.75 miles long, enclosing an area of 358 hectares: this included the citadel, itself covering 24 hectares and situated at the south-west corner of the city. The stele set up in a deep recess near the exit from the throne-room of the North-West Palace, covered by the debris of fallen bricks, had been overlooked by Layard: in its 154 lines it gives a full account not only of the vast banquet given then (879 BC) to 69,574 guests, of whom 65,000 formed the population of the refounded city, but also of the various buildings erected by the king, including nine temples, four of which have been located.

Inscriptions and reliefs of different Assyrian kings have left evidence of the enormous scale of their building works and of the many workmen needed for their execution, military campaigns being waged partly with the purpose of supplying this manpower from prisoners of war. The construction of the perimeter wall of Nimrud must have required millions of mud-bricks, the daily average total laid by one man being one hundred bricks. These walls seem to have lasted two centuries, being reinforced by Esarhaddon (681–669 BC) with a mud-brick outer casing and with ashlar foundations. Such great building works, with the mobilization of large task forces to make, transport and lay the mud-bricks, deserve comparison with the pyramids of Old Kingdom Egypt, and must be seen in the context of the most plausible estimate of the population of Nimrud in the time of Assurnasirpal II as being not less than 92,000. This estimate is based on the stele inscription and on seventh-century BC evidence

Pl 26. Marlik can hardly be mentioned without brief reference to the ritual vessels, the finest of which is a gold beaker with design in repoussé of two winged bulls on their hind legs with their heads in the round, flanking a stylized palm tree. This vessel, also betraying Assyrian influence, is of a simpler design, and may date to the fourteenth century BC, the earliest phase of Marlik. The cemetery could have been in use for six centuries (*c.* 1400–800 BC).

Pl 27. Opposite: Urartian tombs were little known until the excavations at Altintepe and Kayalidere, after which it became evident that the rock-cut chambers in the precipitous south side of Van citadel, seen here, must be described not as shrines but as tombs. Only one of the three major tombs can be identified from inscriptions, that of Argishti I, approached by rock-cut steps along the cliff face. Its main room has rectangular niches in the walls, for offerings or lamps, and was decorated with bronze stars of Assyrian pattern; the burial chamber was on the left on entry.

from a census of Harran, the old city on the western limit of Assyria proper. This figure allows for children: Assyrian families were small, perhaps not entirely because of high infant mortality. It has been questioned whether any attempt to estimate population is justifiable except simply from the area of any city, large or small; but this caution seems excessive. By the time that Nineveh had become the capital (from 705 BC) the Assyrian homeland must have had a population of between 250,000 and 500,000 in all, not necessarily much less in the early ninth century BC. The eventual diminution of this population, masked by the introduction of subject peoples, was one of the factors leading to the downfall of this ruthlessly efficient but vulnerable state.

It is well to emphasize that the Assyrian kings saw themselves as the shepherds of their people, a concept possibly dating back to the period of the earliest Assyrian rulers, described in the king-lists as living in tents: certainly it is illustrated by a statue in the round of Assurnasirpal II, a mace in his left hand and a crook in his right. They sought to improve their homeland, not least by erecting new or restoring old palaces. They had a strong sense of their own past history, spurring them to surpass the achievements of their predecessors, though more in scale than in kind. Such innovations as appeared did not significantly affect the strong cultural continuity, especially evident throughout the Late Assyrian period. Without this the sense of national identity which ensured the survival of the state would not have so long endured.

It is worth turning again to the inscription on the stele in the North-West Palace, for it tells of the peaceful activities of Assurnasirpal II. All was not war and flaying alive of prisoners. He dug a canal, to which he gave the name 'Ditch of Abundance', to bring water from the Zab river to irrigate the land between that and Nimrud, as far as the Tigris. The old line can still be followed, showing that it was cut as far east from the Tigris as possible, to give the greatest area for cultivation. The most remarkable of Assyrian canals was that engineered by Sennacherib to bring additional water to Nineveh, with an aqueduct at Jerwan comprising five stone-built ogival arches, one of which survives, a precursor of Roman achievements.

Assurnasirpal II, like his successors, found his chief recreation in hunting: he mentions the slaughter of lions, bulls and ostriches. These species, as well as apes, he also captured and kept in zoological gardens, allowing them to breed. He followed the precedent set by Tiglath-Pileser I (c. 1114–1077 BC), by collecting different trees, seedlings and plants on campaigns, as tribute or through trade. From as far as south Arabia came frankincense, probably by the route secured in Solomon's time. Many types of wood had an importance in Assyrian architecture suggested by the naming in the stele inscription of seven of the eight wings of the palace after box, mulberry, cedar, cypress, pistachio, tamarisk and poplar respectively. Mulberry and pine are among the species of wood distinguished from samples excavated. Besides timber for construction and embellishment of the palace there was a wide variety of fruit trees, including quinces, figs and vines, suggesting the richness of Assyrian horticulture.

The North-West Palace, like the later palaces, has left a threefold record of Assyrian civilization, in its plan, inscriptions and decoration, the last principally as reliefs forming a dado along the walls of the most important rooms. Not all the inscriptions were designed for mortal eyes, for some were cut on the reverse side of sculptured orthostats; but more usual was the writing of long accounts of the king's campaigns and of his building works and scores in hunting, the lines of cuneiform often extending in a band right across the reliefs. Such disregard

of aesthetic effect is surely but one indication that the record came before the artistic impression, as in all art in the ancient Near East. The reliefs, a genre of Assyrian art probably first appearing in the North-West Palace, hint at one of the most demanding of the king's functions, as chief priest, but were primarily concerned to impress visitors and his own subjects with his personal military prowess and the invincible efficiency of the army, overcoming every natural obstacle of mountain, river or marsh, and battering every recalcitrant city into submission [132].

Many of the reliefs and the vividly painted designs covering the upper wall faces and ceilings, including the coffered ceiling of the throne-room, must have been seen only in a very dim light, for in Assyria, as elsewhere in the Near East, darkness was associated with coolness. This may explain the bold colours—mainly red, blue, black and white—used in the painted mural decoration, with similarly bright colours in friezes of glazed tiles. The colours of stone and timber contrasted with the shining bronze sheeting which covered the doors, and which, in this and the next reign, might be used as a medium for commemorating the king's victories in bands of repoussé relief.

The North-West Palace must have appeared at its most imposing when approached by river: excavations have revealed a mud-brick perimeter wall nearly 15 m. thick along this west side, standing about 6.5 m. high, behind and overlooking a stone quay wall along the Tigris. On the east side the perimeter wall of the citadel was no less than 37 m. thick. The dimensions given by Xenophon, who marched with the Ten Thousand up the left bank of the Tigris, its course by then (401 BC) shifted two miles to the west, suggest a height of 15 m. for the walls of the North-West Palace, which accords well with their thickness, the certain evidence of an upper storey and the scale appropriate to its rooms. In plan the palace followed the usual pattern of the Near East, in that it comprised a number of courts surrounded by rooms, which opened into them and received their light thence. The same needs for light, air and circulation obtained as in the days of the palace of Mari. The arrangement of rooms in the central and south wings reveals several pairs, such as Room B (the throne-room) and Room F, in which the reliefs were principally concerned with wars and with magical ceremonies respectively, the latter exclusively the Nisroch figure, as Layard termed the bird-headed genii, after the biblical reference to Sennacherib's assassination 'in the House of Nisroch' (681 BC): they hold a bucket and fir-cone, and touch the sacred tree [132, 133].

The north façade of the central wing, facing the great square, was evidently

132. Most of the reliefs in the throne-room (B) at Nimrud were military, though that in the recess behind the throne itself depicts Assurnasirpal twice on either side of the sacred tree, one of the recurring themes of Assyrian art. He is receiving the authority of kingship from the national god Assur, represented as usual in a winged sun-disc; behind the king stands a winged genius, with bucket and fir-cone, sprinkling him with holy water. Such must be the meaning of this standard subject, rather than any suggestion of pollenating the sacred tree. From its position this relief obviously had a special importance.

the main frontage, with the two doors into the throne-room (Gates D and E) serving as entrance and exit for those seeking audience, the entrance being the further removed from the throne. Each doorway was flanked by colossal sculptured figures, monsters part man, part lion and part bird, with a kid in the right hand and a plant of life in the left. In addition there stood winged bull men, with the belly of fish and wearing fish-hoods, symbolising Ea, the god of magic. These sculptures were all in soft gypsum, which must have necessitated some protective roofing, evidence for which has not been recovered. Between Gates D and E ran a long frieze of figures in relief, over life-size, of the king receiving a procession of captive tribute-bearers and vassal rulers from north Syria and probably also from Anatolia and elsewhere, led by his commander-in-chief. These were reburied by Layard, and can now be seen with the colossi, once more exposed to view *in situ*. Winged monsters flanked many other passages and doorways, their forms part human and either part leonine or part bovine, the benevolent *lamassu*, guardians of the gates. As a further protection, small bronze dogs were buried under the thresholds, to bark at evil spirits: one such was inscribed: 'Don't stop to think, bite him!' Thus Assyrian fears of the forces of evil and of the unknown were partly assuaged. These fears ever lurked behind the brash self-confidence of reliefs and paintings alike.

The lifetime of the North-West Palace as the principal residence of the Assyrian kings probably spanned three reigns, including those of Shalmaneser III (859–824 BC) and Shamshi-Adad V (824–810 BC). This was an unusually long time, for the kings of the ancient Near East were never so concerned with maintaining their predecessors' palaces as with erecting their own. This reflects both a desire for self-glorification and the ready command of building materials

Pl 29. It is usually possible to discern the most likely spot for an Urartian fortress, built for both military and governmental functions. The standard plan first appeared in the reign of Menua, by whom the fortifications of Van citadel were probably built, still standing in this impressive stretch: this plan comprised a massive perimeter wall with buttresses of uniform size at regular intervals and with a pronounced batter on the wall face. The foundations rested on ledges quarried out of the bedrock, in some places the sole surviving evidence of the line of the defences. One such site is Bostankaya ('the garden rock') near Malazgirt, north of Lake Van.

Pl 28. Opposite: An Urartian royal tomb without inscription on the south side of Van citadel.

169

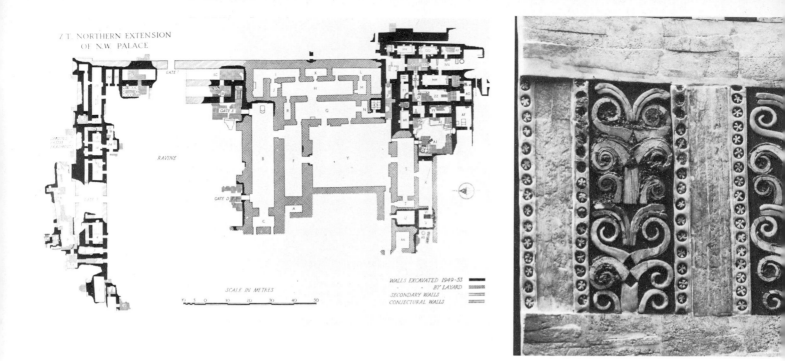

RAVINE

GATE E

GATE D

SCALE IN METRES

WALLS EXCAVATED 1949-55
BY LAYARD
SECONDARY WALLS
CONJECTURAL WALLS

133. The North-West Palace at Nimrud comprised not only the public and domestic wings but also a great parade ground or public square with the rooms of the ziggurat terrace (ZT) forming a north wing, next to the ziggurat itself and its associated temples. The complete facade was 200 m. long from north to south, with a width of 120 m. from east to west, thus covering nearly 2½ hectares. There were altogether more than 70 rooms, with 23 in the central wing and over 20 in the domestic south wing.

and labour. Special care was taken to ensure a good supply of clean water for the palace by the digging of wells. One of these, in Room NN, was the main water supply for the domestic wing, its cleanliness protected by raising its head above the surrounding pavement with a well-made platform of bricks laid in bitumen: here, at the top of a flight of six steps, the great capstone was still *in situ*. In the excavations water first appeared at a depth of 15.15 m., or 205 brick courses, below the well-head; bedrock was eventually reached at a depth of 331 courses.

To the west of the palace stood the group of temples overlooked by the ziggurat, at the north-west corner of the citadel. This ziggurat, originally some 20 m. high and mounted by a vanished staircase on its east side, was closely connected with the chief temple, that dedicated to Ninurta, patron of Nimrud and god of war and hunting, later described as 'Lord of the month appointed for the gathering of armies and the formation of camps'. A feature of the ziggurat is a pilastered north façade of burnt bricks with limestone masonry at its base. The priests of Ninurta used the ziggurat for their observations of the heavens. At its foot stood this god's temple, between the ziggurat and the north wing (ZT) of the palace: from the main entrance the chief sanctuary was approached through an antechamber, on a transverse axis. To the south-east a room with a recessed niche at its east end served either as an audience hall or as a second sanctuary. The temple store-rooms contained rows of jars probably for oil and two inscribed stone tanks sunk into the original floor. The stele and other inscriptions give a summary of the wealth of the principal shrines which Assurnasirpal II built in his capital; the other temple which he records as having been founded, not merely restored, by him was that of Enlil, head of the Sumerian pantheon, not yet located. After mentioning the cedar beams and doors, bronze statues and booty of gold in the temples, the commemorative stele goes on to describe the gold and lapis lazuli inlays, the raging serpents of gold and the

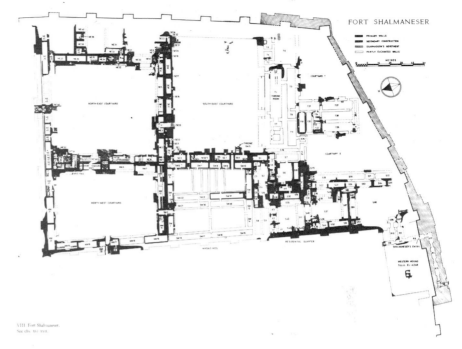

VIII Fort Shalmaneser.
See chs. XV-XVI.

134. Ivory bed-head from Room SW7 of Fort Shalmaneser. One bed-head had Aramaic or Phoenician signs as fitter's marks on the reverse side.

135. The finest example of the use of glazed bricks is the great panel found fallen from above a doorway in the throne-room wing, the public rooms, of Fort Shalmaneser. The impact was immediate, due to the use of white, black, green and yellow bricks on a blue ground.

136. An inscription of Esarhaddon from Nineveh, written in cuneiform on clay in the form of a prism, describes such buildings as Fort Shalmaneser as 'for the ordinance of the camp, the maintenance of the stallions, chariots, weapons, equipment of war and the spoil of the foe of every kind'.

137. Ezida, the name given to all temples dedicated to Nabu, the god of writing and son of Marduk, marks the introduction of stronger Babylonian elements into the religion of Assyria in the time of Adad-nirari III. This building had two wings, with twin sanctuaries of Nabu and his consort Tashmetum in the south wing.

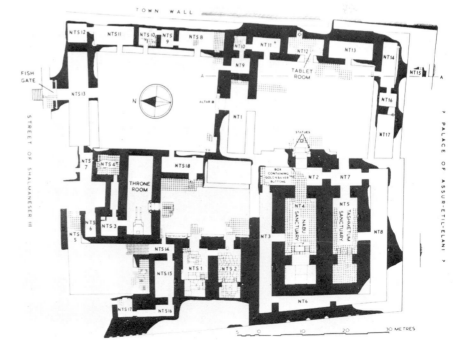

Pl 30. A fine red-polished ware, with shallow bowls and stemmed goblets the most characteristic forms, came into use in Urartu during the eighth century BC; bowls with folded rim, found at Altintepe and at Bastam north-west of Lake Urmia, appear in the seventh century BC. Among varieties of storage jars, or *pithos*, one with sunken squares and triangles is widespread and characteristically Urartian.

statue of the king of red gold and semi-precious stones in the temple of Ninurta. Thus the inscriptions unearthed by the archaeologists can be an invaluable source of information on those aspects of material civilization which have perished either through the depredations of looters or by the natural processes of decay.

The next king, Shalmaneser III (859–824 BC), continued his father's expansionist policy and the aggrandizement of his capital city with the profits of tribute and loot. He brought Assyrian power to a new zenith, only to face internal rebellion at the end of his reign, after which decline set in. The North-West Palace continued in use, and much of the work on the ziggurat dates to this reign. Perhaps the best known monuments of Shalmaneser III are to be seen today in the rearranged Assyrian galleries of the British Museum: these are the Black Obelisk, in fact a stele, from the central building on the citadel of Nimrud and the Bronze Gates from the small palace of Balawat, the royal country residence twelve miles north-east of Nimrud. The 'obelisk' depicts in twenty small reliefs the payment of tribute from five conquered regions, and also pro-

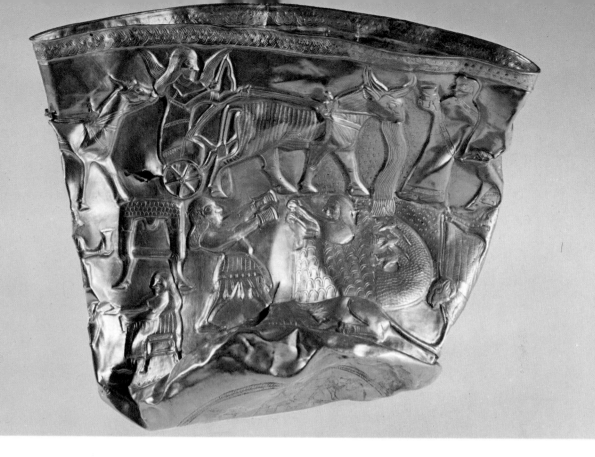

vides the final edition of the annals, covering almost the whole reign (years 1–31). As such these are especially valuable, since the later years of any reign are invariably less frequently recorded than the earlier. The principal items of tribute were gold, silver, lead, copper, ivory, horses and camels. From one region in north Syria, Musri, elephants were sent: these were soon to become extinct there, with drastic consequences for the ivory-carvers' industry, at its zenith in the ninth and eighth centuries BC. Jehu of Israel also sent tribute, as did the Syro–Hittite ruler Karparunda of Hattina (the Amuq Plain); and likewise the ruler of Gilzani, perhaps the Reza'iyeh Plain on the west side of Lake Urmia, a horse-breeding country; and so too the ruler of Suhi in Babylonia. The Assyrian reliefs are an incomparable source of evidence of the dress and manufactures of the various widely scattered peoples who brought tribute to successive kings, as in a later age were the reliefs of Persepolis. Comparison with the Black Obelisk and the bronze bands decorated in repoussé and nailed to the great wooden doors of the palace of Balawat is provided by the reliefs carved on the sides of the throne-base found *in situ* at the east end of the great throne-room (T1) in Fort Shalmaneser. These reliefs include events down to the thirteenth year of the reign, indicating its completion *c.* 845 BC, whereas the Balawat gates recount only the first nine years. The throne-base demonstrates the abandonment by Shalmaneser III of the carving of bas-reliefs on the large scale of the previous reign in the North-West Palace. The talents of the Assyrian artists seem to have found new expression in mural painting, fragmentarily preserved in the throne-room of Fort Shalmaneser, and also in glazed bricks. This latter Assyrian tradition of architectural decoration, originating perhaps in Middle Assyrian murals, was to recur later in Babylon and Susa [135].

Pl 31. The Hasanlu bowl seems to depict the myth of Kummarbi, in which the ultimate victory went to the storm god Teshub, here depicted leading two other chariots in one drawn by a bull, the animal associated with this deity. The technique used on the bowl is repoussé, the details being chased; the general effect is one of a rather crude overcrowding. The antecedents of this gold bowl can be understood only by reference to the ritual vessels from Marlik, discussed in the last chapter.

Fort Shalmaneser, not discovered until the expedition under Mallowan and Oates, was a vast complex laid out on a systematic plan to serve the functions of barracks, arsenal, storehouse and palace [136]. It comprised four quadrants, a residential wing and a throne wing for public audiences. The south-west quadrant had one narrow gateway leading to rooms ranged round four courts: these were all magazines, some full of wine jars, others with jars of corn. The fort has yielded evidence of the life and equipment of the Assyrian army, the quarters for officers of the royal guard being provided with bathrooms. The wide north gate into the south-east sector originally had double doors, with a surviving strip of tarmac bearing the marks of chariot wheels, a reminder of the significance of the vehicles so frequently depicted in the reliefs. Chariots were dismantled and stored in Fort Shalmaneser. An earlier king had boasted of increasing the output of chariots. Bricks 48 cm. square are the hallmark of the original building period, though this great depot remained in use till the very end of the Assyrian state [134].

Although Assyria went into a period of decline after the death of Shalmaneser III (824 BC) until the seizure of the throne by Tiglath-Pileser III (744 BC), two major buildings at Nimrud, the Burnt Palace and Ezida, date to c. 800 BC. The Burnt Palace, with its characteristic throne-room suite, stood immediately west of Ezida, on the opposite side of a street [137].

URARTU

The origins of the kingdom of Urartu, in the highlands around Lake Van, are uncertain in both the archaeological and the written record. It could well be that many petty princes and tribal chiefs gradually allied with one another, either for the exploitation of economic resources such as iron or in face of a common enemy, as the Medes were later to unite against Assyria. This is perhaps implied by the account left by Tiglath-Pileser I of his campaign against the twenty-three rulers of Nairi (then equivalent to the lands immediately west and north of Lake Van): he set up a stele at Yoncalu in the heart of this region. But the earliest detailed references in the Assyrian annals date to the first three years of Shalmaneser III; and the earliest representation of people of Urartu is on the bronze bands of the gates at Balawat. The use of the cuneiform script by the Urartian kings, who styled themselves princes of the city of Turushpa and of the land of Biaina (Van), is itself proof of their debt to Assyrian civilization; and when to this is added the use of the Assyrian language this is doubly stressed. Yet it would be mistaken to claim that Urartu had no cultural character of its own. It would be remarkable if this had been so, given the very different natural environment compared with the Assyrian homeland. In that country of long, hard winters Sarduri I was the first king of Urartu to have left his own inscriptions; they still survive. He founded his capital at Van, after that of his predecessor at Arzashkun had been sacked by Shalmaneser III. The large blocks used for a structure at the foot of the west end of the citadel rock of Van, the end nearest the lake, can only have been brought there by barge. This building was probably designed to protect the water supply, although, with the possibility that Lake Van then extended to the castle rock, it may perhaps have served as a quay for ships.

It was not till the onset of the temporary decline of Assyria that Urartu began to expand, becoming a major power under Menua (c. 810–786 BC), to whom may be attributed a systematic programme of military construction, comprising fortresses sited to protect the main approach roads to Van, with others farther afield. This same king also made an irrigation canal, later attributed to Semiramis (the Assyrian queen Sammuramat, contemporary with Menua's early years), to bring water to Van more than fifty miles from the Hoşap valley to the south-east. The emphasis on irrigation and cisterns throughout Urartu may imply a period of abnormal drought or, more probably, a much larger population than is found in most of these areas today.

The official character of much about Urartian civilization is suggested by its uniformity over most of the kingdom, since the advent of Urartian rule was accompanied by a recognizably standard range of artefacts and architecture, perhaps most clearly apparent in the fortresses and temples. Such a standardized culture would hardly have appeared but for the backwardness of these highlands before the late ninth century BC, with little or no tradition of permanent settlement and strong government, and consequently the scantiest of archaeological evidence. In those regions where Urartian administration was imposed on a people with well-established material civilization in a mixed urban and village economy, as in north-west Iran and the Elaziğ region (formerly Isua), the Urartian element is archaeologically much less readily distinguishable.

There was one city, Musasir, which seems to have exerted a special influence on the formative period of Urartu, or at least on its state religion. This is suggested by the long inscription of Meher Kapisi ('the door of Mithra'), set in a frame carved in a rock face near the citadel of Van and even closer to the later one of Toprakkale, the focal point of a small shrine and dating to the reign of Ishpuini (c. 822–810 BC). Musasir is put first of three cities, more important than Tushpa (Van), their respective gods and goddesses listed with their appropriate sacrificial offerings, male or female animals. Linguistically this inscription and the contemporary Urartian text at Kel-i-shin are slightly different from other Urartian inscriptions, a pointer to the influence of Musasir, confirmed by the association of the god Haldi with this city before he is known to have become the chief of the Urartian pantheon. Like Arzashkun the site of Musasir remains undiscovered, although its mention in the bilingual stele of Kel-i-shin, of Ishpuini, and in the later one at Topzaua, of Rusa I (c. 735–714 BC), suggests a location in the mountainous Iraq–Iran frontier region, possibly near Ruwanduz. The difficulties facing anyone attempting solutions to problems of historical geography in this period are underlined by these bilingual incriptions, where Musasir in the Assyrian version is Ardini in the Urartian. Musasir was clearly a prosperous religious centre, if nothing more, from Assyrian accounts commanding quite a wide territory. Its origins are unknown before the reference in Assurnasirpal II's stela (879 BC); its history was apparently brought to an abrupt end with its sack by Sargon II on his famous eighth campaign (714 BC). The list of booty, including statues of Haldi and three Urartian kings and a wide variety of equipment and furniture from the temple, gives a clear indication of the wealth of a city long held in respect by Assyria as well as Urartu.

The best known record of Musasir is the representation of its temple on a relief from Sargon II's palace at Khorsabad. Though the spearhead on the apex of the roof and the cauldrons flanking the doorway might be thought to suggest Urartian affinities, it is neither a temple of the normal Urartian design nor a *megaron* with connections farther to the west. Musasir was close to the region most likely to have had a decisive influence on Urartian civilization, the Urmia basin of north-west Iran.

The earliest excavated Urartian temple is that at Patnos, thirty miles along the road north-west from Erciş on Lake Van, on the summit of Aznavur. This

Pl 32. The date of some pieces of the Ziwiye treasure may be considerably earlier than their burial in the disturbed period of the establishment of Mĕdian rule under Cyaxares and the flight of Scyths back to their original homeland in the south Russian steppes. A hare, a crouching lynx and the head of a bird of prey appear on this large silver dish from Ziwiye, with concentric design: this decoration, and couchant stags and goats in an Urartian setting on another piece, display Scythian workmanship.

139. Opposite below: round-topped niches occur in the Urartian tomb at Kayalidere, with two bottle-shaped pits, probably for the main burials, and also in the masonry tombs built into the hillside at Altintepe and containing basalt sarcophagi with curved lids.

contained mural paintings and the annals of Menua, two copies each covering two blocks of the temple masonry. A smaller temple stands on the long ridge of Çavuştepe in the lower Hoşap valley, with an inscription dating it to the reign of Sarduri II (*c.* 765–735 BC). The temple of Altintepe, on the large flat summit of a hill twelve miles east of Erzincan, near the north-west frontier of Urartu, is rather later, probably of the reign of Argishti II (714–*c.* 685 BC). A more roughly constructed temple with the same plan as Altintepe was found at Kayalidere, on the Arsania (Murat) River, as usual on the highest point of the site. These temples are a distinctive feature of Urartu [**138**].

Open-air shrines, cut out of the rock, were another element in Urartian religion, in Van and elsewhere. The annals of Sarduri II were inscribed on stelae set in high round-topped niches at the foot of the north side of Van citadel, in a shrine sadly mutilated in the years following its excavation by a Russian expedition (1916–17) but now preserved for the visitor. Finely dressed but uninscribed stelae were set up in an area probably serving as a shrine beside the tombs in the hillside of Altintepe.

The tombs at Altintepe have a false vault, carved to resemble an arch but in fact corbelled and resting on projecting blocks; each tomb has at least three chambers. Rock tombs of Urartian type, many set inaccessibly in a cliff face, are found quite widely in the provinces, including the Urmia basin. Cemeteries of more modest cist graves occur at Ernis on Lake Van and at Iğdir in the Araxes Plain below Mount Ararat [**139**, *Pls 27, 28*].

The palaces of the Urartian kings are known only from provincial centres, for no excavations have been conducted in the ruins of their capital at Van, which is presumably concealed beneath those of the Turkish city destroyed in

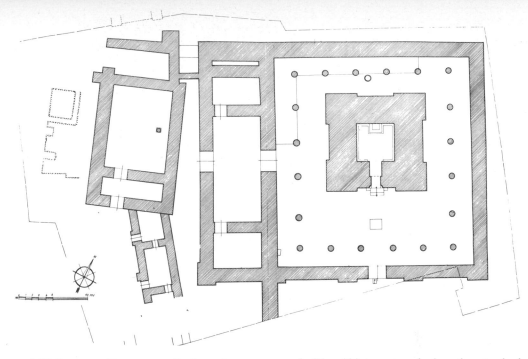

1916. The small mud-brick palace of Giriktepe at Patnos, a mile from Aznavur, has a hall with doubly recessed niches, similar to the burnt buildings of Hasanlu IV (c. 1100–800 BC) just south of Lake Urmia. A closer parallel is apparent in the occurrence at both sites of the skeletons of young women in a context suggesting ritual sacrifice: at Hasanlu they were found with bronze lions with iron pin attachments. Its earlier date indicated the direction of influence as from Hasanlu. The palace at Giriktepe is most probably attributable to Menua, given the presence of his annals in the Aznavur temple; and he may well have destroyed Hasanlu. Argishti I, son of Menua, founded the citadel of Erebuni (Arinberd), modern Erevan, as an inscription in the wall beside the gate testifies. This was no doubt designed as the administrative centre of the fertile Erevan Plain; and it was well placed to control the sensitive north-eastern frontier of Urartu, through the bleak highlands near Lake Sevan. The palace had a throne-room with two doors and a court with wooden gallery supported by fourteen wooden columns on stone bases. Mural decoration in a formal style, including lions, bulls and target motifs, is found on the walls both of the palace at Erebuni and at Altintepe. The official style was not the only outlet for the mural painters of Urartu, as fragments of hunting scenes from Erebuni in a livelier, naturalistic manner show. These owe much less, if anything, to Assyrian art. The parapeted superstructure of Urartian palaces is represented in basalt reliefs from Kef kalesi, overlooking the north-west shore of Lake Van, and in a fragmentary bronze model from Toprakkale [140].

The fortresses are the most widespread monuments to Urartian rule over territories from the upper Euphrates eastwards to Lake Urmia and north to Lake Sevan. They were invariably well built, of the most massive blocks practicable, with a preference for basalt if locally available, this stone beng especially popular for temples and inscriptions. The dimensions of their walls, as visible from surface remains or at excavated sites, on the whole correspond to those given in the detailed letter to the god Assur from Sargon II concerning his eighth campaign (see p. 175). Quality of masonry varied from very rough cyclopean through regular 'bellied' or convex blocks to fine, smoothly dressed ashlar

138. The Altintepe temple has the standard Urartian plan, square with wide shallow corner buttresses and massive walls, suggesting comparison with the 'Cube of Zoroaster' at Naqsh-i Rustam, the royal cemetery of Persepolis. The masonry of these temples was of finely cut and dressed basalt, the superstructure of mud-brick. Two small sockets on either side of the door of the Altintepe temple suggest the spears represented on the Musasir relief. These are appropriate to Haldi, god of war, who accompanied the Urartian kings on campaign, just as spearheads were set up by victorious Assyrian kings. Silver spearheads were among the finds from the temple of Altintepe, clearly votive.

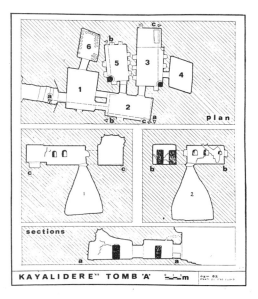

KAYALIDERE" TOMB 'A'

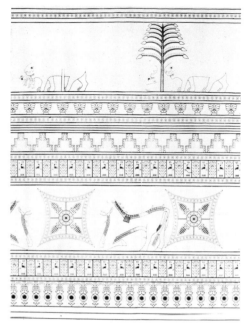

140. At Altintepe the palace was decorated with murals in the court style of Urartu. Here a columned hall, 43.7 × 24.7 m. in area with six rows of three mud-brick columns with stone bases almost 1.5 metres in girth, stands next to the temple with its surrounding court and colonnade. This has been suggested rather improbably as a prototype of the Hall of One Hundred Columns at Persepolis.

141. The curious grid plan of Zernaki Tepe, almost certainly Urartian and of military function, was never completed or occupied.

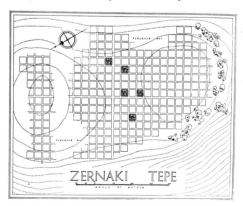

ZERNAKI TEPE

at one site, Çavuştepe. The contours of each site determined the precise perimeter of its defences. Fortresses were sited to command a natural road or a fertile plain, often on a spur projecting from higher ground [142, Pl 29].

Körzüt, near the north-east corner of Lake Van, has a wall of convex dressed blocks with bosses for lifting into position and a gateway wide enough to admit chariots. Menua built other strongholds, some to protect newly won frontiers, such as Qalatgah, overlooking the Ushnu Plain twenty miles west of Hasanlu. Argishti I may have been responsible for the small frontier forts commanding the south-west shore of Lake Sevan, supposed, surely incorrectly, by some Soviet archaeologists to be of Bronze Age date: they are typically Urartian in appearance. The one major citadel attributable to Sarduri II is Çavuştepe, whose fine masonry puts it in a class of its own in Urartu, suggesting it may have been one of this king's principal residences. It seems only a faint possibility that masons may have been specially imported from north Syria, for the Aznavur temple shows the capabilities of Urartian craftsmen fifty years earlier [141, 143].

Some very roughly built strongholds represent places of refuge rather than planned military posts, and may date to the period of rivalry between the Alarodians, the remnant of the Urartian population, and the incoming Armenians in the early Achaemenid empire.

Store-rooms were a principal component of all major Urartian citadels, normally with three rows of huge jars up to two metres high for wine or corn. These have been found at Kayalidere and at later fortresses, with cuneiform or pictographic inscriptions denoting contents and capacity. Sargon II made a point of looting the 'store city' of Ulhu, perhaps Haftavan Tepe in the Salmas Plain at the north-west corner of Lake Urmia, and thus destroying the resources collected by the provincial Urartian administration.

Urartian civilization is distinguished not only by its architecture but also by a wide range of craftsmanship in pottery, metal, ivory and stone. While Assyrian 'palace ware', a thin, highly fired pottery with dimples made by finger impressions, is light in colour and unburnished, in the general Mesopotamian tradition, Urartian pottery is classifiable within the Anatolian tradition of burnished wares, not all wheel-made. The whole range is recognizably different from that in use beyond the frontiers of Urartu [Pl 30].

Bronzeworking seems to have been a particularly flourishing tradition in Urartu, manifest in vessels, furniture and military equipment. Yet it has to be admitted that little of Urartian craftsmanship of any kind survives from the early phases before contact with north Syria began with the western campaigns of Menua. The roles of itinerant craftsmen and of trade in finished articles can be reasonably well understood only with the help of written sources. Bronze components of furniture, including double spiral elements such as had appeared on Assurnasirpal II's chair and foot-stool in reliefs at Nimrud, were found at Kayalidere. These were not so much Urartian as part of the cosmopolitan stock-in-trade of the furniture industry of the Near East in the early first millennium BC. Decorated helmets, shields and quivers demonstrate the wide range of ceremonial military equipment, much of it from Karmir-Blur, taken thither from the earlier, neighbouring citadel of Arinberd. Cavalry and chariotry represented in repoussé on bronze quivers from Karmir-Blur and a fragment of a hunting scene, also in repoussé, from Kayalidere exemplify the importance of horsemanship, confirmed by Assyrian and Urartian written references and by such finds as horse-bits from the tombs at Altintepe. The cire perdue technique of bronze casting is exemplified by two lions from Kayalidere and Patnos [144].

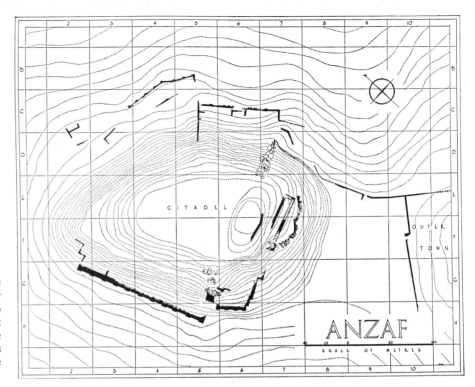

142. At Anzaf, ten miles from Van along the road east to the northern Urmia basin, a lower fort of simple rectangular plan probably dates to Ishpuini, since a column-base with his short building inscription was found next to it. The much larger upper fortress illustrated here has building inscriptions of Menua, and is of the standard plan.

Gold and silver have not survived in great quantity from Urartu, certainly not on the scale of the 393 silver pans and twelve silver shields mentioned by Sargon II as coming from the temple of Musasir. Silver spearheads from Altintepe and a granulated gold earring from Giriktepe deserve mention.

The glyptic art of Urartu is distinctive, including stamp-cylinders, a combination of the stamp- and cylinder-seal.

The debt of Urartian art as a whole to Assyrian, particularly to the formal

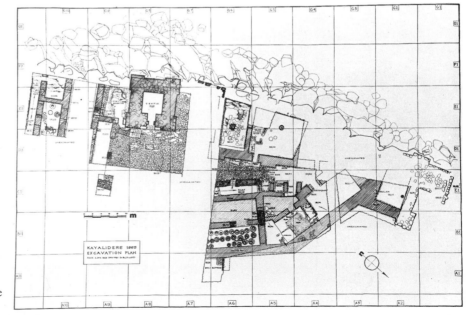

143. The upper citadel at Kayalidere, with the temple (top left) and store-room (lower right).

144. Cauldrons with riveted attachments in the form of a bull's head or a male or female human head are widespread in Urartu and beyond, the best surviving one being from a tomb at Altintepe, on its tripod with feet in the form of bulls' hoofs. Cauldrons of identical type except for the addition of heavy rings occur at Gordion.

145. A lion from Altintepe is the best example of ivory-carving from Urartu, in a style perhaps distinctive of that kingdom.

style of the ninth century BC, was very great. This court style existed side by side with a freer vernacular style, just as the cuneiform script of official inscriptions existed beside pictographs possibly constituting an indigenous script antedating the introduction of cuneiform from Assyria.

THE REVIVAL OF ASSYRIA

Conflict between Urartu and Assyria took a new turn with the seizure of the Assyrian throne by Tiglath–Pileser III (744–727 BC), who by a series of brilliant campaigns rapidly restored the waning power of Assyria. His first objective was to regain control of the trade route to the Mediterranean. To secure this he had first to oust Urartu from its position under Sarduri II of hegemony over an anti-Assyrian alliance. At Kishtan and Halpi on the Euphrates he defeated the Urartian army and its allies; and a few years later he even marched through Van itself (735 BC). The other region of confrontation between the two powers, north-west Iran, was the objective of three seasons of campaigning by Sargon II (716–714 BC), in which he made use of the native Mannaean chieftains against Urartu and the nascent power of the Medes, then allied with Rusa I.

Tiglath–Pileser III has left less behind in the archaeological record than might have been expected. His palace at Nimrud was used as a quarry by Esarhaddon for one of his own: consequently his surviving reliefs are relatively few. His best preserved residences are in Syria, at Til Barsip and at Arslan Tash (Hadatu), which have a traditional Assyrian plan. He reorganized the administration, introducing direct rule through governors over former tribute-paying vassal states. Thus began, with the sack of cities and the more efficient taxation, the accumulation of ivories and other treasures in the palaces of Assyria, a process extended by Sargon II. Under Tiglath–Pileser III the Assyrian army for the first time became largely a regular force, with partly new types of equipment. Chariots were heavier, now having eight- instead of six-spoked wheels, as illustrated on a mural painting at Til Barsip. Crested helmets, perhaps introduced from north Syria where they occur on the Long Wall at Carchemish, and man-size shields turning over at the top for protection against missiles from the defenders during sieges are among new features. Auxiliaries included slingmen, and were generally less well protected than the regulars.

Sargon II decided on a virgin site for his palace, at Khorsabad, not far north-east of Nineveh, with a consequent decline in the status of Nimrud. Never finished, Khorsabad included a large town area of almost one square mile, enclosed by a defensive wall with seven gates and Palace F, probably the house of Sennacherib the crown prince [146]. The palace formed a high bastion overlooking a temple of Nabu (Ezida), with its twin sanctuaries, and four major buildings, each in its plan a miniature palace. The largest (Residence L) is identified by an inscription across the decorated stone threshold, resembling a carpet, as that of Sinahusur, the little known brother and vizier of Sargon II. Residence K was decorated with wall-paintings in the formal Assyrian style.

Khorsabad was decorated with reliefs of war as well as the bull-men and other hieratic themes presumably intended to overawe visitors to the court. The war scenes are now known only from the drawings by Flandin, the artist with the French expedition of Botta and Place: it is generally thought that the sculptures themselves were accidentally sunk in the Tigris. Ninety years later excavations were resumed by Loud, of the Oriental Institute of Chicago, the results of the French expedition being mostly confirmed. Overlooked by the triple entrance to the palace was a great public square, the centre of the whole

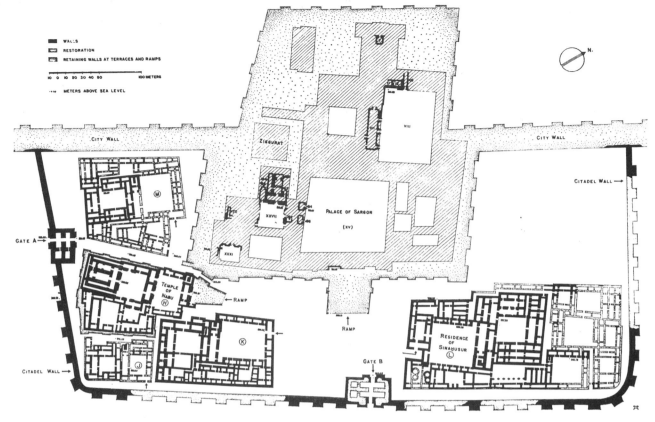

city, whence visitors to the palace ascended a broad ramp, giving access to a large court. From the north-west corner admittance could be gained, through two rooms, to a second large court, whence the throne-room on the south-west side was reached through the huge portals flanked by winged bulls with human heads, the protective *lamassu* previously appearing in the North-West Palace at Nimrud: here at Khorsabad they have five legs, for viewing from front or side. This court was decorated with orthostats depicting Sargon II and his courtiers, larger than life size, an aggrandizement of scale if not of character when compared with earlier reigns. Other state rooms, beyond the throne-room, were grouped round a small inner court. Khorsabad was abandoned for ever on the death of Sargon II in battle: traces of fire hint at violence.

146. Within the main citadel area at the north-west end of the town of Khorsabad stood the king's palace and its associated complex of six temples at the south corner, the latter believed by the French excavators of the nineteenth century to have been the harem.

147. The temple of the moon god Sin, in the Khorsabad palace complex, had a frieze of glazed bricks as a dado right across its facade, standing 1.5 m. high and projecting one metre. It comprised identical processions on either side of the entrance, with the helmeted king and bareheaded vizier on the return of the frieze to the wall face and with a lion, eagle, bull, fig-tree and combined plough and grain-seeder.

THE PHRYGIANS

The civilization of the Phrygian kingdom, centred on the great city of Gordion on the river Sakarya (Sangarius), nowadays easily accessible from Ankara, had features readily distinguishing it from the contemporary civilizations of the late eighth century BC elsewhere in the Near East. It cannot, however, be considered in isolation from the rest of the Anatolian plateau west of the upper Euphrates and the territories of Urartu. Nor is the term 'Phrygian' synonymous with 'Iron Age' in Anatolia. There was throughout a strong underlying legacy from the cultural traditions of the Hittite New Kingdom and its neighbours, especially evident in the confederacy of Tabal. This is known principally from the Assyrian annals, where it appears as a buffer state between Mushki (Phrygia) and Assyria, caught up in an alliance with Urartu against Sargon II. The period of disorder and cultural retrogression in Anatolia, a dark age also in the lack of contemporary evidence, lasted from the twelfth at least into the ninth century BC. Indeed it is possible that the distinctive painted pottery of the so-called 'Early Phrygian' style, characterized by stags with feathery antlers and concentric circles and in due course influencing East Greek pottery, did not appear before the eighth century BC. The evidence against so late a dating, however, includes the sequence of building levels at Büyükkale, the citadel of Boğazköy, where Level II was first established among the ruins of the Hittite capital.

Civilization no doubt survived, if in attenuated form, in scattered strongholds; but there is little of written sources and no coherent archaeological pattern before the late eighth century BC. Archaeological surveys and excavations indicate a radical change in settlement patterns since the second millennium BC, with the foundation of innumerable hilltop sites and the desertion of most, though by no means all, of the earlier settlements in the plains, now each forming a mound (hüyük). Clearly the paramount need for security dictated this change to a distribution of settlements largely continuing into Graeco-Roman times. Earlier hilltop strongholds of the Bronze Age were often reoccupied. At Porsuk, just south of Ulukişla, near the Cilician Gates, massive fortifications of the eighth century BC, contemporary with Alişar IV in the Halys bend of central Anatolia, were preceded by earlier defences. A much larger city was at Göllüdag in the province of Niğde, on a hilltop 2,143 m. high with a crater lake. Its area of three square kilometres, its wall with three surviving gates, its regularly laid out buildings and streets and its central complex with twin-headed lion statues at the entrance, sphinxes on the inner portal and column-bases with four lions all indicate its importance. The burning of the city in the eighth century BC is possibly to be associated with Phrygian expansion eastwards. Another impressive Iron Age citadel is that of Havuz Köy, south of Sivas, with a dressed stone glacis as part of its defensive perimeter: this must have taken a long time to construct, and thus cannot have been built against any sudden incursion, such as that of the Cimmerian raiders from the south Russian steppes, soon after 715 BC.

The excavations at Gordion have revealed a succession of relatively humble occupation levels, yet indicating continuity of settlement, preceding the apogee of the Phrygian kingdom in the eighth century BC, and its subsequent destruction by the Cimmerians (variously dated between 696 and 676 BC, traditionally to 685 BC). The city of Gordion was defended by a massive mud-brick wall: its gateway was of masonry of modest sized stones, with a slight batter and set diagonally to the alignment of the streets within, suggesting the possibility of a star-shaped plan, as depicted on an Assyrian relief of an Anatolian town. Within the Phrygian city the Terraced Building comprised a series of large galleried rooms, each with its anteroom, thus repeating the traditional Anatolian *megaron* plan. Timber was extensively used in the buildings of the eighth century BC at Gordion, with mud-brick or stone. Vertical and horizontal beams and cross-ties were used in one building, the West Phrygian House. The *megaron* reached its full development in Phrygia, *Megaron* 3 being 9.74 m. wide. Gabled roofs are well attested: by the carved façades of rock-cut shrines in the highlands at the source of the Sakarya river; and at Gordion by graffiti on buildings and especially by the wooden chamber of the great tumulus.

Among the outstanding achievements of Phrygian civilization was woodworking, in buildings and in furniture. No fewer than six different kinds of wood were used for the tomb-chamber and contents of Tumulus P at Gordion: the chamber itself was constructed of black pine, while boxwood, yew, pear, maple and poplar were used for the furniture and other wooden artefacts. Of these only pine and poplar are common in the region today. Logs of Syrian juniper and cedar also occur at Gordion. The double-pitched roof of the chamber of the great tumulus, when opened in 1957 found to be still supporting the superimposed mound of clay and the immediately overlying layer of stones, was in its turn supported by three gables, one at the centre and one at each end. In this design and in the careful squaring and mortising of its planks it seems to have resembled contemporary wooden houses in the villages if not also in the city. The squared planks of the chamber walls were enclosed in an outer casing of juniper logs, two feet square in secton; outside these was a layer of rubble, contained by a strong retaining wall [148].

The continuation of the Phrygian skill in making furniture is evident from a reference to men of Sardis as making inlaid woodwork for a palace of Darius I at Susa (*c.* 490 BC): this was but one of the legacies of the Phrygian kingdom to its Lydian successor.

A variety of textiles—carpets, tapestries and garments—is attested in Phrygia by surviving examples and indirect evidence, including a mosaic floor of coloured pebbles in geometric patterns. Up to twenty layers of linen and wool were found over the bed in the chamber of the great tumulus; and traces of purplish material on the bed and the seat of the throne in Tumulus P could suggest the association of this colour with royalty even in this period. Linen and hemp were woven, and mohair from the wool of the Ankara goat. Sheep provided a stable element in the economy of Phrygia, not least for their wool, which external trade alone could never assure.

Not only the skill but also the prosperity of Phrygia in the late eighth century BC is attested by its arts and craftsmanship. In addition to woodwork and weaving, the products of the bronzesmiths exhibit a facility in mass production, especially in the cast bronze bowls with countersunk (omphalos) base and petal pattern. Such bowls need not have been of Phrygian origin, since they were represented on Assyrian reliefs; but present evidence suggests they probably were. Heavy safety-pin brooches, commonly called fibulae, were in general use, as illustrated by the figure of king Urpalla of Tyana on the Ivriz rock relief and by the hoard of 146 from the great tumulus at Gordion. Cauldrons with protomes were imported, using rings for ease of carriage, either from north Syria or, more probably, from Urartu.

Oriental influences are apparent in the great tumulus in two bronze situlae, or drinking cups, probably imported from the Assyrian empire, one with a

148. Wooden chair-back from the great tumulus at Gordion. Joints were made by mortising, for the planks of the tomb chambers, or by small dowels, doubtless reinforced by glue, for the beds, chairs, tables and screens found with the burials. The likeliest explanation for the absence of nails is a long tradition of carpentry rather than any dearth of iron or bronze, in whose working the Phrygians were also expert. The inlaid patterns on the furniture are dominated by a distinctively Phrygian motif, the meander. One of the large bronze cauldrons from the tumuli shows clear signs of wear: otherwise the furniture, portable and elaborate but rather flimsy, might seem to have been made for the tomb only.

149. The Midas Monument and the other early shrines of the Phrygian period reproduce more faithfully than later groups the representation of the facade of a gabled building. The rectilinear pattern employed as ornamentation on the Monument of Midas seems to represent terracotta tiles, although an ultimate derivation from inlaid woodwork or textiles is probable. A similar origin in textiles may be sought for the remarkable pebble mosaic floor in one of the *megara* of Gordion. Though the cult of water divinities may have played its part, the dominant role in Phrygian religion and thus in these rock-cut shrines was that of the Great Mother.

150. A bronze bowl with a smear of wax bearing a Phrygian inscription shows how much must have perished, perhaps also from Anatolian regions outside Phrygia; and it recalls the waxed ivory writing boards used in Assyria and found at Nimrud.

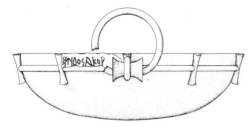

ram's and the other with a lion's head: the eyes are inlaid with white paste, the pupils are of black stone. At Khorsabad servants are depicted filling cups with wine from cauldrons of this form. In Tumulus P three blue faience vessels and a bowl of clear glass, with omphalos and imitating the standard types of bronze bowl at Gordion, are probably imports. Syro-Hittite influence is evident in relief-carved orthostats from the city; but sculpture seems not to have been one of the outstanding skills of Phrygia.

The habit of burying members of the royal dynasty in tumuli or barrows, of which there are eighty at Gordion, was derived from the south Russian steppes and became widespread in Anatolia during the Iron Age, when other concentrations occur, such as one in Kazova in the Pontic region. Tumuli can indeed be taken as an indicator of Iron Age settlement. The evidence from Gordion, however, shows the heterogeneous nature of burial customs in this period. Cremation, the invariable rule in the cemeteries of Carchemish (Yunus) and Hamath, became more universal in western Anatolia between the Cimmerian invasion (traditionally dated 685 BC) and the Persian conquest of Lydia (547 BC). It was not the royal custom at Gordion; but of three minor tumuli in the cemetery area south-east of the great tumulus one had a wooden burial chamber, another a cremation and another a plain cist-grave dug into the earth. Cist-graves and urn-burials might contain inhumations or cremations. In the royal tombs the body and offerings were inserted from above, before the chamber was roofed over and the mound of the tumulus piled over it. This greatly varied in size: the great tumulus at Gordion—containing the extended burial of an old man of short stature, lying on a bed, tentatively identified as king Gordios—stood some 55 m. high; but the vast majority are much smaller. Wooden markers were used at Gordion to mark the location of the chamber beneath the mound.

The Phrygians were instrumental in the diffusion of the alphabet westward from its original Phoenician home, the surviving examples of their script being no later than the most archaic Greek inscriptions of the eighth century BC. Phrygian inscriptions of Mita (Midas) occur at Midas City (Yazilikaya), south-west of Gordion, and as far east as Tyana (Bor) [150].

Phrygian religion centred largely round the cult of the Great Mother, the Luvian Kubaba, Phrygian Kubila and Lydian Kybele or Kybebe, and thus had its roots in the Anatolian past. Close to a large Phrygian hilltop town, the Midas City, was the concentration of rock-cut religious monuments and tombs often given the general name of Phrygian Yazilikaya. These shrines and tombs, as well as the Midas City, date to two periods of the height of the Phrygian kingdom (late eighth century BC) and of the Lydian supremacy (late seventh and early sixth centuries BC). The interval was a time of decline, the result of the Cimmerian raids from the sack of Gordion to that of Sardis (652 BC). Early travellers erroneously described all the rock monuments as tombs, whereas the finer façades are almost all of shrines. The greatest tomb of the high Phrygian period is Arslan Taş, whose two great lions on either side of the small doorway have been described as being in the Hittite tradition, yet in a more vigorous and less conventional style. Humbler rock-cut chamber tombs are typical of Phrygian citadels in this and other regions of Anatolia [149].

In architecture, arts, technology, music and writing Phrygia was ahead of Greece, not in her debt. Earlier Anatolian and contemporary Assyrian and Urartian influences were, however, significant. Metalwork of Anatolian origin—including cauldrons, bowls, stands, fibulae and belt clasps—occurs in Ionian contexts in the late eighth century BC at Heraion in Samos, Emporio in Chios, Ephesus, Smyrna and Mytilene. These finds could suggest contacts simply between the Phrygian hinterland and the Ionian coast. Overland trade from farther east through Phrygia is most clearly indicated by cauldron attachments from Samos. The degree of isolation of Phrygia in the time of its greatest prosperity and power from the Greek cities is more marked than any evidence of contact.

NORTH-WESTERN IRAN

North-western Iran in the Iron II period, now dated c. 1100–800 BC, underwent a diversification into local cultural provinces after the widespread disruption caused by the first Iranian incomers in the Iron I period. Urban life revived in some parts, most notably at Hasanlu (Period IV). At Haftavan the mound was largely occupied by cemeteries. No other site in western Iran is yet known to have enjoyed as early as the eleventh century BC a prosperity comparable with that of Hasanlu IV. The development of the citadel continued, however, into the ninth century BC, until the final holocaust, perhaps the work of the Urartian king Menua (c. 800 BC). He or his son Argishti I seem to have been responsible for the fortifications, comprising a wall of large thin slabs of local stone, with two buttresses between each pair of large towers.

In common with Haftavan and other sites, the mound of Hasanlu comprises a higher citadel and a surrounding lower town, the general contours having been determined before the Iron II period, when the public buildings stood on the citadel. Two protected roads led up from the outer town below, the home of most

151. Phrygian pottery was indigenous, most typical being the Iron Age grey ware of western Anatolia, whose forms are in part found also in the painted pottery of central Anatolia and the Pontic region, termed Alişar IV ware and found as far south-east as Arslantepe (Malatya). The pottery generally indicates a cultural division between the truly Phrygian lands and those lying to the east, in part briefly annexed in the eighth century BC.

152. Five main buildings have been distinguished at Hasanlu, four of them facing on to the Lower Court, reached by a road from the West Gate, which in turn gave access to steps up to the Upper Court, flanked by Burned Building I East and West. While the interpretation of Burned Building II as a temple remains possible, it seems more likely, from their common basic plan, that all these buildings were palaces or at least important residences, Building V ending its days as a stable. Perhaps the buildings should be interpreted as components of one architectural complex, elaborated after the first fire by the addition of porticoes, but retaining their columned hall, anteroom, staircase and store-rooms.

of the inhabitants and of their cemeteries. Public buildings of comparably impressive scale, and approximately of the same period, have been excavated at Kortlar, between Reza'iyeh and Lake Reza'iyeh (Urmia). Hasanlu had been the principal settlement in the Solduz Plain, immediately south of Lake Urmia, for several millennia [152].

Burned Building I at Hasanlu, later and larger than the others, centred round a hall with four rows of columns, having a small open light-well with paved floor and drainage into a storage jar, a wide bench in the north-west corner, a central raised platform for the fireplace and at the back of the hall a brick platform with two steps up to it, perhaps a throne-base. The long life of this building is demonstrated by the replastering of the fireplace over one hundred times. Burned Building II had a hall with two rows of four free-standing columns, and here were found the skeletons of twenty-one young women, a similar phenomenon being found at the Urartian palace of Giriktepe, near Patnos: each was grasping one of the bronze lions with an iron peg long known to be characteristic of Hasanlu. At the west end of the façade stood one stele, facing three others up to 4.5 m. high, the other stelae being in front of Burned Building IV on the opposite side of the Lower Court. All these stelae are quite undecorated and uninscribed. Behind Burned Building II was a kitchen area, just inside the later Urartian perimeter wall. In the middle of its entrance was a stone platform or dais. The skilful use of timber is demonstrated by the very wide entrances to these buildings of Hasanlu IV, with three pairs of wooden columns set on stone slabs supporting the lintel. Burned Building III closely reproduced the plan of the Period V (Iron I) building mentioned in the last chapter. In Burned Building V were four horses, and outside it remains of bronze horse-trappings, one of many examples of the prominence of horsemanship in north-western Iran, further attested by Assyrian references to tribute of horses from this region.

The greater proportion of valuable artefacts from Burned Building I was found in debris belonging to the upper storey, suggesting that the principal living quarters in these buildings were upstairs; there may even have been a third storey in Burned Building I, including an arsenal, hinted at by a quantity of iron lanceheads and sword-blades. The variety of vessels and weapons from the citadel and graves of Hasanlu and of personal ornaments from graves there and at Haftavan bears ample witness to the versatility of the Iron II culture. The jewellery of Hasanlu includes clustered gold earrings larger than, but similar to, examples from two cemeteries to the east, at Khorvin and Sialk B. By the ninth century BC Assyrian imports, including cylinder-seals and glazed wall tiles of white, black, yellow and blue, have appeared at Hasanlu; but, given its geographical proximity to Assyria, the weakness of Mesopotamian influence is remarkable. Hasanlu was in an altogether different world from Nimrud.

The pottery of Hasanlu IV, developing from Iron I forms, includes jars with horizontally bridged spout: this is the most readily recognizable Iron II form throughout north-western Iran, found in grey ware or, at Haftavan IV, in red ware. The 'palace ware' of Hasanlu, giving a variety not found at minor Iron II sites, betrays the strong influence of metal vessels, as in the use of gadrooning. Bronzesmiths had attained their highest skill and productivity; iron, though becoming commoner, was still valuable enough to be used for personal ornaments, such as bracelets for a girl buried at Haftavan, and not to be spared for arrowheads. Not till the eighth century BC did iron come into more general use in Iran.

Ivory work from Hasanlu suggests contacts with Hamath in Syria. Less certain is the Assyrian influence on a silver beaker, with figures inlaid in electrum, including two soldiers in a horse-drawn chariot: the style is not unlike that of the reliefs of Assurnasirpal II. The famous gold bowl is generally agreed to date to a period well before the sack of Hasanlu IV (c. 800 BC); and the one plausible interpretation of its crowded scenes is in terms of the Hurrian myth of Kummarbi [Pl 31].

In Trans-Caucasia the cultures of the late second millennium BC, which had interacted with the Iron I culture of north-west Iran, continued largely unchanged in the ninth century BC. The Koban-Colchidic culture in the west, with its metal industry, still flourished; and the Gandja–Karabagh culture in the central areas and the Kayakent–Chorochoi culture in the east, along the western shores of the Caspian Sea and in Daghestan, persisted, beyond the orbit of Urartian influence [153].

The Urmia basin during the eighth century BC is most clearly documented by the longest and most detailed of all surviving Assyrian military records, the letter to the god Assur setting out the events of Sargon II's eighth campaign (714 BC). This refers to numerous towns, among them Ulhu, perhaps identifiable with Haftavan III, with its Urartian governmental building or civilian citadel. To the south the frontier was extended beyond the lake, with an Urartian fortress at Qalatgah commanding the fertile Ushnu valley and a small fort or police post at Agrab Tepe, close to Hasanlu, itself newly fortified. The indigenous cultural traditions of Iron II largely persisted; but the impact of the Urartian administration is the one clear feature in the archaeologically obscure landscape.

The bronze industry of one region of western Iran, Luristan, first became known as the result of local tomb-robbing about 1932, since when it has achieved exaggerated prominence. The long continuity of metalworking, influenced at times variously by Mesopotamia and Elam, can now be demonstrated by grave-groups from the mid-third millennium BC onwards. The distinctive 'Luristan bronzes' as such belong to a relatively short period, equivalent to Iron II and IIIA (tenth–seventh centuries BC), when local traditions were best able to flourish unhampered by external influences. The chronological evidence rules out the theory of a Cimmerian origin, since those nomads did not appear before the eighth century BC. The metallurgical evidence likewise indicates the indigenous background of this industry, which cannot accurately be termed 'Luristan'. Nomadic intrusions there certainly were, and variations between different parts of Luristan. But cultural continuity persisted until the upheavals of the end of the seventh century BC, the destruction of Elam and the rise of Media [154].

THE LEVANT IN THE NINTH AND EIGHTH CENTURIES BC
In the Levant in the ninth and eighth centuries BC there was a remarkable conjunction of different cultural traditions. This was brought about partly by the military penetration of the region by Assyria, with brief Urartian intervention in north Syria brought to an end by Tiglath–Pileser III (c. 743 BC), but more significantly by trade. In this the Phoenicians played the leading role, but with Greek colonists at Al Mina (Posideion) establishing a foothold at the mouth of the Orontes (c. 825 BC). Al Mina ended the virtual Phoenician monopoly of Levantine maritime trade. In Cyprus, though there is no historical reference to Phoenician control before the late eighth century BC, Black-on-Red ware flasks and other pottery suggest Phoenician settlers or at least traders in the south-east

153. Elaborately decorated bronze axes, of which this is an unusually fine specimen, and bands or belts are typical of late Koban burials, perhaps being made first in the Koban area of the north Caucasus and diffused thence throughout Trans-Caucasia. Associated with these belts are iron daggers and fibulae of simple bow type, the latter supporting a dating to the eighth century BC, both for the late Koban burials and for the Iron Age cemeteries of Trialeti, where cist-graves have been found at Maralyn Deresi and elsewhere. Here contacts with Luristan are demonstrated by swords with double splayed pommel. Urartu could conquer much of the region, but could not destroy its indigenous craftsmanship.

154. The distinctive products of the workshops in and around Luristan comprised elaborate votive pins, iron swords, bronze standard-finials and a wealth of horse-trappings, including harness-rings and decorated cheek-pieces for horse-bits as shown above.

of the island from the late ninth century BC. The arrival of the Greeks brought about commercial rivalry, and eventually the Phoenicians were willing to serve as naval forces for the Achaemenid Persian empire against Greece; but in many places, both on the mainland and in Cyprus, a blending of these two cultures took place, the strongest influence being from east to west. This is perhaps most significant in the adoption by the Greeks of the Phoenician alphabet, in its turn derived from the Canaanite script of *c.* 1000 BC and thus from cuneiform, first written alphabetically at Ugarit.

The dating evidence for the Greek colony of Posideion (Al Mina) rests mainly on two classes of pottery, Black-on-Red and Red Slip wares. The occurrence, even if in small quantities, of Black-on-Red ware along the coast from Al Mina southwards—at Tell Sukas, Tell Abu Hawam, Ashkelon and elsewhere—suggests a rapid extension of Greek trade, once its revival after the 'dark age' became established. Red Slip ware had had a very wide distribution, from Jordan and Hamath north to the Amuq Plain and across the Euphrates to Tell Halaf (Guzana), being imported to Nimrud by the time of Sargon II [155].

Among the beneficiaries of the growth of maritime trade were the petty rulers of Cyprus, of whom ten are named by Esarhaddon of Assyria (681–669 BC). One is Damusi, king of Karti-Hadasti, probably to be identified with Kition, just outside Larnaca. The height of prosperity in Cyprus is represented by the rich burials in masonry tombs with a wide, gently sloping entrance passage (*dromos*) at Salamis, five miles north of Famagusta. The very position of this town, on the east coast of Cyprus, stresses the economic and cultural links with the Phoenician homeland, comparable with those of Enkomi, situated nearby, until its final desertion (*c.* 1050 BC). The Late Bronze Age cities of Cyprus, including Enkomi and Kition, were finally destroyed by an earthquake (*c.* 1075 BC). Yet there seems to have been some continuity of settlement, however attenuated, since remains of the early eleventh century BC have been found at Salamis, which began its history as a modest port. These early centuries fall within the Cypro-Geometric period.

In the eighth century BC (Cypro-Geometric III) Salamis expanded greatly, the old cemetery being built over and a new one founded much farther west. The major tombs were equipped with a variety of pottery, metalwork, furniture, horses and chariots, dating to late eighth and early seventh century BC. Phoenician influence is especially clear in the ivory-work.

All too little is known of the Phoenician homeland in the ninth and eighth centuries BC; but the impact of Phoenician culture is nowhere more apparent than in the kingdom of Israel, less so in its small southern neighbour, Judah. The division of Solomon's kingdom was in due course followed by the removal of the capital of Israel to the new site of Samaria (880 BC), from Tirzah (Tell el Farah) not far to the east. The Old Testament relates the religious conflict of the prophetic party, leading the followers of Yahveh, against the insidious Phoenician influence, as they saw it, of the royal entourage, especially in the reign of Ahab (874–852 BC).

Samaria has proved to be not only historically significant but especially important in clarification of the complexities of Iron Age archaeology in Palestine, these being largely created by archaeologists themselves. More firmly than Hazor or Megiddo, Samaria can be related to chronological fixed points. Thus the first six periods fall within the lifetime of the kingdom of Israel (880–720 BC), from the foundation of the city to its capture by the Assyrians. Periods I–II are distinguished by masonry of the fine quality and Proto-Aeolic capitals readily attributable to imported Phoenician builders, with the same origin for the ivories. These form one of the few groups, from Ahab's 'House of Ivory', securely dated to the ninth century BC, like those from Arslan Tash in north Syria. The later building phases at Samaria show a marked deterioration in the standard of masonry, commonly attributed to the employment of less skilled Israelites. The ceramic sequence for Samaria, including Period VII (720–587 BC), correlated with that from the contemporary levels at Hazor, gives the framework for other sites in Palestine, with modifications for those in Judah.

Substantial buildings were erected in Ahab's time in Hazor VIII, which had a rock-cut water system, comparable with that of Late Bronze Age date at Megiddo. Provision of water was a major problem for most towns in Israel and Judah. Hazor VIII was refortified to include the whole citadel mound; there was also a building with monolithic piers. The size of towns was modest: Megiddo covered thirteen, Lachish eighteen and Tell Beit Mersim only seven and a half acres. A quasi-circular perimeter occurs both at Tell Beit Mersim A, as in the earlier Stratum B, and at Beth Shemesh IIB, west of Jerusalem.

A period of prosperity was enjoyed by both Israel and Judah under Jeroboam II and Uzziah in the mid-eighth century BC, when Uzziah imposed stricter control over the Negev than since the days of Solomon, with construction of a chain of forts, some large strongholds and a number of terraces and cisterns to develop agriculture, a foretaste of the work of the Nabataeans in this arid region. Rough masonry walls have been located in many places. The smelter and trading-post of Ezion-Geber (Elath) was revived in Stratum II, plausibly attributed to Jehoshaphat (873–849 BC), the contemporary of Ahab, whose attempt to re-establish the Red Sea trade was frustrated by the wreck of his ships in a storm. Uzziah (779–740 BC) is recorded as having rebuilt Elath and having restored it to Judah: to him therefore may be ascribed Stratum III, when the settlement first grew into a real township, with houses occupying the whole walled area not taken up by the smelting furnace. The Judaean hold on Elath was never very secure, however, and it was probably in the reign of Uziah's grandson Ahaz (c. 735 BC) that the Judaeans were for ever expelled thence by their constant rivals, the Edomites. To them, therefore, may be attributed the remains of Stratum IV, which with three sub-phases continued into the Persian period. The cultural and ethnic connections of the population, partly evident from their pottery, lay more with the east than with the lands west of the Dead Sea and the Wadi Arabah.

Hazor, in the extreme north of Israel, suffered a series of disasters necessitating rebuilding. The pillared building of Hazor VIII was surrounded by a residential quarter in VII, destroyed perhaps by the Aramaeans from Damascus (c. 800 BC). Then Hazor VI, of the time of Jeroboam II, was destroyed by earthquake (c. 760 BC). There is a correlation between written and archaeological evidence in the destruction of Hazor V by Tiglath-Pileser III (732 BC). Thereafter the town became impoverished. Megiddo III has a grid plan quite atypical of Palestine: it could belong to the period of Jeroboam II, in which case it was at least partially destroyed by Tiglath-Pileser III (734 BC). The prosperity of this building level at Megiddo fits better into this period than into that of the Assyrian occupation, probably represented by Megiddo II, with a fortress as its only important structure.

The prosperity of both kingdoms was all too short-lived, for the power of renascent Assyria was not to leave them long undisturbed. From 734 BC onwards Israel was absorbed, first in part, then, fourteen years later, in entirety into the

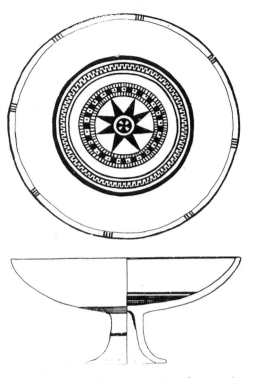

155. Black-on-Red ware remains of uncertain affinities—a problem in the archaeology of the ninth and eighth centuries BC in the north-east Mediterranean. Sheer quantity of finds and degree of attention by archaeologists have tended to over-emphasize the role of Cyprus, where this pottery appeared suddenly: it was evidently imported, Cypriot products being of second-class quality. One possible source is the Lebanon; but the wide distribution in Anatolia, eventually as far north as the Pontic region, with the continuity of Aegean influence in Cilicia and the presence of a factory at Tarsus, tend to support an Anatolian origin.

Assyrian empire. The new overlord exerted cultural influence as far south as Buseirah, capital of the Edomite kingdom in south Trans-Jordan. Northern types of pottery, especially the wheel-burnished bowls, penetrated into Judah, and can be regarded as a hall-mark of its later period, first under Assyrian suzerainty and finally under attack by the Neo-Babylonian forces.

The underlying continuity of ceramic development in Palestine, in spite of successive imports, can perhaps be taken as symptomatic of a relatively backward, conservative material culture.

Jerusalem remained in Jebusite hands until captured by David; and the Middle Bronze Age defences, built *c.* 1800 BC, were in use for a thousand years. The first rebuilding of these has vanished, the most important discovery of the period being a cave outside the line of the wall, containing a deposit of intact pottery suggesting a date of *c.* 800 BC, and indicating a shrine presumably of one of the unorthodox cults mentioned in the Bible [157].

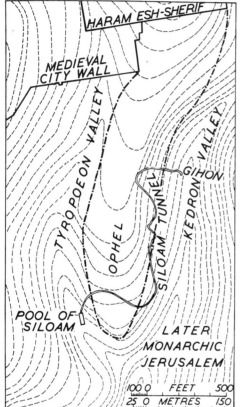

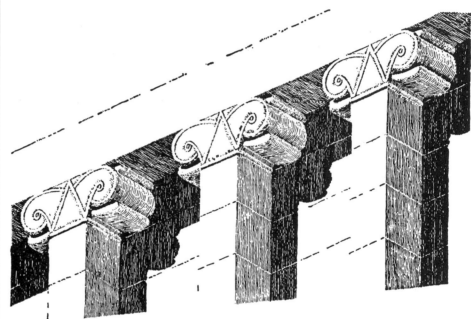

157. Remains of the rebuildings of the defences of Jerusalem, including work attributable to Hezekiah. His most famous achievement was the cutting of the Siloam tunnel, to bring the water from the spring Gihon to a roofed cistern, concealed from any enemy and thus safe, even though not within the walls. The growing threat from Assyria demanded drastic measures.

156. The entrance to the Israelite capital of Samaria, decorated with proto-aeolic capitals. Samaria was planned with the whole plateau within the defences laid out as a royal quarter, found badly preserved owing to later damage. This was the one town of any size founded by the Israelites, who elsewhere reoccupied older settlements, often, as at Hazor, on a scale not approaching that of the heyday of Canaanite civilization.

7

The Near East in a New Era: from the Last Years of Assyria

Sennacherib (705–681 BC) began his reign by rebuilding and enlarging Nineveh, henceforth the Assyrian capital. He stabilized the northern and eastern frontiers, but campaigned as far as Judah in the reign of Hezekiah (700 BC). Assyrian difficulties with Babylonia came to a head in this reign. The far south had its ancient cities largely isolated by Chaldaean tribes, though urban communities remained strong in Babylonia proper, with the citizens of Babylon looking to Assyria for help. Normally the Assyrian kings tried to control populous Babylonia only indirectly. Anti-Assyrian sentiments were always latent, and finally brought a violent reaction from Sennacherib, culminating in the sack of Babylon (689 BC). After a period of peace, the 'brothers' war' ended in the fall of Babylon to Assurbanipal (648 BC): in some respects this had been a civil war, Babylonian resistance being stiffened by Assyrians. This, with the losses in Babylonian campaigns, inevitably weakened the state.

Meanwhile Urartu, under Rusa II (c. 685–645 BC), enjoyed a cultural and military revival. Relations with Assyria were peaceful. Soon afterwards, however, the Scythian hordes invaded Urartu, passed south as far as Palestine and ended Assyrian rule west of the Euphrates. This allowed Josiah of Judah to achieve a brief restoration of the kingdom of Solomon, at the same time enforcing the centralization of the cult of Yahveh in Jerusalem and the abolition of idolatrous sanctuaries.

Assurbanipal (668–627 BC), the last great Assyrian king, campaigned repeatedly against the old enemy, Elam, finally obliterating it and sacking its ancient capital, Susa (c. 640 BC). This removed a buffer between Assyria and the rapidly growing power of the Medes, held in check by the twenty-eight-year rule of the Scyths in 'Upper Asia' (653–625 BC), as recounted by Herodotus. The overthrow of the Scythian power eliminated the last obstacle to the downfall of Assyria under the attacks of Babylonian and Median armies (614–612 BC).

The old Mesopotamian world lingered on, even reviving under the Neo-Babylonian dynasty. When its empire, including Susiana, fell to the new power of Cyrus the Persian, he was greeted—by Babylonians as by the Jews—with good reason as the harbinger of a new era (539 BC).

SENNACHERIB AND NINEVEH

The reign of Sennacherib is sometimes looked on as the golden age of Assyria. There is a certain truth in this, since his predecessors had expanded and secured the limits of Assyrian rule on almost every front. Only Babylon remained a problem, and one which Assyria was never for long to solve, driving Sennacherib eventually to depart from the wiser policy of tolerance by the destruction of the city itself and the removal of the statue of its chief god, Marduk (689 BC).

158. **158.** On the walls of his 'Palace without a Rival', Sennacherib caused to be depicted the hauling of colossal bull-men for his palace portals on sledges towed by gangs of workmen, and others shown here slowly climbing the citadel mound to empty their baskets of stones and earth, overlooked by a line of the royal guard with spears, round wickerwork shields and crested helmets.

The first two years of his reign were spent by Sennacherib in rebuilding and enlarging the ancient city of Nineveh, where he established the capital, as it was to be till the fall of Assyria (612 BC). It is unusually fortunate that a record of this building activity survives not only on the ground, in the excavated palace and other structures and in the city defences, but also in inscriptions and reliefs, notably among the many reliefs from Sennacherib's 'Palace Without a Rival'— the South-West Palace excavated by Layard in the mid-nineteenth century [158]. Layard was primarily interested in extracting the greatest number of carved orthostats from this palace, where, as he himself stated: '. . . I had opened no less than seventy-one halls, chambers and passages, whose walls, almost without exception, had been panelled with slabs of sculptured alabaster recording the wars, the triumphs and the great deeds of the Assyrian king. By a rough calculation about 9,880 feet or nearly two miles of bas-reliefs, with twenty-seven portals, formed by colossal winged bulls and lion-sphinxes, were uncovered in that part alone of the building explored during my researches.' At least he left a record of his discoveries; nor were all these slabs removed. Later excavations, in the inter-war period, revealed that little but the kitchen quarters had been untouched by Layard and his associate Rassam.

Even today much remains to be investigated at Nineveh. The ruins are substantially of Sennacherib's work, with extra, unfinished defences along the vulnerable east side, thrown up perhaps shortly before the final assault by the Medes and Babylonians. The perimeter of the main wall of Nineveh was nearly eight miles long, of masonry with a mud-brick superstructure, having stone stepped parapets, like those at Ashur, and towers. The outer defences comprised two large ditches and walls, placed alternately. Layard estimated the main north gateway to have stood 33 m. high: it comprised two chambers and three gates, the inner and outer one formed by human-headed bulls. A similar but unsculptured gateway was later found in the inner wall on the east side, its two guard-rooms being about 26 × 7.5 m. in area, including the roadway through the centre.

There was thus much more to the rebuilding of Nineveh than the palace alone. The defences had to be built to enclose an area large enough for the population of the city, plausibly stated in the Old Testament (Jonah IV, 11) to have numbered 120,000. As Assurnasirpal II had done for Nimrud, Sennacherib secured a reliable water supply for Nineveh, of which he has left an account in a rock inscription at Bavian. In constructing one of the canals bringing water from the hills iron pick-axes were used, and Sennacherib achieved an engineering feat more in keeping with Roman than Assyrian times: this was the acqueduct spanning a valley at Jerwan, about 300 m. long, with a maximum width of about 25 m. There were five ogival arches, one of which survives; and the water channel was constructed of well-jointed slabs coated with cement as waterproofing.

Sennacherib's inscriptions repeatedly stress his repair and enlargement of the city, especially the foundation platform of the palace, and thus of the whole citadel of Kuyunjik, the larger of the two citadel mounds; the other, Nebi Yunus, was chosen for a palace and arsenal by Esarhaddon. Water was brought primarily for the gardens of the people of Nineveh and for the park which Sennacherib planted, 'like Mount Amanus, wherein were set out all kinds of herbs and fruit trees. . . .' Cotton, the 'wool-bearing tree', was now introduced. The king had the work on his palace recorded thus: 'Lest in the passing of days its platform should give way before the floods of high water, I set up great slabs of limestone around its walls, and strengthened its structure; over these I filled in the terrace to a height of 170 courses of brickwork, I added to the site of the former palace . . . Thereon I had them build a palace of ivory, maple, boxwood, mulberry, cedar, cypress, spruce and pistachio, the "Palace without a Rival", for my royal abode.' In another inscription we read that '. . . Portals, patterned after a Hittite [i.e. north Syrian] palace, I had constructed in front of the doors; with beams of cedar and cypress, whose scent is pleasant, products of Amanus and Sirara the snow-capped mountains, I roofed them. Door-leaves of cedar, cypress and spruce I bound with a band of silver and copper and set them up in their doorways . . . the dark colour of the roofing timbers in the chambers I brightened [painted?] . . .'.

In Assyria the position of the king was more assured than in Babylon. He did not have to undergo the annual coronation, or the taking the hands of Bel. He was the high priest of his people, and his ritual duties loomed large, dictating

159. Assyrian relief carving was destined to reach its highest level in the poignant lion-hunting scenes from the palace of Sennacherib's grandson Assurbanipal, seen here. But already in the earlier reign the strict adherence to registers, recording each successive phase of a victorious campaign in strips, was frequently abandoned in favour of a freer rendering, even with a rudimentary representation of the landscape background. This is discernible, for example, in the reliefs of Sennacherib's siege of Lachish in Judah (700 BC) and also in those of his campaign against the marsh-dwellers at the mouth of the Tigris—Euphrates, to be seen in the British Museum. The use of registers, however, was never wholly superseded.

the lay-out of palace and temples. But he never claimed divinity, as the Pharaohs of Egypt did; and he is shown little more than life size in the reliefs. The gods of Assyria, save for Assur in his winged solar emblem drawing his bow to aid the Assyrian army, seldom appear in the reliefs. They are more frequent in the designs of the royal cylinder-seals. Therefore two rock reliefs in the hills near Nineveh of the reign of Sennacherib, at Maltai and Bavian, are particularly interesting for their representation of processions of gods and goddesses. Not all are indisputably identifiable, partly owing to changes in the order of precedence. Each deity is mounted on an animal, his or her particular attribute, following the traditional iconography of Hurrian origin manifest at Yazilikaya [159, 160].

Sennacherib was one of the Assyrian kings especially interested in acquiring a royal library, including copies of Sumerian and Akkadian tablets which would otherwise have been utterly lost to posterity. These were made by the scribes employed by the king, who seems to have taken a deep interest in the art of tablet-writing. It was Assurbanipal who achieved most in collecting together a library, now largely in the British Museum. His claim to complete mastery of cuneiform must have been exaggerated, for a very lengthy and sustained training was required. The scribes specialized in temple, priestly, medical, business or military affairs. These highest achievements of Assyrian cuneiform literature came at a time when Aramaic had come to be widely used as a spoken language in Assyria, and Aramaic inscriptions on tablets occur in the reign of Sennacherib. At the same time Sumerian was zealously studied, though long a dead language, and Sumerian names were given to the palace and gates of Nineveh.

Assyrian civilization was thus still developing, in the visual arts and in literature alike, at the very time when external forces and internal weaknesses were about to bring about decline and ultimate downfall.

URARTU

During the early seventh century BC Urartu made a remarkable recovery from the setbacks and disasters inflicted by Assyria and by the raiding Cimmerians

coming through the Caucasus (715 BC) and irrupting all over Anatolia. In part only, this recovery was the outcome of détente with Assyria in the face of the common danger from the northern steppes. Under Rusa II (c. 685–645 BC) there seems to have been extensive administrative reorganization of the kingdom. A new royal city, Rusahinili, on the spur called Toprakkale ('earth castle') three miles east of Van citadel, was founded, as well as the fortress of Kefkalesi overlooking from a high hill the north-west shore of Lake Van at Adilcevaz. Both may have had equal importance as royal residences, though the scale and decoration of its buildings suggests Kefkalesi as the more significant centre. Though not far west of Toprakkale, it would have been a little closer to the western frontier, where campaigns towards central Anatolia and north Syria, Mushki and Hate, are recorded by Rusa II in an inscription perhaps significantly found at Adilcevaz. The other frontiers were not, however, neglected. To the north of the Urmia basin the great fortress of Bastam was constructed, with buildings outside the walls and gateways at each end, at the foot of the high rock. Rusa II may not have been the first to build at Bastam, for a date in the eighth century BC is possible for a columned hall near the north gate. Other fortresses found in this region, guarding the Urartian frontier south of the river Araxes, may also belong to this reign, perhaps including Behr Ahram, with a temple and an area of 750 × 300 m. The north-eastern frontier region was reorganized by moving the seat of government from Argishti I's palace at Arinberd (Erebuni) to a new citadel a few miles away at Karmir-Blur (Teishebaina), whose Armenian name ('red hill') derives from the burning of the final destruction. Irrigation works were carried out in this region.

Outside Karmir-Blur citadel there was a town extending up to four hectares south and west of the citadel. A grid plan, less regular than at Zernaki Tepe, is suggested by the excavated area, with blocks of up to five houses, each having a

160. At Maltai the reliefs are on a cliff in the south side of the Dehok valley, by the road from Assyria to the upper Zab valley. All four panels depict the same procession: seven divinities are flanked by two figures of the king in the usual attitude of prayer, his right arm raised, his left hand grasping a mace. Assur, the national god and leader of the pantheon, heads the procession, standing on a dragon and a horned lion; then comes his consort Ninlil, seated on a throne mounted on a lion; there follows Enlil (the old head of the Sumerian pantheon), Sin (moon god), Shamash (sun god), Adad (storm and weather god) and Ishtar (goddess of fertility and love). Unlike the king, the gods and goddesses wear the horned crown, since Sumerian times the attribute of divinity.

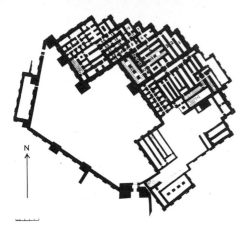

161. Plan of Karmir-Blur, which has proved to be a very rich site in its yield of artefacts, including decorated shields, helmets and quivers as well as inscribed bronze bowls, the best pieces antedating its construction and transferred from Arinberd. The excavated plan comprises the store-rooms of the ground floor: the living quarters must have been in the upper storey. The citadel overlooked an irregularly shaped parade ground with two entrances, the main gateway and the facade being defended by towers about 12 m. wide, with buttresses between, a design perhaps to be regarded as a slight advance on that of earlier reigns in Urartu.

court and two rooms, divided by streets. The store-rooms, with their huge jars, are characteristic of all major Urartian fortresses, though it is those of the time of Rusa II whose contents have survived best. The jars at Karmir-Blur, Kefkalesi and Bastam usually have either pictographic or cuneiform inscriptions, indicating contents or capacity or both. Urartian cuneiform tablets have been excavated at Karmir-Blur and Bastam [161].

The temple of Haldi, chief god of Urartu, at Toprakkale is significant in the history of stoneworking for its platform of rusticated limestone masonry, each block having smoothly dressed edges but a rough central boss. Basalt and limestone were inlaid in concentric circles as architectural decoration. Next to the temple were store-rooms and other buildings, now indicated only by their foundation ledges cut in the rock. A tunnel with spiral staircase led down to a large subterranean cistern, water being brought along the hillside by a channel from a spring. The throne of Haldi has been reconstructed from seventeen bronze components. Figures and other parts were all cast by the *cire perdue* method. Parallels with furniture represented on Assyrian reliefs from the ninth century BC onwards underline the long duration and cosmopolitan character of fashions in this craft. Some of the contents of this temple date later than Rusa II.

A hint that this period was one not merely of renaissance but also of innovation in Urartu is provided by the appearance of sculpture in relief, on a small scale in the repeated design from the citadel of Kefkalesi. The fragmentary relief found near the shore of Lake Van, in the ruins of a medieval castle, Adilcevaz, is larger and of finer quality. The Adilcevaz relief may suggest how much has perished of art in the form of ornately patterned textiles. Urartian art shared with the later art of Achaemenid Iran the ability to borrow and adapt more than to invent [162].

THE CIMMERIANS AND SCYTHS: DECLINE OF ASSYRIA

The threat to Urartu and then to Assyria in the late eighth and seventh centuries BC from the Cimmerians and their Scythian cousins is reflected in scattered archaeological traces. The presence of nomadic peoples is often difficult, if not almost impossible, to discern in the material record: tented camps leave little or no lasting relics. Artefacts have to be portable, so that the art of woodcarving, for example, may flourish, and much care be lavished on horse gear, while sculpture is not at all in evidence. The Urartian and Median kingdoms undoubtedly began with a predominantly mobile population, becoming more settled only as political conditions changed. The Cimmerians and Scyths left little trace of their passing, and never put down permanent roots. In the name Crimea (Krim) the name of the Cimmerians survives; and they left a trail of destruction after their raids across Urartu and their victories over Urartian armies (715, 707 BC), destroying first Gordion (at a date between 696 and 675 BC) and later Sardis (652 BC). The memory of the Scythian rule in 'Upper Asia' (probably 653–625 BC) survives in the name of the town of Sakkiz, south of Lake Urmia, their name in the Old Persian records being Saka. The obscure but devastating incursion of the Scyths into the Levant (c. 637 BC) is recalled in the Hellenistic town of Scythopolis (Beth Shan).

If the Cimmerians can be associated with the Catacomb culture of the eastern Ukraine and the Don basin, with its pit graves, they must have been expelled thence in the later second millennium BC, and must have had a subsequent homeland near the Caucasus, for which there is historical evidence (c.

735 BC). Possibly the cemetery of Samtavro, near Mtskheta in the Georgian S.S.R., may be Cimmerian. The problem of identification of Cimmerian and Scythian remains is that these people adopted and disseminated the art of the Caucasus and the steppes to the north, but there is nothing which they can be proved to have originated. The treasure buried at Ziwiye, near Sakkiz (*c.* 600 BC), was a motley hoard which has aroused much discussion and which indeed demonstrated the juxtaposition of Assyrian, Urartian, Scythian and local Mannaean workmanship [*Pl 30*]. The 'animal style', however, whether at Ziwiye or on the contemporary Luristan bronzes, can be traced back to the third millennium BC north of the Caucasus, and is only erroneously attributed to Scyths and Cimmerians alone. The tumuli of Sé Girdan, close to Dinkha Tepe and west of Hasanlu, may be Scythian.

A generally accepted hall-mark of the Scyths is the arrowhead with a hook on the tang, found in large numbers in the ruins of Karmir-Blur. The cemetery of Mingechaur in the Azerbaijan S.S.R. includes burials, some in graves roofed with slabs, containing many iron weapons, red pottery and a variety of jewellery. This was a provincial reflection of the wealth of the Scythian royal tombs, including Kostromskaya and Kelermes, in the Kuban valley and dating to the sixth century BC. The design of those tombs, with a wooden chamber surmounted by a barrow (*kurgan*), is typical of the south Russian steppes. The contents betray the military activities of the Scythian chiefs, at Kostromskaya the weapons of war being supplemented by the sacrifice of twenty-two horses. Oriental influences reveal the effects of the Scythian sojourn in Iran; Greek influence became more marked later, from contacts with Greek colonies on the north coast of the Black Sea, tolerated by the Scyths for purposes of commerce.

The seeds of the downfall of Assyria were sown in western Iran, with the rise of the Medes in the late eighth century BC and thereafter, whose civilization is discussed below (see p. 201). But other factors assisted this process, among them the overstraining of Assyrian resources by Esarhaddon in the invasion of Egypt, culminating early in Assurbanipal's reign in the sack of Thebes. Though but an episode in Egyptian history, this brief period of Assyrian rule is commemorated on a stele of Esarhaddon found at Zincirli recording his victorious campaign (671 BC) and in sphinxes inscribed with Egyptian hieroglyphs of the Pharaoh Taharka. These stood in the palace of Esarhaddon on the smaller of the two citadel mounds of Nineveh, Nebi Yunus, still little excavated. Written references indicate that he also built here an arsenal. Restoration work was also carried out at Nimrud, where he had a palace on the citadel. The rebuilding of Babylon was begun, in accord with a policy of conciliation; but little trace of the Assyrian presence was found in the excavations, save for paving stones inscribed with the name of Sennacherib.

The circumstances of Esarhaddon's accession, after his father's assassination (681 BC), led him to make careful provision for the succession, expressed in the treaties imposed on his Median vassals and no doubt on others too. Copies of some of these survive in rectangular cuneiform tablets, the largest preserved anywhere, impressed with the royal cylinder-seal. Assurbanipal was to succeed Esarhaddon to the throne in Nineveh and his brother Shamash-shum-ukin in Babylon.

This arrangement was ultimately to prove fatal to relations between Assyria and Babylon, which never recovered from Sennacherib's sack of the city (689 BC). The archaeological record of successive campaigns, especially from *c.* 651 to *c.* 640 BC, against Babylon and its allies the Chaldaean tribes of Mesopotamia,

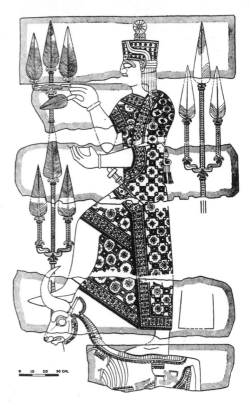

162. This relief from Adilcevaz represents either the sun god of Urartu, Shivini, as suggested by the solar emblem on the god's crown, or Tesheba, storm and weather god, since he is standing on that god's animal, a bull. His elaborate garment suggests the brocaded vestments put over the divine statues in the temples. He is shown in the act of sprinkling the sacred tree with holy water, thus adopting an Assyrian theme for a distinctively Urartian composition. A similar theme, with griffin holding a bucket, is one of a wide repertoire, including soldiers with a chariot, appearing on seal impressions from Toprakkale and Karmir-Blur. Stamp-cylinders are a distinctively Urartian form of seal.

the Arabs and, most serious opponents of all, the Elamites, is contained in the annals and other inscriptions and in the crowded reliefs from the palace of Assurbanipal (669–c. 627 BC) at Nineveh. The Elamite wars are depicted in gruesome detail, the inscriptions no longer running across the reliefs in one band, as in the ninth century BC, but scattered in short passages set beside each recorded incident. Amid this fighting there was time for lion hunting, represented in this reign in the most poignant and lifelike of all the Assyrian reliefs, bearing comparison with Greek art at its best.

In spite of the fall of Babylon (648 BC) and the final destruction of Elam, with the desecration of the royal tombs at Susa (640 BC), Assyria was doomed. Vulnerably small in population, weakened by the long involvement with the populous cities of Babylonia and the wars with Elam, rent by recurrent internal dissension, the declining state was a prey to its disaffected subject peoples. As soon as Medes and Babylonians allied against their common enemy the end was inevitable. The general rejoicing is vividly expressed in the Book of Nahum. The archaeological record shows that, while remnants of the population returned, for example, to Nimrud, and used much the same pottery as that of the last years of the Assyrian empire, the homeland of Assyria had received a lasting blow and urban life vanished for centuries.

SYRIA, PHOENICIA AND PALESTINE
Syria, Phoenicia and Palestine under Assyrian supremacy have left an archaeological record suggesting the economic stagnation often associated with the absorption of small states and cities into larger empires. The independence of the Syro-Hittite cities of Hamath (720 BC), Carchemish (717 BC) and their smaller neighbours had finally been ended with their annexation by Sargon II and the appointment of Assyrian governors. Syro-Hittite civilization now succumbed to that of the all-powerful Assyrian state. Small citadels, presumed to be official residences, were built on the summit of mounds such as Hamath D, Megiddo II and Hazor III. The independence of the Phoenician cities was impaired by Esarhaddon, when Sidon was destroyed, a new town founded and the territory reduced to the status of an Assyrian province (676 BC). Yet the wrath of Assyria was brought down on the Phoenicians only when they refused to pay tribute: otherwise their commercial freedom was preserved.

To the south, Judah was perforce a vassal of Assyria, compelled in the reign of Manasseh to accept the installation of the state cult of the god Assur within the very temple of Yahveh in Jerusalem. In the end, however, this religious centralization helped Josiah of Judah (c. 637–608 BC) in his efforts to impose the cult of Yahveh throughout his enlarged kingdom and to suppress the many idolatrous sanctuaries. Josiah's death in the battle of Megiddo weakened Judah; and soon came successive attacks by the Babylonians (598, 587 BC). These brought town life to an end, and recovery under Persian rule was slow, in spite of the policy of toleration of indigenous religions. Not all the Jews wished to leave the 'fleshpots of Babylon'. The temple was rebuilt by Zerubbabel by c. 516 BC, on the lines of the temple of Solomon; but nothing has been found of this. Archaeological confirmation of the biblical account of the rebuilding of the walls of Jerusalem by the governor Nehemiah (c. 445–433 BC) is, however, available: the extension of the city down the steep eastern slope was abandoned in favour of an easier line along the crest, while on the west side the old line was retained. A smaller city was adequate for the reduced population; but the completion of the work in fifty-two days was nevertheless remarkable.

Archaeology tends to illustrate much but prove little of the events recorded in the Old Testament. Yet there is much material evidence surviving from sites in Judah from the last years of the seventh century BC, if only because these levels were sealed by the debris of the Babylonian destruction. Almost all the buildings excavated in Jerusalem were on the eastern slope, and it was mostly their foundations which survived. Fertility figurines of the mother goddess type have been found in Jerusalem and at many other sites, including Tell Beit Mirsim. Here, in Stratum A, was recovered the major part of the plan of a small town in the hill country, where stone dye-vats suggest a thriving textile industry, the wool being dyed before weaving. Eight miles to the north-west stood Tell ed Duweir (Lachish), larger but only partially excavated, where the presence in tombs of terracotta figurines of the Astarte type, with model doves, symbol of that goddess, and model chairs, beds and rattles tends to confirm the prophet Micah's denunciation of that city as the beginning of sin in the land. The deposition of offerings, the universal practice among the common people, was in itself contrary to the Deuteronomic Law.

Pottery being fragile, most of that from excavations in Judah can be dated around 600 BC. The most obvious development is of bowls with wheel-burnished surface and folded rim and of juglets with vertically applied burnish, found at Tell Beit Mirsim A and imported from the north or at least imitating northern prototypes. For wheel burnish had appeared at Samaria as early as Period I, though then no vessel was purely wheel-burnished; and by Period VI this surface treatment was in general use. But many of the principal seventh-century forms, such as the bowls with thickened rim, do not occur. These evidently arrived in the wake of the Assyrian conquest of Israel, emphasized by a sharp change in the pottery of Samaria from Period VI to VII. An alien form in Samaria VII, a round-based bowl with marked carination and high, flaring rim, is comparable with the 'Assyrian dinner service' from Tell Jemmeh, near Gaza. This includes jars with dimple decoration and bowls of thin 'eggshell' ware, found among the palace ware at Nimrud and there dated to c. 750–700 BC.

Ramat Rahel, not far north of Jerusalem, casts light on the Judaean monarchy in its closing years. In Level VB was an early citadel and village, of the eighth and seventh centuries BC. At Engedi, by the west shore of the Dead Sea, the buildings of Level V were of the time of Josiah, those of Level IV of the Persian period. Ramat Rahel VA comprised a small upper citadel of 50 × 60 m. and a lower town covering about two hectares. This building period probably included the palace of Jehoiakim (608–597 BC), criticized by Jeremiah for using forced labour, and taken into exile with the nobility after the first Babylonian attack on Jerusalem. Documents perhaps connected with a court martial were found in the ruins of a small room under the eastern outer gate tower at Lachish, part of the city's main defences, dating to the burning of Level II, the later of the two destructions. These eighteen inscribed sherds, or ostraca, known as the Lachish Letters, provide vivid evidence almost certainly to be associated with the very last days of resistance to the Babylonians (587 BC). One letter refers to watching for the signal-stations of Lachish.

Jewish independence had vanished, and a long decline in terms of material culture ensued. More important to Babylon than Judah were the Phoenician ports as commercial outlets, as the Median power in the east obliged the Neo-Babylonian empire to look west. When Tyre fell to Nebuchadnezzar after a siege of thirteen years Phoenician independence had likewise finally ended (572 BC). The later revival came under Persian rule.

GREECE AND THE NEAR EAST AND LYDIA

Greek contacts with the Near East, based on trade and the foundation of colonies on the east Mediterranean and Black Sea coasts, led to the appearance of certain Near Eastern influence in Greek art, from the mid-eighth century BC onwards. Slavish imitation was unusual, however, and it has been claimed that Hittite (i.e. Syro-Hittite) and Syrian prototypes stood behind the earliest Greek sculptures. Whether it is justifiable to state that the Greeks had little interest in Assyrian and Egyptian products is perhaps more open to question. The early colonies, such as Al Mina (Posideion) on the Syrian coast, where a date of *c.* 825–720 BC for the earliest levels (X–VIII) seems more probable than the excavator's suggested *c.* 750–650 BC, and Sinope on the Black Sea coast (812 BC), from which the colony of Trapezos (Trebizond) was established (756 BC), must have been the means of cultural as well as purely commercial relations between east and west. At Al Mina Greek potters set up shop, and contacts between Greeks and Cypriots were especially close. The difference between the eighth and seventh centuries BC can be summed up as the slow change from east–west influences to a more balanced exchange, eventually leading in the sixth century BC to the first extension of Hellenic influences, into Lydia, Cyprus and, partly through Greek mercenaries, even into Egypt.

Cyprus enjoyed a period of peace in the Cypro-Archaic I period, the seventh century BC, marked by the proliferation of rural sanctuaries, of which one on the north coast, at Ayia Irini, deserves mention. Originally built in the Late Bronze Age (*c.* 1200 BC), it was frequently destroyed and restored.

Greek influence on the Anatolian hinterland cannot be reckoned very significant before the Persian period. The archaeological record suggests, on the contrary, that earlier traditions persisted, in spite of the disruption caused by the Cimmerian raids and the consequent fall of Phrygian power. In central Anatolia, Büyükkale, the citadel of the old Hittite capital of Boğazköy, was refortified in the early seventh century BC with defences including a stone glacis; and the area within the walls was gradually built over, until by the early sixth century BC the town had extended outside the walls. The first imported Greek pottery found here is Proto-Corinthian (*c.* 650–625 BC), like other Greek imports significant less for their quantity than their evidence for dating, since the preponderant local wares do not yet provide a precise chronology. Graffiti in the Phrygian alphabet and language point to cultural connections with the lands west of the Halys. Architecture, pottery and evidence of cult practices may all indicate a dominant Phrygian element, culturally if not also numerically, at Boğazköy as late as the fifth century BC. Identification of this city with Pteria, in the Median sphere after the fixing of the frontier with Lydia on the river Halys (585 BC) but subsequently conquered by Croesus of Lydia, seems reasonable. Phrygian cultural influence appears to have become most widespread after the political decline of the kingdom centred on Gordion; but the use of pottery in Iron Age Anatolia to demonstrate Phrygian culture is fraught with pitfalls, the terms 'Phrygian' and 'Iron Age' being by no means synonymous. The religion of the Bronze Age seems to have survived, even the official shrine of Yazilikaya still being visited, as seventh- and sixth-century BC pottery shows. The Phrygian contribution is most vividly discernible in the south-east gate of the citadel, in a cult niche containing three statues: a goddess wearing a tall *polos* (headdress) is flanked by two boys in short trousers, one playing a seven-stringed kithara and the other a double flute. The goddess must be Kubaba of eastern origin and at the same time Kybele, whose cult statues appear at Gordion, Ankara and elsewhere, with the rendering of her garment indicating western influence, derived from East Greek art of the early sixth century BC.

Gordion was to revive very soon after the Cimmerian destruction, though the citadel mound remained in ruins till the advent of Persian rule. There was an extensive outer city, immediately east of the citadel, enclosed by a massive brick-built defensive wall with an elaborately designed gateway almost opposite the stone-built gate of the pre-Cimmerian Phrygian city. Three phases have been distinguished, two in the seventh and one in the early sixth century BC: the amount of charcoal in the bricks of the first phase suggests it was built from the burnt debris of the destruction. The citadel was rebuilt in the first years of Persian rule (from *c.* 546 BC).

While Phrygia enjoyed a period of revival under Lydian supremacy, Lydia had suffered less from the Cimmerians. Its centre lay not far inland, with access to the sea and thus more readily to foreign trade; and it had the advantage of the gold from the bed of the Pactolus, the river of Sardis. The excavations at Sardis have revealed three Lydian periods in a market quarter with shops, the earliest level being violently destroyed, presumably by the Cimmerians (652 BC).

Apart from stonecutting the Lydians had other talents, not revealed in the archaeological record, for example, music. External relations are illustrated by the sequence of pottery from the Lydian levels at Sardis. Beneath the floor of a Lydian potter's shop Greek Proto-Geometric and Geometric pottery was found, as well as types paralleled in Cyprus, Cilicia and south-west Anatolia. Later, in the shop, was a mixture of Geometric and Orientalizing types then in fashion in Lydia (*c.* 600 BC).

THE MEDES

Although the Medes had very probably entered Iran as one of several tribal groups in the Iranian migrations beginning in about the fourteenth century BC, the first historical reference to them occurs in the annals of Shalmaneser III of Assyria (836 BC). They seem to have remained a loosely knit family of clans, only under Assyrian pressure driven towards gradual unification, centred on the Hamadan region. Herodotus states that the Median ruler Deioces (Daiaukku) founded Ecbatana and built many smaller strongholds. He was exiled by Sargon II to Hamath in Syria after defeat in the seventh campaign (715 BC).

Archaeological evidence at first hand of Median civilization is now available from three excavated sites, Godin Tepe and Tepe Nush-i Jan between Hamadan and Kermanshah, and Baba Jan in north Luristan. At all three are buildings which can plausibly be associated with a local khan or clan chief, anxious to protect his own authority and at the same time to ape the tastes of the nearest city known to him, no doubt Ecbatana (Hamadan). The ordinary people must still have been tent-dwellers. In Godin Tepe II, probably founded *c.* 750 BC, the main building comprised three columned halls, including a throne-room with a mud-brick throne seat in the north wall and benches on four sides. The fortifications had key-shaped arrow-slots, still preserved. The columned hall, first manifested farther north at Hasanlu, is a common factor with Tepe Nush-i Jan and Baba Jan, where the older building on the central mound is described by the excavator as a fortified manor house, in Level 2 having eight towers, one serving as a gateway, and probably of late ninth century BC date. Two rectangular rooms were prototypes of the columned hall in the 'fort' on the east mound of Baba Jan, next to the 'painted chamber' of the eighth century BC. This was distinguished

163. Elaborate blind windows of the Fire Temple of Nush-i-Jan decorate the walls of the sanctuary. The altar, of mud-brick, steps out in four stages at the top, to a height of 85 cm. The fire bowl on top is so shallow that it seems likely that the flame was rekindled before each ceremony. The implications of this temple for the early history of Zoroastrianism are far-reaching. Long mud-brick struts were used for vaulting, a technique appearing in the fortifications at Persepolis and in later periods in Iran. Then the Fire Temple, still in good repair, was very carefully filled with six metres' depth of shale chips, then with alternate layers of chips and mud and finally with mud-brick. The ramp is about eight metres high, with three complete turns preserved.

by its heavy wall tiles with decorative designs painted in red, probably imitating textile hangings and unparalleled elsewhere.

Tepe Nush-i Jan is undoubtedly the most impressive Median site so far excavated, for its position on a natural hill near Maliyar and its remarkable preservation, the outside walls standing up to eight metres high. Apart from some Parthian village occupation, it is a one-period site. The central of the three buildings, and probably the oldest, has a plan described as a stepped lozenge, comprising entrance room, antechamber, spiral ramp and large triangular sanctuary with a free-standing altar, whose form justifies description of this as the Fire Temple. Immediately east of the Fire Temple stood the Fort, with guardroom, spiral ramp and staircase and four magazines. West of the Fire Temple stood the Hall, about 19 × 15 m. inside, probably with three rows of four columns [163].

Tepe Nush-i Jan will help to provide a sequence of Median pottery, especially for the seventh century BC, including a secondary phase. At Baba Jan the ceramic sequence suggests that Godin Tepe II is later than Tepe Nush-i Jan. The earlier phases of Baba Jan have yielded spouted and deep jars of painted pottery in the 'genre Luristan' style. A silversmith's hoard of over two hundred small objects, including double and quadruple spiral beads and over a hundred scraps of metal, attests the wealth of Media. Those pieces not jewellery seem almost certain to have been valued as bullion, and thus to provide significant evidence of ingot currency, such as seems to have existed in Assyria in the seventh century BC, and which assuredly was in use in the Achaemenid empire, when Greek silver coinage was gaining in popularity.

The closing decades of Urartu are even obscurer than the final years of Assyria. The few written references point to a decline setting in soon after the death of Rusa II (c. 645 BC), when Sarduri III may have accepted Assurbanipal's claim to titular overlordship. The Scythian raid (c. 637 BC) must have damaged Urartu seriously. A bronze shield of Rusa III (c. 635–609/585 BC) from Toprak-kale is decorated with lions in a curiously attenuated style, perhaps a hint of the decadence of Urartian art in its final phase. Karmir-Blur fell at some date not later than c. 585 BC; but the *coup-de-grâce* had been administered to Urartu as much by the arrival of newcomers from the west, the Armenians, as by Scyths or Medes. Archaeology tells nothing of the early Armenian settlements. The Alarodian survivors of Urartu were driven to take refuge in roughly built mountain strongholds above Lake Van, while, according to Xenophon, the Armenian incomers occupied the more fertile, low-lying pasture lands. A long obscurity had descended on the old homeland of Urartu.

EPILOGUE: BABYLON, LYDIA AND PERSEPOLIS

In some ways the sheer scale of political developments after the fall of Assyria (612 BC) until the death of Alexander the Great in Babylon (323 BC), together with the survival of historical sources covering these three centuries in some detail, at least in certain aspects, renders the task of outlining the material civilization very difficult. Much is now known of a few great centres, yet all too little of the life of the ordinary people of Mesopotamia, Persia or Lydia.

The great city of Babylon, brief as its imperial power proved to be, was rightly the wonder of travellers, of whom Herodotus in the mid-fifth century BC and Ctesias, court physician to Artaxerxes II, have left the best accounts. The walls and public buildings within their eight-mile outer perimeter were of kiln-fired bricks, an innovation of the Neo-Babylonian period (626–539 BC), to which nearly all the buildings belong. The inner rampart extended for three miles on the east side of the Euphrates and two and a quarter miles on the west bank, where the 'new town' remains unexcavated. Eight gates gave entry to Babylon, including the famous Ishtar Gate on the north, the most complex in plan, with rows of lions, bulls and dragons in relief on glazed bricks, a development of an art originating in Assyria. Six lower rows of animals were probably always concealed below road level, exemplifying the magical function of so much Near Eastern art. The royal palace, or Southern Citadel, included the great throne-room with startlingly bold decoration in glazed bricks, very far in style from anything Assyrian. Next to the domestic quarters of the palace stood, most probably, the 'Hanging Gardens' of Babylon, of which only the massive supporting brick barrel vaults remain; it is said that Nebuchadnezzar built these gardens to remind his queen of her native Median trees and mountains. South of the palace stood the chief temple of Babylon, dedicated to Marduk, within a precinct about one quarter of a mile square, with twelve gates. Near the west side stood the great ziggurat, the principal landmark of Babylon, almost 90 m. high. There were probably eight stages, the height of the first two corresponding exactly with the horizontal measurement of the main staircase, thus fitting a Babylonian canon of design. Outside Babylon itself extensive building works were carried out, including the renovation of the sacred precinct of Ur by Nabonidus, last king of Babylon. He exalted the cult of the moon god Sin, whose crescent appears on all his surviving stelae; and he sought to establish a new capital at Teima, in an oasis in the north Arabian desert about one hundred miles east of the Gulf of Aqaba. Both innovations incurred the enmity of the priests of Marduk, the state god, and led to the Babylonian welcome to Cyrus the Persian as a liberator (539 BC).

In western Anatolia, the land of Phrygia enjoyed a period of revival under Lydian supremacy. Lydia had suffered less from the Cimmerians. Its centre lay not far inland, with access to the Aegean and thus more readily to foreign trade. Gold refining developed as a source of wealth, with the alluvial gold from the bed of the Pactolus, the river of Sardis, the Lydian capital. It was in stonecutting and dressing that Lydian skill was particularly marked, equalled only by the Ionians. The masonry of the Acropolis wall at Sardis, of the Pyramid Tomb and the Gyges Tomb and other chamber tombs in the Bin Tepe cemetery three miles north of Sardis is all of the same appearance, with finely picked centre and drafted margins four or five centimetres wide on four sides, without trace of the toothed chisel. Double clamps of fishtail and dovetail forms were used, for example, in the burial chamber ascribed to Alyattes. The Lydians may well have been the tutors of the Ionian builders and sculptors, who in the sixth century BC themselves took the leadership in these arts.

Lydian and Ionian architecture must have made a profound impression on the Persian conqueror, reflected beyond doubt in the masonry of the new capital founded by Cyrus the Great, Pasargadae. There is now ample evidence that the toothed chisel was not yet in use in the reign of Cyrus, though it had appeared in Greece as early as *c.* 570 BC, where it was used on sculpture before masonry. It came into use, however, very soon after the death of Cyrus, whose tomb comprises a gabled chamber of very modest size on a high podium or plinth of six receding tiers. Greco-Lydian participation in the building of Pasargadae was a relatively brief episode in early Achaemenid art and architecture, the sculpture always being integrated into the overall architectural design. The whole was surely the outcome of Iranian direction with foreign advice and craftsmanship.

Achaemenid architecture appears in its purest form at Persepolis (Parsa), for at Susa something of Mesopotamian traditions survived in the plan of the palace: the glazed brick relief figures of the imperial guard, the Immortals, in the palace of Artaxerxes II (404–359 BC) are in the Assyro-Babylonian tradition; and rooms were grouped round internal courts. The terrace of Persepolis, covering thirteen hectares, is partly cut out of the mountain and partly artificial. The buildings date to the reigns of Darius the Great, Xerxes and Artaxerxes I (i.e to *c.* 518–460 BC), and comprise public halls and residential palaces, rather loosely related to one another. The function, recently much discussed, of Persepolis centred probably round a rather brief annual residence by the king over the period of the great New Year spring festival. The reliefs emphasize the international character of an empire whose civilization has been all too much belittled by the bias of philhellenic western scholars unwilling to look for once westwards through eastern eyes, instead of always vice versa. The reliefs of the Audience Hall, or Apadana, demonstrate the cosmopolitan character of the empire which embraced Egypt and Bactria, Ionia and India. The design of the Apadana shows the innovation of columnar architecture, a major contribution of the Achaemenid kings. When Persepolis went up in flames at the feast of the Macedonian conqueror, a world lasting several millennia finally expired.

Further Reading

The following recommended books are accompanied by a selection of articles from the most important and accessible journals dealing wholly or in part with the archaeology of the Near East. It is not possible to include all reports on excavated sites mentioned in the text; but many books and articles listed below include ample references.

Among the most useful and widely relevant journals are:

USA	*American Journal of Archaeology* (*A.J.A.*) (with summary [Ed. Mellink] of field work in Turkey)
UK	*Anatolian Studies* (*A.S.*) (with summaries of major excavations in Turkey)
UK	*Antiquity*
USA	*Archaeology*
TK	*Belleten* (*Türk Tarih Kurumu*) (Turkish with English, French or German)
NL	*Bibliotheca Orientalis* (*Bib. Or.*) (largely comprising reviews)
USA	*Biblical Archaeologist*
USA	*Bulletin of the American Schools of Oriental Research* (*B.A.S.O.R.*)
USA	*Current Anthropology* (*C.A.*)
UK	*Illustrated London News* (*I.L.N.*) (with frequent archaeological articles)
UK	*Iran* (with full survey of surveys and excavations in Iran)
France	*Iranica Antiqua*
UK	*Iraq*
Israel	*Israel Exploration Journal* (*I.E.J.*)
USA	*Journal of the American Oriental Society* (*J.A.O.S.*)
USA	*Journal of Cuneiform Studies* (*J.C.S.*)
UK	*Journal of Hellenic Studies* (*J.H.S.*)
USA	*Journal of Near Eastern Studies* (*J.N.E.S.*)
UK	*Levant*
France	*Paléorient*
UK	*Palestine Exploration Quarterly* (*P.E.Q.*)
UK	*Proceedings of the Prehistoric Society* (*P.P.S.*)
France	*Revue Biblique* (with summaries of excavations in Palestine)
France	*Syria*
UK	*World Archaeology* (whole issues devoted to one topic)

* Largely or mainly linguistic and historical in emphasis, though *J.N.E.S.* was at one time largely archaeological.

GENERAL WORKS ON ARCHAEOLOGY, ART AND ARCHITECTURE

Ehrich, R. W. (Ed.), *Chronologies in Old World Archaeology*, Chicago 1965.
Bannister Fletcher, *A History of Architecture on the Comparative Method* (18th edition), Chapter II by C. A. Burney, London 1974.
Frankfort, H., *The Art and Architecture of the Ancient Orient*, Harmondsworth 1954.
Lampl, P., *Cities and Planning in the Ancient Near East*, London 1968.

Maxwell-Hyslop, R., *West Asiatic Jewellery*, London 1971.

Schaeffer, C. F. A., *Stratigraphic Comparée et Chronologie de l'Asie Occidentale*, Oxford 1948.

GENERAL WORKS ON THE HISTORY OF THE ANCIENT NEAR EAST

Cambridge Ancient History, (*CAH*), Vols. I–II (revised edition); a few fascicles being listed below, and Vol. III, *The Assyrian Empire*.

Conteneau, G., *Everyday Life in Assyria and Babylon*, London 1954. (English Trans.)

Frye, R. N., *The Heritage of Persia*, London 1962.

Gurney, O. R., *The Hittites*, new ed., London 1975.

Hallo, W. W., and Simpson, W. K., *The Ancient Near East–A History*, New York 1971.

Noth, M., *History of Israel*, London 1958.

Oppenheim, A. L., *Ancient Mesopotamia*, Chicago 1964.

Roux, G., *Ancient Iraq*, London 1964.

Saggs, H. W. F., *The Greatness That Was Babylon*, London 1962.

CHAPTER 1

Books, including final excavation reports:

Anati, E., *Palestine before the Hebrews*, London 1963.

Dikaios, P., *Khirokitia*, Oxford 1953.

Braidwood, R. J. and Howe, B., *Prehistoric Investigations in Iraqi Kurdistan*, Chicago 1960.

Garstang, J., *Prehistoric Mersin*, Oxford 1953.

Hole, F., Flannery, K. V., *et al.*, *Prehistory and Human Ecology of the Deh Luran Plain*, Michigan 1969.

Masson, V. M,. and Sarianidi, V. I., *Central Asia–Turkmenia Before the Achaemenids* (Chapters IV and V, with bibliography), London 1972.

Mellaart, J., *Çatal Hüyük*, London 1967.

Mellaart, J., *Excavations at Hacilar*, Edinburgh 1970.

Mellaart, J., *The Neolithic of the Near East*, London 1975 (detailed and authoritative treatment, up-to-date and amply illustrated).

Prausnitz, M. W., *From Hunter to Farmer and Trader*, Jerusalem 1970.

Singh, P., *Neolithic Cultures of Western Asia*, London 1974 (with very full bibliography, up-to-date till 1972).

Ucko, P. J., and Dimbleby, G. W., (Ed.), *The Domestication and Exploitation of Plants and Animals*, *DEPA*, London 1969 (with several useful articles on the Near East).

Articles:

Angel, J. L., 'Ecology and population in the Eastern Mediterranean' in *World Archaeology*, 4, 1972–73, pp. 88–105.

Braidwood, R. J., 'The early village in south-western Asia' in *J.N.E.S.*, XXXII (1973), pp. 34–9.

Flannery, K. V., 'Origins and ecological effects of early domestication in Iran and the Near East' in *D.E.P.A.*, pp. 73–100.

Garrod, D., 'The Natufian culture: the life and economy of a Mesolithic people in the Near East' in *Proceedings of the British Academy*, XLIII (1957), pp. 211–27.

Kenyon, K. M., 'Excavations at Jericho, 1957–8' in *P.E.Q.*, 1960, pp. 1–21.

Kirkbride, D., 'Five Seasons at the Pre-Pottery Neolithic village of Beidha in Jordan' in *P.E.Q.*, 1966, pp. 8–72.

Kirkbride, D., 'Early Neolithic village life south of the Dead Sea' in *Antiquity*, XLII (1968), pp. 263–74.

Lamberg-Karlovsky, C. C., 'Prehistoric Central Asia: a review' in *Antiquity*, XLVII (1973), pp. 43–7.

Mellaart, J., 'Excavations at Çatal Hüyük', first to fourth preliminary reports in *A.S.*, XII (1962), pp. 41–65; XIII (1963), pp. 43-103; XIV (1964), pp. 39–119; XVI (1966), pp. 165-91.

Moore, A. M. T., 'The Late Neolithic in Palestine' in *Levant*, V (1973), pp. 36–68.

Oates, J., 'The background and development of early farming communities in Mesopotamia and the Zagros' in *P.P.S.*, XXXIX (1973), pp. 147–81.

Renfrew, C., Dixon, J. E., and Cann, J. R., 'Obsidian and early cultural contact in the Near East' in *P.P.S.* XXXII (1966), pp. 30–72.

Smith, P. E. L., and Young, T. C., 'The evolution of early agriculture and culture in Greater Mesopotamia: a trial model' in Brian Spooner (Ed.), *Population Growth: Anthropological Implications*, Cambridge, Mass., 1972, pp. 1–59.

Vita-Finzi, C., and Higgs, E. S., 'Prehistoric economy in the Mount Carmel area of Palestine: site catchment analysis' in *P.P.S.*, XXXVI (1970), pp. 1–37.

Wright, G. A., 'Origins of food production in south-western Asia: a survey of ideas' in *C.A.*, XIII (1971), pp. 447–73.

Zeist, W. Van, 'Reflections on prehistoric environments in the Near East' in *DEPA*, pp. 35-46.

CHAPTER 2

Books, including final excavation reports:

Adams, R. McC., *Land Behind Baghdad*, Chicago 1965.

Adams, R. McC., and Nissen, H., *The Uruk Countryside*, Chicago 1972.

Amiet, P., *La Glyptique Mésopotamienne Archaique*, Paris 1961.

Childe, V. G., *New Light on the Most Ancient East*, London 1952.

Delougaz, P., and Lloyd, S., *Pre-Sargonid Temples in the Diyala Region*, O.I.P., LVIII, Chicago 1942.

Delougaz, P., *Pottery From the Diyala Region*, O.I.P., LXIII, Chicago 1952.

Frankfort, H., *Stratified Cylinder-Seals from the Diyala Region*, O.I.P., LXXII, Chicago 1956.

Gadd, C. J., *The Cities of Babylonia*, CAH I–II, fasc. 9, 1964.

Kramer, S. N., *From The Tablets of Sumer*, Colorado 1956.

Mallowan, M. E. L., *The development of cities from Al-'Ubaid to the end of Uruk 5*, 2 parts, CAH I–II, fasc. 58, 1967.

Mallowan, M. E. L., *The Early Dynastic period in Mesopotamia*, CAH, I–II, fasc. 62, 1968.

Parrot, A., *Archéologie Mésopotamienne*, II, Paris, 1953.

Parrot, A., *Mari–Capitale Fabuleuse*, Paris 1974.

Parrot, A., *Sumer* (The Arts of Mankind), London 1960. English translation.

Perkins, A. L., *The Comparative Archaeology of Early Mesopotamia*, S.A.O.C., 25, Chicago 1949 (typology of prehistoric periods: for reference only).

Tobler, A. J., *Excavations at Tepe Gawra II*, Philadelphia 1950.

Woolley, C. L., *Ur Excavations II: The Royal Cemetery*, London and Philadelphia 1934.

Ucko, P. J., Tringham, R., and Dimbleby G. W., (Ed.), *Man, Settlement and Urbanism* (*M.S.U.*), London 1972.

Articles:

Adams, R. McC., 'Patterns of urbanization in early southern Mesopotamia' in *M.S.U.*, pp. 735–49.

Gibson, McG., 'Population shift and the rise of Mesopotamian civilization' in C. Renfrew (Ed.), *Models in Prehistory*, London, 1973, pp. 447–463.

Helbaek, H., 'Samarran irrigation agriculture at Choga Mami in Iraq' in *Iraq*, XXXI (1972), pp. 35–48.

Lloyd, S., and Safar, F., 'Tell Hassuna' in *J.N.E.S.*, IV (1945), pp. 255–89.

Lloyd, S., and Safar, F., 'Eridu . . .' in *Sumer*, IV (1948), pp. 115–27.

Lloyd, S., and Safar, F., 'Tell Uqair . . .' in *J.N.E.S.*, II (1943), pp. 131–158.

Lloyd, S., 'Ur-Al'Ubaid, Uqair and Eridu' in *Iraq*, XXII (1960), pp. 23–31.

Mallowan, M. E. L., and Rose, J. C., 'Excavations at Tell Arpachiyah, 1933' in *Iraq*, II (1935), pp. 1–178.

Moorey, P. R. S., 'The "plano-convex building" at Kish and early Mesopotamiam palaces' in *Iraq*, XXVI (1964), pp. 83–98.

Pecirlova, J., 'Recent views on the emergence and character of the earliest states in southern Mesopotamia' in *Archiv Orientalny*, 43 (1975), pp. 131–45.

Postgate, J. N., 'The role of the temple in the Mesopotamian secular community' in *M.S.U.*, pp. 811–25.

Young, T. C., 'Population densities and early Mesopotamian urbanism' in *M.S.U.*, pp. 827–42.

CHAPTER 3

Books, including final excavation reports:

Driver, G. R., and Miles, J. C., *The Babylonian Laws*, Oxford, 1952 (data on feudalism etc.).

Gadd, C. J., '*The Dynasty of Agade and the Gutian invasion*', CAH I–II, fasc. 17, 1966.

Gadd, C. J., 'Babylonia, *c.* 2120–1800 BC,' CAH I–II, fasc. 28, 1965.

Gadd, C. J., 'Hammurabi and the end of his dynasty', CAH I–II, fasc. 35, 1965.

Kramer, S. N., *The Sumerians: their History, Culture and Character*, Chicago 1963.

Kupper, J. R., *Les Nomades en Mésopotamie aù Templs des Rois de Mari*, Paris 1957.

Leemans, W. F., *Foreign Trade in the Old Babylonian Period*, Leiden 1960.

Oates, D., *Studies in the Ancient History of Northern Iraq*, London 1968.

Parrot, A., and Dossin, G., (Ed.), *Archives Royales de Mari*, I–XVI, Paris 1950.

Parrot, A., *Le Palais: (1) Architecture (2) Peintures Murales*, Mission Archéologique de Mari II (1) and II (2), Paris 1958.

Woolley, C. L., *Ur Excavations V: The Ziggurat and its Surroundings*, London & Philadelphia 1939.

Woolley, C. L., *Excavations at Ur: a Record of Twelve Years' Work*, London, 1954.

Articles:

Kraus, F. R., 'Le rôle des temples depuis la troisième dynastie d'Ur jusqu'à la première dynastie de Babylone' in *Cahiers d'Histoire Mondiale*, I (1953–54), pp. 518–45.

Malamat, A., 'Mari' in *Biblical Archaeologist*, XXXIV (1971), pp. 2–22.

Mallowan, M. E. L., 'The Mechanics of ancient trade in western Asia' in *Iran*, III (1965), pp. 1–7.

Moorey, P. R. S., 'Pictorial evidence for the history of horse-riding in Iraq before the Kassite period' in *Iraq*, XXXII (1970), pp. 36–50.

Oppenheim, A. L., 'Seafaring merchants of Ur' in *J.A.O.S.*, LXXIV (1954), pp. 6–17.

CHAPTER 4

Books, including final excavation reports:

Robert, J., and Braidwood, L. S., *Excavations in the Plain of Antioch I*, O.I.P. LXI, Chicago 1960.

Culican, W., *The First Merchant Venturers*, London, 1966.

Drower, S. M., *Ugarit*, CAH I–II, fasc. 63, 1968.

Dunand, M., *Fouilles de Byblos*, Paris, 1926.

Kenyon, K. M., *Amorites and Canaanites*, London 1963.

Kenyon, K. M., *Archaeology in the Holy Land*, London 1969.

Kenyon, K. M., *Excavations at Jericho I–II*, Jerusalem 1960–5.

Kenyon, K. M., *Digging up Jerusalem*, London 1975.

Kupper, J. R., *Northern Mesopotamia and Syria*, CAH I–II, fasc. 14, 1963.

Schaeffer, C. F. A., *Ugaritica I–IV*, Paris 1939–62.

Schaeffer, C. F. A., and Nougayrol, J., *Le Palais Royal d'Ugarit (Mission de Ras Shamra)*, Vols. VI, VII, IX, Paris 1955–7.

Seters, J. van., *The Hyksos: a new Investigation*, Yale U.P. 1966.

Woolley, C. L., *Alalakh—An Account of Excavations at Tell Atchana in the Hatay, 1937–1949*, Oxford 1955.

Yadin, Y., *Hazor*, London 1972 (including chapter on Megiddo).

Articles:

Gelb, I. J., 'The early history of the West Semitic peoples' in *J.C.S.*, XV (1961), pp. 29–47.

Hestrin, R., and Tadmor, M., 'Report on hoard of E.B.A. tools at Kfar Monash' in *I.E.J.*, 13 (1963), pp. 265–88.

Matthiae, P., 'Ebla nel periodo delle dinastie amorree e della dinastia di Akkad: scoperti archeologiche recenti a Tell Mardikh' in *Orientalia*, 44 (1975), pp. 337–60.

Prag, K., 'The Intermediate Early Bronze–Middle Bronze Age: an interpretation of the evidence from Trans-Jordan, Syria and the Lebanon' in *Levant*, VI (1974), pp. 69–116.

Rainey, A. F., 'Foreign business agents at Ugarit' in I.E.J., 13 (1963), pp. 313–21.

Speiser, E. A., 'The Hurrian participation in the civilizations of Mesopotamia, Syria and Palestine' in *Cahiers d'Histoire Mondiale*, I (1953–54), pp. 311–27.

Ussishkin, D., 'The Ghassulian' temple in Ein Gedi and the origin of the hoard from Nahal Mishmar' in *Biblical Archaeologist* XXXIV (1971), pp. 23–38.

CHAPTER 5

Books, including final excavations reports:

Akurgal, E., *The Art of the Hittites*, London 1962. (German first edition: Munich, 1961)

Alkim, U. B., *Anatolia I*, Geneva 1970.

Bittel, K., *Hattusha–Capital of the Hittites*, Oxford 1970.

Blegen, C., *Troy I, Troy II, Troy III, Troy IV*, Princeton 1950–58.

Burney, C. A., and Lang, D. M., *The Peoples of the Hills*, London 1971.

Deshayes, J., *Les Outils de Bronze de l'Indus au Danube, IVe au IIe Millénaire*, Paris 1960.

Dyson, R. H., *The archaeological evidence of the second millennium BC on the Persian plateau*, CAH I–II, fasc. 66, 1968.

Garelli, P., *Les Assyriens en Cappadoce*, Paris 1963.

Garstang, J., and Gurney, O. R., *The Geography of the Hittite Empire*, London, 1956.

Ghirshman, R., *Persia–From the Origins till Alexander the Great*, London 1964.

Ghirshman, R., *Fouilles de Sialk, prés de Kashan I–II*, Paris 1938–39.

Hinz, W., *Elam*, London 1972.

Larsen, M. T., *Old Assyrian Caravan Procedures*, Istanbul 1967.

Lloyd, S., and Mellaart, J., *Beycesultan I–II*, London 1962–65.

MacQueen, J. G., *The Hittites and their Contemporaries in Asia Minor*, London 1975.

Matheson, S., *Persia: an Archeological Guide*, London 1976 (excellent bibliography).

Melaart, J., *Anatolia, c. 4000–2300 BC*, CAH I–II, fasc. 8, 1965.

Mellaart, J., *Anatolia before c. 4000 BC and c. 2300–1750 BC*, CAH I–II, fasc. 20, 1964.

Mellaart, J., *The Chalcolithic and Early Bronze Ages in the Near East and Anatolia*, Beirut 1966.

Articles:

Beale, T. W., 'Early trade in highland Iran: a view from the source' in *World Archaeology*, 5 (1973), pp. 133–48.

Bittel, K., 'The Great Temple of Hattusha-Bogazköy' in *A.J.A.*, 80 (1976), pp. 66–73.

Caldwell, J. R., 'Pottery and cultural history on the Iranian plateau' in *J.N.E.S.*, XXVII (1968), pp. 178–83 (openly avowed emphasis on Tal-i-Iblis).

Diamant, S., and Rutter, J., 'Horned objects in Anatolia and the Near East and possible connexions with the Minoan "horns of consecration"' in *A.S.*, XIX (1969), pp. 147–77.

Emre, K., 'The pottery of the Assyrian colony period according to the building levels of the Kaniš Karum' in *Anatolia*, VII (1963), pp. 87–99.

Goff, C. L., 'Luristan before the Iron Age' in *Iran*, IX (1971), pp. 131–52.

Guterbock, H. G., 'Yazilikaya: a propos a new interpretation' in *J.N.E.S.*, XXXIV (1975), pp. 273–7.

Herrmann, G., 'Lapis lazuli: the early phases of its trade' in *Iraq*, XXX (1968), pp. 21–57.

Lamberg-Karlovsky, C. C., 'Urban interaction on the Iranian plateau–excavations at Tepe Yahya 1967–1973' in *Proceedings of the British Academy*, LIX (1973).

Lamberg-Karlovsky, C. C., 'Trade mechanisms in Indus-Mesopotamian inter-relations' in *J.A.O.S.*, XCII (1972), pp. 222–9.

Lamberg-Karlovsky, C. C., 'Archaeology and metallurgical technology in prehistoric Afghanistan, India and Pakistan' in *American Anthropologist*, LXIX (1967), pp. 145–62.

Lamberg-Karlovsky, C. C., and Tosi M., 'Shahr-i-Sokhta and Tepe Yahya: Tracks on the earliest history of the Iranian plateau' in *East and West*, 23 (1973), pp. 21–53.

Mallowan, M. E. L., 'Elamite problems' in *Proceedings of the British Academy*, LV (1969), pp. 255–92.

Mellaart, J., 'The end of the early Bronze Age in Anatolia and the Aegean' in *A.J.A.*, 62 (1958), pp. 9–33.

Mellaart, J., 'Anatolian chronology in the Early Middle and Bronze Age' in *A.S.*, VII (1957), pp. 55–88.

Mellaart, J., 'Notes on the architectural remains of Troy I and II' *A.S.*, IX (1959), pp. 131–62.

Moorey, P. R. S., 'Prehistoric copper and bronze metallurgy in western Iran (with special reference to Luristan)' in *Iran*, VII (1969), pp. 131–53.

Muhly, J. D., and Wertime, T. A., 'Evidence for the sources and use of tin during the Bronze Age of the Near East: a reply to J. E. Dayton' in *World Archaeology*, 5, 1973, pp. 111–22; cf. *World Archaeology*, 3 (1971–2), pp. 49–70.

Özgüç, T., 'The art and architecture of ancient Kanesh' in *Anatolia*, VIII (1964), pp. 27–48.

Piggott, S., 'The earliest wheeled vehicles and the Caucasian evidence' in *P.P.S.*, XXXIV (1968), pp. 266–318.

Sulimirski, T., 'The Neolithic of the U.S.S.R.' in *University of London Institute of Archaeology Bulletin*, VI (1967), pp. 94–129.

Tosi, M., 'Early urban evolution and settlement patterns in the Indo-Iranian border-land' in Colin Renfrew (Ed.), *Models in Prehistory*, London 1973, pp. 429–46.

Weiss, H., and Young, T. C., 'The Merchants of Susa: Godin V and plateau-lowland relations in the late fourth millennium B.C.' in *Iran*, XIII (1975), pp. 1–17.

Wheeler, T. S., 'Early Bronze Age burial customs in western Anatolia' in *A.J.A.*, 78 (1974), pp. 415–25.

Wright, H. T., Neely, J. E., Johnson, G. A., and Speth, J., 'Early fourth millennium developments in southwestern Iran' in *Iran*, XIII (1975), pp. 129–47.

Young, T. C., 'A comparative ceramic chronology for western Iran, 1500–500 BC' in *Iran*, III (1965), pp. 53–85.

Young, T. C., 'The Iranian migration into the Zagros' in *Iran*, V (1967), pp. 11–34.

CHAPTER 6

Books, including final excavation reports:
Akurgal, E., *The Birth of Greek Art*, London 1968.
Barnett, R. D., *Catalogue of the Nimrud Ivories in the British Museum*, London 1975.
Barnett, R. D., *Assyrian Palace Reliefs*, London 1970.
Burney, C. A., and Lang, D. M., *The Peoples of the Hills*, London 1971. (Chapter V.)
Crowfoot, J. W., and Kenyon, K. M., *Samaria-Sebaste I–III*, London 1938–39.
Fugmann, E., *Hama: L'architecture des Périodes Pré-Hellénistiques*, Copenhagen 1958.
Harden, D. B., *The Phoenicians*, London 1962.
Karageorghis, V., *Salamis in Cyprus*, London 1969.
King, L. W., *Bronze reliefs from the Gates of Shalmaneser King of Assyria*, London 1915.
Loud, G., and Altman, B., *Khorsabad, Parts I–II*, Chicago 1936–38.
Luckenbill, D. D., *Ancient Records of Assyria and Babylonia*, 2 vols, Chicago 1926.
Madhloom, T. A., *The Chronology of Neo-Assyrian Art*, London 1970.
Mallowan, M. E. L., *Nimrud and its Remains*, 2 vols. & plan folder, London 1966.
Mellink, M. J., (Ed.), *Dark Ages and Nomads*, Istanbul 1964.
Moorey, P. R. S., *A Catalogue of the Persian Bronzes in the Ashmolean Museum*, Oxford 1971.
Piotrovskii, B. B. (trans. P. S. Gelling), *Urartu–the Kingdom of Van and its Art*, 1967.
Porada, E., *Ancient Iran*, 1965. (English Trans.)
Parrot, A., *Nineveh and Babylon* (The Arts of Mankind), London 1965 (English Trans.)
Van Loon, M. N., *Urartian Art*, Istanbul 1966.
Yadin, Y., *The Art of Warfare in Biblical Lands*, London 1963.

Articles:
Brinkman, J. A., 'Foreign relations of Babylonia from 1600–625 BC: the documentary evidence' in *A.J.A.*, 76 (1972), pp. 271–81.
Burney, C. A., 'Urartian fortresses and towns in the Van region' in *A.S.*, VII (1957), pp. 37–53.
Burney, C. A., 'Measured plans of Urartian fortresses' in *A.S.*, X (1960), pp. 177–96.
Burney, C. A., 'A first season of excavations at the Urartian citadel of Kayalidere' in *A.S.*, XVI (1966), pp. 55–111.
Dyson, R. H., 'Problems of Protohistoric Iran as seen from Hasanlu' in *J.N.E.S.*, XXIV (1965), pp. 193–217.
Frankfort, H., 'The origin of the *bit hilâni*' in *Iraq*, XIV (1952), pp. 120–31.
Graham, A. J., 'Patterns in early Greek colonisation' in *J.H.S.*, XCI (1971), pp. 35–47.
Guterbock, H. G., 'Carchemish' in *J.N.E.S.*, XIII (1954), pp. 102–14.
Hallo, W. W., 'From Qarqar to Carchemish: Assyria and Israel in the light of new discoveries' in *The Biblical Archaeologist*, XXIII (1960), pp. 34–61.
Hansman, J., 'Elamites, Achaemenians and Anshan' in *Iran*, X (1972), pp. 101–25.
Hawkins, J. D., 'Building inscriptions of Carchemish' in *A.S.*, XXII (1972), pp. 87–114.
Klein, J. J., 'Urartian hieroglyphic inscriptions from Altintepe' in *A.S.*, XXIV (1974), pp. 77–94.
Levine, L. D., 'Geographical studies in the Neo-Assyrian Zagros', I, in *Iran*, XI, (1973), pp. 1–27; and II in *Iran*, XII (1974), pp. 99–124.
Mallowan, M. E. L., 'Carchemish: reflections on the chronology of the sculpture' in *A.S.*, XXII (1972), pp. 63–85.
Maxwell-Hyslop, K. R., 'Assyrian sources of iron' in *Iraq*, XXXVI (1974), pp. 139–54.
Maxwell-Hyslop, K. R., 'Urartian bronzes in Etruscan tombs' in *Iraq*, XVIII (1956), pp. 150–67.

Meade, C. G., 'Luristan in the first half of the first millennium BC' in *Iran*, VI (1968), pp. 105–34.

Mellaart, J., 'Iron Age pottery from southern Anatolia' in *Belleten*, XIX (1955), pp. 115–36.

Moorey, P. R. S., 'Towards a chronology for the Luristan bronzes' in *Iran*, IX (1971), pp. 113–29. .

Muscarella, O. W., 'The oriental origin of siren cauldron attachments' in *Hesperia*, XXXI (1962), pp. 317–29.

Oppenheim, A. L., 'Essay on overland trade in the first millennium BC' in *J.C.S.*, XXI (1967), pp. 236–54.

Saggs, H. W. F., 'Assyrian warfare in the Sargonid period' in *Iraq*, XXV (1963), pp. 145–54.

Stronach, D. B. 'The development of the fibula in the Near East' in *Iraq*, XXI (1959), pp. 181–206.

Tarhan, M. T., and Sevin, V., 'The relation between Urartian temple gates and monumental rock niches' in *Belleten*, XXXIX (1975), pp. 401–12.

Turner, G., 'The state apartments of Late Assyrian palaces' in *Iraq*, XXXII (1970), pp. 177–213.

Winter, I. J., 'Phoenician and north Syrian ivory carving in historical context: questions of style and distribution' in *Iraq* XXXVIII (1976), pp. 1–22.

CHAPTER 7

Books, including final excavation reports:
Cook, J. M., *The Greeks in Ionia and the East*, London, 1962.

Haspels, C. H. E., *The Highlands of Phrygia: Sites and Monuments*, 2 vols, Princeton 1971.

Jettmar, K., *The Art of the Steppes*, London 1967. (English Trans.)

Macqueen, J. G., *Babylon*, London 1964.

Nylander, C., *Ionians in Pasargadae*, Stockholm 1971.

Özgüç, T., *Altintepe I and II*, Ankara 1966–69.

Schmidt, E. F., *Persepolis I: Structures, Reliefs, Inscriptions*, Chicago 1953.

Schmidt, E. F., *Persepolis II: Contents of the Treasury . . .*, Chicago 1957.

Schmidt, E. F., *Persepolis III*, Chicago 1970.

Wilber, D. N., *Persepolis: the Archaeology of Parsa, Seat of the Persian Kings*, London 1969.

Articles:
Barnett, R. D., 'The treasure of Ziwiye' in *Iraq*, XVIII (1956), pp. 111–6.

Barnett, R. D., 'Median Art' in *Iranica Antiqua*, II (1962), pp. 77–95.

Birmingham, J. M., 'The overland route across Anatolia in the eighth and seventh centuries BC' in *A.S.*, XI (1961), pp. 185–95.

Phillips, E. D., 'The Scythian domination in western Asia' in *World Archaeology*, 4 (1972–3), pp. 129–38.

Stern, E., 'Israel at the close of the period of the monarchy: an archaeological survey' in *Biblical Archaeologist*, XXXVIII (1975), pp. 26–54.

Stronach, D. B., 'Urartian and Achaemenian tower temples' in *J.N.E.S.*, XXVI (1967), pp. 278–88.

Thureau-Dangin, F., 'Les reliefs rupestres de Maltai' in *R.A.*, XXI (1924), pp. 185–97.

Turner, G., 'Tell Nebi Yunus: the *ekal mašarti* of Nineveh' in *Iraq*, XXXII (1970), pp. 68–85.

Wiseman, D. J., 'The vassal treaties of Esarhaddon' in *Iraq*, XX (1958), pp. 1–100.

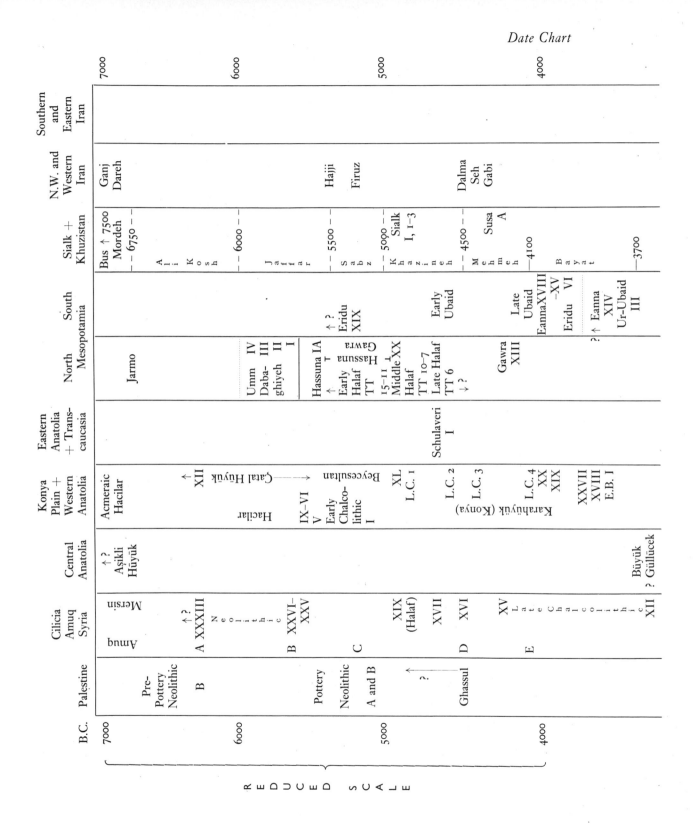

Comparative chronological chart (regions across columns; dates in B.C. from 3500 at top to 1595 at bottom).

B.C.	Palestine	Cilicia Amuq Syria	Central Anatolia	Konya Plain + Western Anatolia	Eastern Anatolia + Trans-Caucasia	North Mesopotamia	South Mesopotamia	Sialk + Khuzistan	N.W. and Western Iran	Southern and Eastern Iran
3500	Proto-Urban	Cilicia F (Tarsus)	Alişar [O–IA]	XVII — ↑ XVIa — ?	↑ ?	Khafaje — Sin I — ↑ II Brak (Eye Temples)	Early Uruk Late Uruk Eanna IVc–IVa ↑	Susa Bd — Ca	Pisdeli	Shahr-i-Sokhte I — Tepe Yahya VA — IA
	E.B. I	E.B. I — G	Late Chalcolithic	Troy XVIb — XVIa — XVb		III Gawra VIII — IV — Sin V →	Eanna III ←	Cb — Susa 4–5		IVC
3000	E.B. II	E.B. II — H	Alişar IB — E.B. II (T A / o i / m c / b a / s)	I XVa — XIVb — XIVa →	Early Trans-Caucasian I		Jemdet Nasr →	Sialk III, 6–7B — Susa Cc	Godin V	II/III
				XIIIc — XIIIb	E.T.C. II	Ninevite 5	E.D. I ←	Susa Da	↑ ? Geoy K1–3	IVB
2500	E.B. III	E.B. III — A — I	Alişar III	XIIIa — VIB — XII — III — XI	↑ ? Maikop	Ashur H — Sin X — Assyrian rulers in tents — Brak	E.D. II ← — E.D. IIIa Royal Cemetery of UR — E.D. IIIb — 2370 Sargon Akkadian Dynasty	Sialk IV — Susa De → Naramsin in Susa	Godin IV ↓ Yanik Tepe and Haftavan VIII	Yahya IVA Shahdad (Late)
	E.B.–M.B.	E.B. IIIa — B — Eb1a — J	Kültepe Karum IV–III	Karahüyük X — IX — VIII — IV — VII — V	Trialeti (Early) Group E.T.C. III	Ashur E Tell Brak	Gutian Rule — Ur III	Ur III	Haftavan VII	
2000	M.B. I	M.B.A. — K — Alalakh VII	Karum II — "IC" — IBIV D IA	VIa — III — V — VI Burnt Palace	Trialeti (Middle) Group	Ashur D Shamshi-Adad I Rimah III	Isin-Larsa — Old Babylonian — 1743 Hammurabi	Old Elamite	Haftavan VI C	Hissar IA — Hissar III C
	M.B. II	L — Kizzuwatna	Hittite Old Kingdom IV C Büyükkale	IV	Trialeti	Ashur C	1595	Susa E	Haftavan VI B ← Dinkha	
	M.B.–L.B.									

L.B. I	Alalakh IV Hittite Rule	Büyükkale IV B / IV A / III B / III A	III	(Late) Group	Middle Assyrian Rimah I	Kassite Dynasty	Untash-Gal Middle Elamite	Yarim Tepe	
L.B. II	— B. of Kadesh (L.B.A.)							VI A ←	
Philistines	Sack of Ugarit Sea Peoples		— Trojan War II	Lchashen: Wagon Burials		↓ c. 1170 —		(Gurgan)	
						Middle Babylonian		Iron I (Hasanlu V etc.)	
Accession of David	Hama F Suhis II		I	Mushki in E. Anatolia				Marlik (early phase)	
	Hama Carchemish E	Phrygian rule I A	Phrygian Kingdom					Iron II (Hasanlu IV)	
880 Samaria Periods I-VI				— Sack of Arzashkun	— 879 Nimrud refounded		Neo-Elamite	First ref. to Medes 836	
					— Fort Shalmaneser			— Sack of Hasanlu IV	
				810	— 744 Tiglath			Nush-i-Jan	
720 Fall of Samaria	720–717 Assyrian Empire		685 Sack of Gordion	786 Menua Urartu	— 727 Pileser III	689 Sack of Babylon	640 Sack of Susa	653 Scythian rule	
700 Siege of Jerusalem Judah		IB		685 Rusa II	705–703 Nineveh rebuilt	626 Neo-Babylonian	Susa refounded	625 Cyrus conquers Media	
587 Exile			547 Persian conquest of Lydia	645	612 Fall of Nineveh	539 Cyrus enters Babylon		550	Achaemenid Empire

The discoveries of the 1974 and 1975 seasons of excavations by the Italian expedition at Tell Mardikh, halfway between Aleppo and Hama in Syria, are sure to revolutionize many preconceptions concerning the political, economic, religious and linguistic patterns of Syria in the later third millennium BC. Many uncertainties await the clarification to be expected from full publication of the tablets, including some 15,000 from the royal archives; and further discoveries can be expected. The site, however, can definitely be identified with Ebla. Two successful campaigns against Mari and trading links with Kanesh (Kültepe) in central Anatolia as well as with Carchemish and Ashur are attested. The language is described by the leading philologist as Palaeo-Canaanite, strengthening the opinion that the population of the Levant in the Early Bronze Age was already largely or even predominantly Canaanite. The tablets included many found fallen from their collapsed wooden shelves. Syllabaries in Sumerian and the local language (Eblaite) bear witness to the debt to Sumerian civilization; but the general impression is of the cultural and economic strength of Syria, especially in the period *c*. 2400–2250 BC. The destruction of Ebla, never again so prosperous, may plausibly be attributed to Naramsin.

List of Illustrations

The author and publishers are grateful to the many official bodies, institutions, and individuals who kindly supplied illustrative material. The publishers have attempted to observe the legal requirements with respect to the rights of copyright holders of illustrations. Nevertheless, persons who feel they may have claims are invited to apply to the publishers.